The Thurber Album

A COLLECTION OF PIECES

ABOUT PEOPLE

BY

JAMES THURBER

818.
5
Thurber

Simon and Schuster

New York

NINTH PRINTING

SBN 671-21014-9 CASEBOUND EDITION
SBN 671-21015-7 TOUCHSTONE PAPERBACK EDITION

To Herman Allen Miller
OCTOBER 25, 1896—APRIL 20, 1949
whose friendship was an
early and enduring inspiration

Foreword

THE PIECES IN THIS BOOK *began, some four years ago, as a kind of summer exercise in personal memory, but before long I began writing letters to people, or calling them up, to verify a name or a date, and in the end I had research material weighing as much as a young St. Bernard: letters, carbon copies, newspaper clippings, magazine tear-sheets, notes, eulogies, poems, photographs, and nearly a dozen books. The writing of the book had turned into a major project for me, which could not have been finished without the generous and unselfish help of a number of men and women who have answered questions, ransacked old trunks, and plodded through old newspaper files.*

I especially want to thank my mother, Mary A. Thurber, Mahlon Taylor, Ruth Taylor Davis, the late Mrs. Joseph Villiers Denney, Thomas Denney, Mrs. William A. Ireland, Lester C. Getzloe, James E. Pollard, George Smallsreed, Ray Evans, Sr., Stafford Taylor, H. T. Webster, Joel Sayre, John McNulty, Charles M. Coffin, R. W. Pence, Adolph Waller, James F. Fullington, Burton E. Stevenson, Hugh

Foreword

Huntington, Bernard A. Bergman, Gerry Turner, Karl Pauly, Mrs. Irma Krieger, Mrs. Agnes Beal Smith, Mrs. Thelma Roseboom, William Allaway, Mr. and Mrs. Clifford R. Fisher, Earl G. Fisher, Mrs. Clarence H. Schwenke, Carl Ziegfeld, William F. Thurber, Robert C. Thurber, David Levy, and Ed Penisten.

All the chapters appear here in book form for the first time except "Adam's Anvil," which was originally printed in My World and Welcome to It, published by Harcourt, Brace, under the title "A Good Man." It has been rewritten and expanded to include new material. All of the stories were published in The New Yorker with the exception of "Conversation Piece," which has not been printed before. Well, one or two of its paragraphs were transposed from "Man with a Rose" to give my grandmother room of her own. Most of the pieces have been changed, a little or a lot, for technical or personal reasons, none of them worth going into, and several titles are new.

One of the most pleasant results of the writing of The Thurber Album has been the letters that I received from Mrs. Dorothy Canfield Fisher. If nothing else had come out of it all, these letters would have amply repaid me for my efforts.

J. T.

WEST CORNWALL
CONNECTICUT
MARCH 29, 1952

Contents

Author's Note

THESE PIECES are arranged in a kind of chronological order, and they also have a certain vague continuity. Some of the people in the early ones pop up now and then later, a little cryptically, perhaps, if they have not been encountered before.

The photograph gallery at the end contains pictures of most of the principal figures in the book, but there are a few unavoidable omissions, in spite of a diligent search through attics. The editor of the Columbus *Dispatch,* and many others mentioned in the Foreword, were of constant help in digging up old photographs for me to select from, and I thank them all again.

"This is good country, the Ohio country, and I have never ceased to be content that here I came to rest."

*The Autobiography of
Judge Stacy Taylor.*

CHAPTER ONE

Time Exposure

I T WAS just a hundred years ago last summer that one John Matheny, industrious farmer, pious husband of the former Lizzie Bell, and father of her four children, was drowned in the Hocking River in Ohio, in his thirty-fourth year One of his three daughters, Katherine, called Kate, married a young farmer named William M. Fisher when she was sixteen and became, among other things, my grandmother. Grandma Fisher never told her grandchildren tales about her father because she was only seven when he was drowned, and she didn't remember much about him. The man she did remember vividly, and told tales about, was her stepfather, a colorful figure in the annals of several families—he was married three times —and the author, some seventy years ago, of a short unpublished manuscript entitled "The Autobiography of Judge Stacy Taylor." This personal history was recently lent me by its owner, Mahlon Taylor of Punxsutawney, Pennsylvania, last surviving child of the judge, who had more than thirty children, counting his stepchildren and the dozen or so boys and girls he adopted when their parents were killed by Indians or died of a plague. The remarkable memory of Mahlon Taylor, who is now ninety-four years old, readily supplies any fact that his father left out of his brief, but exciting and sometimes bloody, memoirs. He not only remembers how his father lifted him up in his arms, eighty-seven years ago, so that he could look on the countenance of Abraham Lincoln when the martyred President lay in state in the rotunda of the State House in Columbus, but he also recalls the name of the owner of the black horses that drew the hearse that day, and the name of the man who owned the hearse, which was nothing more than a farm wagon draped in black bunting. The Sage of Punxsutawney, furthermore, can repeat the words of a gentleman who quieted and dispelled a group of men that threatened to lynch the members of a theatrical company then playing in Columbus.

Stacy Taylor was born in Virginia, one hundred and forty-six years ago, within a carriage ride of the nation's capital and the town of Alexandria, and when he was nineteen he drove his seventeen-year-old wife, Mary Hollingsworth Taylor, to Alexandria, on the

Time Exposure

Fourth of July, 1825, to hear President John Quincy Adams speak proudly of the Republic's past and confidently of its future. After the ceremonies, Stacy and Mary shook hands with President Adams, and with four ex-Presidents of the United States: John Adams, Thomas Jefferson, James Madison, and James Monroe. (John Adams and Jefferson, incidentally, died exactly one year after that day, on the Fourth of July, 1826, and Monroe died on another Fourth of July, in the year 1831.) Young Taylor was not thrilled by the nearness of Washington, D.C., where formal history was being made and immortals were to be seen walking along the streets, for he was a restless and adventurous youth who dreamed of the Northwest Territory, the Western Reserve, and the Indian country, and he was determined to seek his fortune there. When he was only twenty, he loaded his wife and the firstborn of their eight children into a wagon, with their household possessions, and set out for the bright streams and deep forests on the other side of the Alleghenies.

Taylor, as he refers to himself in his autobiography, "came to rest" in the town of St. Marys, Ohio, in the summer of 1826, when two future Presidents from that state were merely toddling about: Ulysses S. Grant, who was then four years old, and Rutherford B. Hayes, who was three going on four. I don't suppose anybody in St. Marys remembers that its first nayor was a young Virginian named Stacy Taylor, but I like to think that the gravestones of his beloved first wife and four of their children can still be found in the town's oldest cemetery. There is no grief or gloom in the memoirs, however, for it is a tale of pioneer action in a period when men had little time for tears. Soon after Taylor settled in St. Marys, he formed a fur-trading partnership with another restless young man, one George Johnson, and for seven years they roamed the wilderness along the banks of the Wabash in Indiana, buying furs from the comparatively peaceable Wyandots, Ottawas, and Senecas, and the touchy and truculent Shawnees, who liked a slashing knife fight when they were full of whiskey. They also liked the soft-spoken Taylor, who neither sold firewater nor got drunk, who dealt with them honestly and never brandished a gun, but was mighty good, when he had to be, on forehand or backhand, with a yardstick, one end of which was weighted with lead. Taylor and his partner paid silver dollars—the Indians didn't like paper money—for mink, otter, fox, wolf, bear, beaver, and raccoon, and the hides of deer. (There is no mention of how much mink cost a hundred and twenty-five years ago, but the Indians sold a good otter pelt for six dollars.) The young traders finally paid as much as two thousand dollars in one transaction, and the Indians welcomed their coming in the trapping season, and often turned to Taylor in their arguments with other white men. He successfully represented one Ohio tribe which had been rudely dealt with in a hasty and unfair federal treaty. He was never molested, even by the Shawnees, but he witnessed a dozen savage knife brawls, and he graphically describes one of the bloodiest, involving three remarkable Indians, one of them known, strangely enough, as McDougle. I set down his account exactly as he wrote it, leaving in his subtitles:

Captain Bright Horn; Big Lewis

During the spring, summer, and fall of 1832 a number of Indians were killed in the immediate vicinity of St. Marys by their own people. There was an Indian among the Shawnees by the name of Captain Bright Horn, who had served in the American army under General Harrison during the War of 1812, and commanded a company of Indians, and who distinguished himself for gallantry in the Battle of Tippecanoe and in other battles with the British and Indians. This Indian was intelligent and civil and was always remarkable for his attachment to the white people with whom he had an acquaintance. There was also another Indian belonging to the same tribe who was named Big Lewis. This man was the largest and strongest man ever known in northwestern Ohio of any race. Some time during the spring before named a large company of Indians came in from their spring trapping with a large quantity of fur skins, which were purchased by Taylor and Johnson, and after they had received their pay they encamped in the immediate vicinity of St. Marys for the night. In this company was Big Lewis and Captain Bright Horn.

A Drunken Fight; McDougle; Death of Captain Bright Horn

During the evening they procured a large quantity of whiskey somewhere (as Johnson and Taylor never sold any liquor, or kept any for sale). Soon they were in a drunken frenzy, and hearing their yells, Taylor and two or three other white men repaired to the scene to see what was the matter. In a few minutes after they arrived at the Indian camp Captain Bright Horn, who was enraged at something some other Indians had said or done to him, attacked with his knife (which was very large) one Indian after another, until he succeeded in killing two, when he attacked the third, by the name of McDougle, who, after receiving a cut in the mouth with Bright Horn's knife, which opened his mouth nearly to his ear, fled and got behind Big Lewis (who always kept sober) for protection. Big Lewis caught Bright Horn as he approached, and told him to stop, he "had killed Indians enough." They stood for a minute facing each other in silence, when Big Lewis said to Bright Horn (in Indian language), "You mad?" Bright Horn in the same language answered, "Yes." In an instant Big Lewis drew his knife and so cut Bright that his bowels came out after the knife, and he fell struggling to the earth. While he was yet struggling in death, McDougle peeped around his protector, and drawing his knife, cried out to the dying man, in the Indian language, "Heap Devil, maybe not dead yet," and sprang at the struggling man and cut off his head. And thus ended in a drunken frolic a brave Indian soldier.

STACY TAYLOR wanted to be a lawyer, and he had brought a set of law books from Virginia, together with the plays of Shakespeare and the poems of Robert Burns, which he read so often that he learned long passages from the plays by heart, and all of the poems. He read his books at night, after going to bed, by the light of a candle whose stick was balanced on his chest. (I tried this myself the other day, and can only conclude that the judge had a longer neck than mine or a great deal more chest.) Studying law by candlelight in the wilderness, while rearing a family of eight and dealing with Shawnees, was a slow process, and he was not admitted to the Ohio bar until he was thirty. If he has his dates right he was elected associate judge of Mercer County when he was only twenty-six, law certificate or no law certificate. Three years later he was a successful candidate for the Whig Party for representative in the state legislature. He rode horseback through the ten counties of his district, telling the voters about the merits of the Miami Canal project and advising against the proposed Northern Railroad. There were other issues, too, long since forgotten, but the intensity of the young Whig's campaign still glows in the pages of his memoirs. After a speech at Fort Recovery, he became lost in a twenty-mile forest,

7

whose foot-wide Indian trail had been obscured by fallen leaves. Darkness came on, without moon or stars, and he took refuge in the crotch of a tree, where for two hours he outsnarled half a dozen "wildcats and catamounts" among the branches. The distant barking of a dog led him at last to a log cabin, whose owner set him on the road back to St. Marys. He was proud of his election as representative, for it came in a strong Democratic year, when the governorship and almost all the other state offices went to Democrats. The autobiography takes a few sharp cracks at Democrats, in the best Whig tradition, including one Judge William L. Helfinstein, whose legal learning and integrity Judge Taylor held in low regard, but the Virginian was a fair man and he admits that his political enemy "did much better than was hoped for or expected" after his election to office.

In one brief sentence, casually tossed into a paragraph, the Judge writes, "With another man Taylor bought for eighty dollars from an Indian chief in Indiana a section of land on which the largest part of the town of Fort Wayne now stands." He seemed well on his way to building up a considerable fortune when he made the mistake of going in for contracting on a large scale, building dams and other ambitious constructions. In a section of the manuscript entitled "Financial Ruin," he tells how he got stuck with a lot of checks of the unsound state treasury of Ohio and had to sell them at a discount of sixty-three per cent. This marked the end of his business enterprises and of his interest in his autobiography. Its last sentence goes like this: "On Taylor's return to St. Marys in 1837 he engaged actively in the practice of law throughout that judicial district, and continued to practice until 1846, when he removed with his four motherless children to Columbus." The narrative of the first forty years of Judge Stacy Taylor's life leaves a lot of loose ends. He does not say what became of his real estate holdings in Indiana, and Mary Hollingsworth is the only one of his three wives mentioned in the manuscript. He was only forty-seven years old when he married Lizzie Bell Matheny and, after that, he still had another forty years to live, but he must have felt that his crowded first four decades were the only ones worthy of permanent record. When he died, in 1893, at the age of eighty-seven, full of scars and honors, still able to recite all the poems of his great idol Robert Burns without a slip, he had lived all but thirteen years of the American nineteenth century. Nobody knows the exact number of his children, stepchildren, and adopted children, or how many of their boys and girls, and grandsons and granddaughters, heard him recite, in his last decades, "Tam o' Shanter" and "The Cotter's Saturday Night," but he had a wonderful old age and he was a welcome visitor in dozens of homes. His son Mahlon, at ninety-four, bewails, now and then, his father's "untimely" death, which he lays to an indiscreet diet. "He could have lived to be an old man," sighs Uncle Mahlon, "but he ate himself into the grave."

Elizabeth Bell Matheny Taylor, the Judge's third wife—I don't know much about his second one—died before I was born, and so I don't know much about her either, but I well remember two wonderful first cousins of hers, known to us children as Dr. Beall and Aunt Mary Van York. They were the son and daughter of a skinker named Sam Bell, who ran a hotel on the banks of the Ohio Canal before the Civil War. Sam was a hardheaded Whig and a practical man, and he didn't understand why his son fancied up the family name by putting an "a" in it, or why the boy had always wanted to be a medico instead of going into the hotel business and getting his sleep. He would be dog, he used to complain, if he didn't think his children were a little quisby. Mary, for instance, smoked chawin' tabacca in her pipe, a chawin' tabacca strong enough to knock a dog off a gut-wagon. And there was that goddam lamp oil that Buddy, the doctor, was always tryin' to make folks take internal, for their ailments. The stuff was meant for lightin' houses, not for treatin' humans, and old Sam would have no part of it. When he lay dying, he refused a tablespoonful of lamp oil held to his lips by his solicitous son. "I'd ruther die like a man than live like a lamp," he said, and he died like a man.

Dr. Beall was a homeopath, with idiosyncrasies of his own—a believer in small doses of mild drugs, a heavy meal three times a day, a good cigar after each one, a little whiskey to regulate the heart, a cheerful disposition to relax the system, a healthy skepticism to clear the mind of notions, and a sane moderation in exercise and bathing, either of which could kill a man if he didn't watch out. His ancient black medical bag held, in neat rows, dozens of phials containing white pills and powders that looked exactly the same. Coal oil, of course, could be drawn from a lamp in any house in the old days, and next to one on a table in his office he kept a teaspoon, a tablespoon, and a wine-glass, and he would fill one or another of them with kerosene, depending on the severity of a patient's ailment. He often took a slug of the stuff himself, and he confounded those who predicted it would kill him by living to be almost ninety.

The old homeopath was a fine skeptic, who doubted practically everything that people tried to foist on him as truth, especially in the dubious areas of medical theory and assumption. He was a tall man, over six feet, and heavy, and we children considered him the best-dressed and most distinguished-looking member of the family. From youth into old age, and from morning till night, he wore the same costume; spike-tailed coat, striped trousers, bat-wing collar, and black bow tie, an outfit that gave his usually negative pronouncements an air of great authority. He made his rounds wearing a plug hat, and when he took it off he revealed a thick shock of white hair that stood straight up on end. He told us that his hair had turned white overnight, after he toppled over during a plague of the Asiatic cholera somewhere in Ohio, and was thrown into the "black wagon" and tossed among the dead in a charnel pit on the edge of town. If a jackanapes or nincompoop informed him that medical science held no record of a man's hair turning white overnight, he would shout amiably, "Tom-fool-er-y," dragging out the syllables for effect, and then add, "Pop-py-cock!" When he stayed at my grandfather's house, its rooms were loud with these words. Once, at Sunday dinner, my grandfather observed that whiskey had kept General Grant toned up and on his toes. "Tom-fool-er-y!" cried Dr. Beall. One of my great-aunts then opined that Grant's drinking had been bad for him. "Pop-py-cock!" roared the doctor, a broad-minded man, who could oppose both sides of an argument. Another time, Cousin Martha Matheny looked out a window of an upstairs room in the Fisher home and was dismayed to see Dr. Beall walking about in the snow in his bare feet. He heard the window sash being raised, but before his woman relative could

scold him he beat her to it by bawling his favorite
words at her. She told him, nonetheless, that he would
catch his death tramping around in the snow at his
age—he must have been eighty then. He explained
that nothing was so good for opening the pores of the
feet as a walk in the snow. The human foot, he added,
was intended by God Almighty to come in contact
with the good earth from time to time.

Dr. Beall often smoked more than one cigar after
each meal, and he worried his female relatives by
smoking in bed. He would sometimes lie down, fully
clothed, after dinner, and doze off with a lighted cigar
in his mouth. I was on hand one evening when my
grandmother smelled cloth burning and dashed into
the doctor's bedroom to find him asleep on a comforter
that was quietly smoldering. "Wake up, Dr. Beall!"
she cried. "You're on fire!" He opened one eye and
gave her, through the smoke, his best skeptical gaze.
"You're on fire," she repeated. "Get up." "Tom-fool-
er-y!" he told her. "Pop-py-cock!" He was right, in a
way. It was the bed that was on fire, and not the homeopath. All of us children missed Dr. Beall, after he
had smoked his last cigar and died quietly in a bed that
was, as luck would have it, not in flames. We would
gladly have exchanged the tranquillity of our grandfather's house, after that, for the burning presence of
Dr. Beall and the booming sounds of his vast but
genial disbelief.

The Thurber Album

Dr. Beall's sister Mary was half as big as he was and twice as spry. A husky youngster of twelve could have lifted her easily, for she was under five feet and weighed less than ninety pounds, but he would have had an armful of spunky vitality. Mary, at any age, could outplay and outwork her brother, and she could outsmoke him, too. Buddy probably consumed some eighty thousand cigars, burning hundreds of comforters and counterpanes in the process, during his eighty-seven years, but Sis smoked, at a fair estimate, about two hundred thousand pipefuls of tobacco during her ninety-three. She was partial to a thick, dark-brown slab of chewing tobacco called Star plug, which came with a little tin star attached to its center. Decades ago, my grandfather once sent her a box of his cigars in the hope of winning her away from the unladylike habit of smoking plug in a clay pipe. It was no good. She promptly chopped up the cigars in a wooden mixing bowl, smoked a few pipefuls of the pallid stuff, threw the rest away, and went back to the pipe she had smoked since she was seventeen. When the world's greatest woman smoker died, her women relatives found, in her drafty apartment in a loft building in central Columbus, a tin box containing a constellation of thousands of little tin stars.

Aunt Mary, as she was called by several generations of admiring children, outlived and outsmoked her two husbands. The first one was an ornery scalawag

named Griffin, who, we were given to understand
when we were young, had gone to hell for his sins.
He used to spank around Columbus, a hundred years
ago, in a smart rig that had yellow wheels trimmed in
red, and carried, like as not, some brazen blond hussy
on those summer evenings when he arrived home late.
This gentleman died young, leaving his worldly goods
to a designing brother and cutting his wife off without
a cent. Her cousin-in-law, Judge Stacy Taylor, who
was forever taking, for nothing, the cases of relatives
and friends, carried this one through the Ohio courts
for two years before he finally succeeded in breaking
the will. The experience didn't embitter Mary. She
married a pleasant, sedentary grocer named Van
York, but he proved to be a sit-by-the-fire, and she was
far too peart for his comfort. They were amicably
divorced, without legal entanglements, and Mary, all
on her own, wandered out to St. Louis, where she
opened a rooming house. It burned down, and she
escaped the flames by sliding down a rope from a
third-story window. Everything she owned, including
God knows how many little tin stars, was destroyed in
the fire. With what money she had left she bought a
train ticket to New Orleans, where she had heard
there was a plague of yellow fever. According to
Mahlon Taylor, the indomitable Mary Van York,
momentarily despondent, had had some idea of getting shed of her troublesome life by catching the

plague, but, being practically indestructible, she survived, and worked heroically as a nurse until medical men got the plague under control. Then she returned, a little anticlimactically, to Columbus and to more than fifty years of life.

I doubt whether either of her husbands shared her liking for snakes, but we children loved to hear her tell how she had adopted a motherless blacksnake when she was a young woman, and made a pet of it. It used to sleep on the foot of her bed at night and it had the run of her home during the day, doubtless making women visitors and gentlemen callers nervous and uneasy. When we asked her what in the world she saw in a horrible snake, she would say, indignantly, "He wasn't horrible. He was a lovely monster, and smarter than a dog." Dogs, she contended, should be in Hell where they belonged, with the late Mr. Griffin. The only dog of ours that ever interested her was Rex, our bull terrier, for whose fine physique she had a certain detached respect. "You're a handsome fiend," she snarled at him one day. He was lying down and, sensing that he was being praised, he began beating his tail upon the floor. "Don't flatter me, you ugly beast!" she snapped, and walked out of the room. It was one of our sorrows that her snake had died long before any of us was born, and that she never got another one. She spent her last years all alone, with her pipe, her memories, and a stack of five-cent novels as high as her head, for Street & Smith must have got almost as many of her nickels as the makers of Star plug. She was an intense admirer of Buffalo Bill, Wild Bill Hickok, Daniel Boone, Davy Crockett, and Young Wild West, among other fictional characters, but in her old age they were all supplanted in her hero-loving heart by Tarzan of the Apes, whose adventures she read in the Columbus *Citizen*. "He's a wonderful wretch," she would tell us, with an admiring light in her eye. Smoking her pipe, sometimes wearing a shawl on her head, and talking in a deep-toned Old Testament voice, a perfect instrument for dark and bloody narratives, she would tell tales of the far West to the children who called on her, sometimes making Tarzan a contemporary of Buffalo Bill, and now and then involving herself in the action of the stories. Her favorite tale was about a Pawnee attack upon a wagon train and the kidnapping of a male white infant. "He grew up to be wicked and beautiful," she would say. "Wicked and beautiful." When we asked her what finally became of him she would say dolorously, "He married this Boston woman." She died well before the advent of radio, thus missing, alas, the adventures of that wonderful wretch, the Lone Ranger, a hero right down the center of her alley.

They came and got her when she was ninety-three—

a bunch of "busybodies" who told her that she was sick and wasn't able to look after herself any longer. Mary Van York explained angrily that she had looked after herself pretty well, please and thank you, for three-quarters of a century, but they wouldn't listen to her. In the hospital, starched hussies and wenches, some of them seventy years younger than she was, told her that she couldn't smoke any more, and took her pipe away. This may not have been the direct cause of her death, but it was certainly the direct cause of her second, and last, loss of interest in living. She questioned, in her best sepulchral tones, the security of a nation whose womenfolks had no desire for the solace of the healthful weed that God had given them. Many of the men and women she had delighted as children called on her. She would gaze at them with dimming eyes and say sorrowfully, "Poor Willie," or "Poor Ruth," for her own life had been a hard one and she was convinced that all her visitors were carrying heavy burdens and crosses. She begged a cigar from one of the men, broke it in two, crumpled up half of it, and chewed it lustily, with a look of great satisfaction on her face. It wasn't Star plug in a pipe, but it was tobacco. The other half she hid under her pillow, but one of the starched snippets found it, scolded her gently, and took it away from her. The end of Mary Van York came not long after that. She died peacefully on a Sunday morning, with the streets quiet all around, except for the good, old-fashioned sound of church bells ringing in the town.

RUTH TAYLOR ("poor Ruth") Davis, one of the most devoted friends of the late Mary Van York, is the daughter of Mahlon Taylor, whose remarkable memory has illuminated many a faraway scene for me, and she has told me about the present days and nights of her father, in Punxsutawney. He is still, although only six years this side of five score, an alert and active man, and if his eyes don't see as well as they once did, they twinkle as much as ever. He washes his shock of white hair, as thick as Dr. Beall's, once a week in Old Dutch Cleanser, on the ground that scouring powder is the best thing in the world to keep a head of hair in healthy condition. Someone described him a few years ago as looking a little like "a benign John Nance Garner," but this didn't please him particularly, for he is as strong a Republican as his father was a Whig, or maybe even stronger. He has been known for years as Punxsutawney's outstanding critic of every Democratic President since Andrew Jackson. When he was well into his eighties he was asked to make an after-dinner speech at a banquet celebrating the successful conclusion of a campaign to raise funds for his church. His family was somewhat uneasy about this, because of his tendency to take Democrats apart, but he promised he would stick to unpolitical anecdotes about itinerant parsons he had known in his youth. (One of these poor devils, he remembered, got more than a ton of turnips at a donation party, and little else.) When he was called on at the banquet, he got to his feet and recited a long and not exactly reverent poem his father had taught him seventy years before, entitled "The Parson and His Barrel of Beer." He didn't forget a single phrase, and his audience loved it. "I guess the wrong spirit moved me," he told his daughter on the way home.

Until recently, Mahlon Taylor went to bed at midnight and read until dawn, but now he has to use a reading glass, and five hours at a stretch is a mite too much for him. During the day he gets through three newspapers (all Republican, of course) and several magazines, including *The New Yorker*, and he takes his favorite books to bed with him: the poems of Burns, the plays of Shakespeare and Aeschylus, and the novels of Dickens, Thackeray, and Tolstoy, whose "Anna Karenina," he wrote me recently, should be read in conjunction with William Dean Howells' enlightening interview with its author. He is also fond of "The Library of the World's Best Literature," and his daughter, in making his bed, often finds as many as half a dozen volumes in it. He can recite almost as much of Burns as his father could, and he applies scores of quotations from Shakespeare to the modern American scene. A few years ago a young woman relative of his sent him a copy of a Shakespeare examination she had taken in college, and he took a whirl at it himself, answering eight out of the ten questions correctly.

He likes to play cribbage, at which he has been an expert since he was a young man, and contract bridge, which he took up in his eighties and mastered in no time at all. In the summer, when the weather is good, he sits in his backyard and listens to baseball games on his portable radio. He thinks it was eighty-five years ago, or possibly eighty-six, that he saw the Cincinnati Red Stockings play another team at the Franklin County Fair, and win by a score of 54-4. His favorite team nowadays is the Cleveland Indians, and he was disappointed when they showed something less than Taylor vitality during the final weeks of the past season. He is confident that they will win the pennant this year, for he holds that Yankee luck can't last forever.

I often find myself thinking about Mahlon Taylor, with something of the sense of repose that the late Bert Leston Taylor—no relation—enjoyed when he contemplated the distant star Canopus. The combined life spans of Judge Stacy Taylor and his son Mahlon cover one hundred and forty-six years of American history, beginning in 1806, when Thomas Jefferson was President of the United States, and extending to the administration of Harry S. Truman. I haven't seen Uncle Mahlon for six years, but nothing serious has happened to him since then, I am glad to say, except the second defeat of Thomas E. Dewey. He went to Columbus in 1946, for my mother's eightieth birthday party. He looked as chipper as when I had last seen him ten years before, but he apparently thought that I had begun to fail. At one point during the festivities, he leaped up from his chair and beckoned to me. "Jimmy," he said, "you look tuckered. Take my seat." He was eighty-eight years old then and I was only fifty. I declined his offer, politely but firmly. His fondest wish is that he may live to see another Republican in the White House. I may not make it myself, since I am considerably more tuckered than I was six years ago, but it wouldn't surprise me if he does. It wouldn't surprise me at all.

CHAPTER TWO

Adam's Anvil

I T WAS about fifteen years ago, just after Mahlon Taylor left Columbus to live in Punxsutawney, that I came across a faded obituary of my great-grandfather, Jacob Fisher, preserved in an old family scrapbook. Jacob, I learned, was born in 1808, one of the eleven children of Michael Fisher, who had built his cabin on the east shore of the Scioto River, south of Columbus, in 1799, the year George Washington died. This Michael was one of the six sons—the most restless one—of Adam Fisher, a blacksmith, of Hampshire County, Virginia, who died there in the year 1782. I have no yellowing eulogy of old Adam, or any other report of him except a copy of his last will and testament, which I found not long ago, while digging into ancient family records. The original will was filed in the Hampshire County courthouse at Romney,

23

which became a part of West Virginia after General George Brinton McClellan smashed across the Ohio River, during the Civil War, and seized the western end of the Old Dominion in the name of the Federal Union. The document disposing of the blacksmith's earthly possessions is dated the 14th day of May in the year of our Lord 1778. It contains some curious spellings which I respectfully preserve.

"In the name of God Amen," it begins. "I Adam Fisher, Black Smith of the County of Hampshire and Colloney of Virginia being weak in body, but of sound mind and memory blessed be God, Do here make this my last Will and Testament in manner and form as follows. That is to say, that it is my desire that in the first place, that after my Decease, I be deacently buried after a Christian manner, and my funeral charges to be paid and all my Just Debts ... Imprimis I do leave and bequeath unto my well beloved Wife Christian Fisher, the benefit of as much of the plantation I now live on (in the manor) as she shall stand in need of during her widowhood, and likewise one Negro wench named Fan, to be hers during her widowhood and no longer, and if she should marry again she is to have what the law allows." The will then goes on to provide for the six sons and two daughters of Adam and his beloved wife, whose name appears three times as "Christian" and once as "Christina." The will was probated in 1783 and it ends in a mysterious renunciation of all rights by Christian, or Christina. She refused to join in the probate, declaring that "she would not accept, receive, or take any Legacy or legacies to her given or bequeathed by this Will or any part thereof and renounced all benefit and advantage which she might claim by the same." It is probable that Christian, or Christina, was married again, or intended to be, for she must still have been a young woman and she was, after all, the mother of only eight children.

I don't know what became of Fan, or of any of the rest of Adam Fisher's "movable property," except his old smithy anvil. Uncle Mahlon tells me that the iron block was bequeathed to Michael Fisher, a blacksmith as well as a farmer, who passed it on to his son Jacob when he died. Jake could shoe a horse as well as his father and grandfather, and Uncle Mahlon, as a boy, used to watch him hammering iron shoes into shape on the anvil. Jake's sons, one of whom, William M. Fisher, became my grandfather, all grew up to be city fellows, and they had no use for an anvil or any knowledge of how to use one. I am sure this did not please old Jake, and it is a fond notion of mine, although I have no facts to support it, that he picked up the anvil one day, in a fit of temper and disdain, and threw it away. For Jake Fisher, as we shall see, was a mighty man, with large and sinewy hands.

Jacob Fisher's death notice, headed simply "Memorial," recorded that he was survived by three sisters and a brother, six of his thirteen children, thirty-two grandchildren, and six great-grandchildren. The rest of the story, except for a single arresting sentence, praised the deceased's homely virtues—a persistent devotion to the Lord, kindliness to his neighbors, and generosity to those in want. The sentence that caught my eye and interest, set austerely apart in a paragraph by itself, read, "In his prime Jacob Fisher was the strongest man for many miles below the city." That was all; no instances were given of my great-grand-father's physical prowess. In the severe and solemn memorials of 1885 in Ohio there was no place for vain glorification of the pitiful and transitory clay. I wondered, when I read the obituary, what lay behind that cautious tribute to the earthly power of old Jake Fisher's flesh. It wasn't until I asked Mahlon Taylor that I found out.

A far lesser breed of men has succeeded the old gentleman on the American earth, and I tremble to think what he would have said of a great-grandson who turned out to be a writer. Perhaps I can make up for it a little by giving the substance of the story that should have followed that topic sentence left hanging mute and lonely in old Jake's obituary. He would have wanted it there in place of the list of his virtues. He didn't care if his neighbors knew that he could heft a bigger load of stone or iron than any other man for miles south of the city, or in any other direction, or that he had once picked up an old locomotive wheel and throwed it thirty-four inches farther than the next strongest man in the countryside; but his acts of kindness and generosity were his own private business, and not to be bragged about. He had a clean conscience, a good appetite, and sound common sense— except for his habit of taking a homemade physic, compounded of bitter roots, that was strong enough to singe a brigadier's mustache—and he stayed young-looking all the years of his long life. "I don't know what old Jake used on his hair," said Mahlon, that Old Dutch Cleanser man, "but it stayed full and black up to his death. Beard turned gray, but his hair didn't. He died with all his own teeth in his head, too—all except one. That'd been knocked out with a brick in a fight."

Jake Fisher fought a thousand fights in his time. In those days, if you went west of the Alleghenies, there was only one way of settling an argument or a difference of opinion. Farther west they wrassled and gouged out eyes with their thumbnails, but in the Northwest Territory they fought standing up, with their fists. Some men would pick up a club or a rock or even a broadaxe, and a few grabbed for their guns, but mostly they slugged it out toe to toe.

"Jake never lost a fight," Mahlon said. "He fought men who were hard on their womenfolks or were cruel to dumb animals, but mostly he fought to back up his political beliefs or to defend the divine inspiration of Scripture. 'There is too goddam much blasphemin' goes on,' he used to say. He was a good man."

Jacob Fisher, born in a log cabin when Jefferson was President, was twenty-one when Andrew Jackson took office. "Your great-grandpa's prime that the fella speaks of," said Uncle Mahlon, "began about then and lasted up to Cleveland's first term. He couldn't go through another Democratic administration, and so he died." Jake's political bias, it seems, was partly determined by an incident of the War of 1812. General Jackson had ordered the execution of a young soldier who had deserted to visit his dying mother. Jake heard about it from his father and he never got it out of his mind. He licked every Jackson man he met, once going up onto the platform of a meeting house to knock down a visiting speaker from the East who praised Old Hickory. Afterward he stopped his buggy beside the man, who was walking along the road, holding his jaw. "Git in the buggy and I'll take you to the hotel," said Jake. The man refused. "Git in the buggy!" roared Jake. The man got in. A fist fight settled an issue once and for all, and subsequent hard feelings were not to be tolerated. If Jake broke a man's ribs or fractured his jaw, he took the man home. Often he sat up all night at the bedside of a vanquished foe, applying arnica or changing bandages. He could assist at the birth of a child, and he had a comforting voice in a house of death. "About all the graves in the old Walnut Hill Cemetery were dug singlehanded by Jake," said Uncle Mahlon. "He never allowed nobody to help him."

Jacob Fisher built one of the first stone houses south of Columbus, and people used to go out from the town to watch him pick up a three-hundred-pound granite sill and set it in place. "He was only a hair over five foot ten," said Uncle Mahlon, "but he weighed a hundred and ninety-eight pounds, most of it bone and muscle. You couldn't lay your finger between his hipbone and his ribs, he was that close-built. He walked so straight he never run his shoes over, heel or sole—they wore out even." Around the house that Jake built grew up a farm of ten thousand acres. Through a part of his vast fields drifted the barges of the Ohio Canal on their way to and from Athens, and across one end of his property the Chillicothe tollpike was cut. Jake owned a great gravel pit and he allowed the road contractor to use all the gravel he needed, with the understanding that Jake would never have to pay toll. When the pike was finished and the tollgate put up, the agreement was forgotten. The pole would be kept in place across the road when Jake drove along in his buggy. "He'd git out and beat up the tollgate keeper," Uncle Mahlon told me, "and then raise the gate and drive on. They kept puttin' bigger and stronger men on the gate. Jake licked eight of 'em all told, and finally his patience gave out and he threatened to go over their heads to their bosses and lick *them,* and after that they didn't molest him. The gatekeeper would h'ist the gate when Jake's rig was still a quarter-mile away."

THE CANAL wove itself into my great-grandfather's saga, too. If you stood on his back porch, you could see the slow boats passing through the land, half a mile away. Once in a while, when a barge came along, Jake would cup his hands around his mouth and bellow, "Git me some whiskey!" On the return trip five barrels would be tossed off onto Jake's land. He didn't drink or smoke or chew, but his hired hands did. When he was not yet forty, Jake had half a hundred Negroes working for him. Each man had a jug and a tin cup and the barrels were set in a lean-to and you could get whiskey whenever you wanted it. If a man got mean drunk or lazy drunk, Jake would whip him sober with a hickory withe. The men learned to drink moderately, out of fear of the big man's lash, and also out of a real devotion to him. "Your great-grandpa," said Uncle Mahlon, "was the first man in Franklin County to sit down at table with a Negro. This caused a stew and a fret in the Presbyterian Church, but Jake just said, 'If a man's good enough to work for me, he's good enough to eat with me,' and that settled that."

Adam's Anvil

One day there was hell and a battle royal along the canal. Jake wandered down to the waterway and witnessed a dismaying spectacle. The bargemen were "whippin' up ducks." Each of the men held in his hand a long-lashed bullwhip. Their sport consisted of casting the whip at ducks floating in the canal in such a way that the end of the lash wrapped itself several times about a duck's neck. Then they would jerk the bird up onto the barge. The bargemen were expert at this curious pastime. They caught a great many ducks. The ducks were Jake's. He ran down to the towpath, grabbed the towrope away from the drowsy boy on the mule, and hauled the boat into shore. Then he leaped on board and began to throw men into the water and onto the land. "He could throw a six-foot grown man as far as twenty-five feet when he was in a rage," said Uncle Mahlon. "A lot of heads cracked and bones broke that day, but nobody was killed. Your great-grandpa never tried to kill anybody—except one Indian. He was a good man."

I asked about the Indian. There were a great many Indians in central Ohio in the first thirty years of Jake Fisher's prime, descendants, perhaps, of the braves who fought at the Battle of Fallen Timbers. They plagued Jake because, although they couldn't outwrassle or outhoist him, they could outrun him. "If I could catch 'em," he used to say wistfully, "I could hold 'em." He never gave up trying. "Once, over by the old deer lick west of the river," Uncle Mahlon told me, "he challenged an Indian to a foot race—see which one could reach an old elm tree first. The Indian won by a couple of strides. Your great-grandpa ran back and got his gun where he had left it and shot the Indian. He wasn't killed, but he was hurt bad. Jake carried him to his own home and nursed him back to life. Old Fisher didn't get more than two, three hours' sleep a night for weeks, sittin' up with that Indian. The fella thought he was going to die, so he confessed to his sins and crimes, which included most of the thievin' and skulduggery that'd gone on in the county for the past five years. Your great-grandpa never gave him away to the authorities. Jake always said the Lord God Almighty disturbed his aim the day he shot that Indian."

Shortly after that, Jake became captain of a horse militia company, whose main duty was to keep order at public hangings. Captain Fisher, in his official capacity, wore a sabre, but he never picked up a gun again, even to face an armed man. There was the November evening when Stambaugh showed up on the road outside the Fisher house. He was a quick-moving, broad-shouldered neighbor, and there was bad blood between him and Milt Fisher, one of Jake's sons. It was suppertime and Jake had just finished saying grace. One of his darkies came running into the dining room. "Stambaugh's come to git Mr. Milt!"

he said. "He got a shotgun in one hand and a broadaxe in t'other!" Jake told Milt and his other sons to sit still. He took his napkin out of his collar and went out the door, empty-handed. "Jake took Stambaugh's gun away from him and broke it in two," said Uncle Mahlon. "Then he snapped the axe handle and throwed the pieces away. He broke that gun and axe in his hands, like you'd break a stick."

WHEN FORT SUMTER was fired on, Jake Fisher, still hard as a boulder, had just turned fifty-three. They wouldn't take him in the Army, so he stayed at home and fought Copperheads and mealymouthed patriots with his fists. "On a market day Jake would lick as many as six, eight men," Uncle Mahlon said. "Mostly men who questioned Lincoln's policies or turned scared after a Rebel victory. Once a fella that was ridin' on a horse yelled something that angered your great-grandpa and Jake ordered him down off his horse. The fella was just takin' off his coat to square away when Jake walked over to the horse. 'We gotta have more room,' he said. 'I don't want you to hit this horse when I throw you.' Thereupon he picked the animal up in his arms and moved it eight or ten feet away. He was used to doing that in his own blacksmith shop—it was easier to move 'em that way than to lead 'em sometimes. Well, when the fella saw that, he took to his heels and ran faster than an Indian."

The Thurber Album

On another occasion during the war years, a friend of Jake's told him that five men, probably Copperheads, were conspiring to beat Jake up. They were in the back room of Frick's saloon, laying plans for a mass assault. Jake jumped on a horse and rode over to the place. "He didn't knock them fellows down," said Uncle Mahlon. "He throwed 'em. Jake only fought with his fists over political or religious questions. He throwed fellas that whipped up ducks or were just plain ornery." It was also during the Civil War, when Morgan's raiders had crossed over into Ohio, that a train of boxcars on its way to Cincinnati stopped in the yards in Columbus. Jake found out that they were crowded with men, Home Guards, on their way to protect the Ohio-Kentucky border. "The goddam Copperheads has cooped them boys up in there without no air!" said Jake. He tore a rail loose from a siding and, swinging it like a tennis racket, beat holes in the sides of each car. The authorities always looked the other way when Jake started out on one of his rampages. "Nobody wanted to arrest a man as good as Jake," Uncle Mahlon said. He kept trying to enlist in the Union army almost up to the day of Lee's surrender, and once demonstrated his fitness to a couple of recruiting officers by pulling a thick oak door loose from its hinges as easily as if it had been a petal he was plucking from a daisy. After the war was over, and Jake was either sixty or sixty-one, Uncle Mahlon can't be sure about that, he throwed his last man, an impudent gatekeeper at a county fair. "It wasn't his best throw," said Uncle Mahlon, "but the fella went a good twenty feet."

In his seventies, Jake Fisher could still lift two hundred pounds' dead weight from the ground and hold it at arm's length above his head. Three years before he died he performed his last exploit in public. The drunken driver of a team of horses on High Street tumbled over onto the doubletree and the horses took off. Jake outran the other men who saw it happen and pulled the team to a stop. "I can still catch 'em," he said proudly, "and if I can catch 'em, I can hold 'em." In his last days he had little respect for the soft race of men he saw growing up around him. When he was taken to see a newborn great-grandchild, a puny boy weighing seven pounds, Jake snorted. "Goddam it," he said, "the next generation of Fishers is goin' to be squirrels."

IN HIS SEVENTY-SEVENTH YEAR, Jake took to his bed for the last time. As he lay dying, the preacher called on him. "Don't you want to forgive your enemies?" he asked. Jake smiled. "I ain't got none," he said. "I licked 'em all."

CHAPTER THREE

Man with a Rose

M Y GRANDFATHER built the first house on Bryden
Road nearly seventy years ago, and until recently a granite carriage stone bearing the carved legend "Fisher, 1884" marked the point of his bold pio-
neering east of Parsons Avenue. I don't know what
became of the stone; perhaps it is buried somewhere
in a city dump, the old iron hitching post festering
near by.

Commerce began to creep eastward in Columbus
a long time ago, following the route of the Great Run
the day the dam broke, and obliterating the quiet landmarks of the carriage years. The last I heard, my
grandfather's house had been cut up into apartments,
and I find it hard to picture the rambling coolness of
the old place quartered and confined. I haven't been
in the house for more than a quarter of a century, be-

cause I want to remember it as it was when I was young and my grandfather was alive. He was married the year the Civil War started, and died, at the age of seventy-eight, the year the First World War ended.

When my grandfather was out of town on a business trip, he always introduced himself to strangers as William M. Fisher, of Columbus, Ohio, a full, resounding identification of which he was incurably fond. He took it for granted that the people he met in the Middle West would have heard of him and his commission house, founded in 1870 and incorporated in 1901 as the William M. Fisher & Sons Co., and he expected everybody to share his pride in the capital of his native state. He liked to let people know who he was, and he presented himself with a flourish, often to the embarrassment of his shy wife. He never went into a hotel or a restaurant without sending for the manager or the maître d'hôtel and announcing for all to hear, "I am William M. Fisher, of Columbus, Ohio." He was at once taken for a connoisseur of food, or a citizen of importance, or a gentleman of large affairs.

William M. Fisher, of Columbus, Ohio, was a man of average height and build, living in a period and a region marked by a dull uniformity of masculine attire, but he managed a visibility all his own, since he had a compelling urge to stand out among men. He had had all his teeth capped with gold when he was still a young man, and their gleam was not only set off by a black beard but vividly accented by a red rose, whose stem he clamped between his teeth like a cigar. In the summertime, he got a fresh rose every morning from his wife's garden. Out of season, he would drop in at a florist's shop for his bright and special ornament. People who knew him would stop him on the street and mention his color scheme of rose and gold and black. Strangers who passed him would turn and look back. He loved it. Several times, he was photographed with the rose in his mouth. He had a passion for having his picture taken, and during his lifetime he became known to scores of studios around the country. He often visited a photographer on his way to a business conference, setting out early enough to have time for multiple poses. Once, he was taken full length, wearing his derby and overcoat and carrying a satchel. An enlargement of this likeness, heavily framed and protected by glass, hung prominently in his living room, and everybody entering the room for the first time was drawn to it. In the lower left-hand corner behind the glass, there was a telegram that read, "Urgent. Do not go to Catawba tonight. Details follow." He explained to people who asked about it— and everybody did—that he had been about to leave his hotel in Port Clinton, Ohio, where he had gone one summer in the eighteen-eighties to buy peaches, when the telegram arrived from his store. If it had come ten minutes later, he said, he would have been aboard a small excursion steamer sailing for Catawba Island that sank with the loss of everyone aboard. Any other man, learning of the disaster and of his close escape, would have gone to a bar for a stiff drink. My grandfather hunted up the nearest photographer.

UNTIL TWENTY YEARS after Gettysburg, Town Street had not ventured past Parsons Avenue, an eastern boundary of polite, middle-class living marked by a tall oak left standing in the middle of the street. Here Town Street suddenly took a jog to the right, as if to avoid the old tree, and proceeded east under its fancy name of Bryden Road. My grandfather owned the first three lots on the right and built his house across from the grounds of what is now the Columbus School for Girls. Behind the iron hitching post and the granite carriage block, the Fisher lawn, constantly trimmed and sprinkled in the dry weather, rose steeply, the better to set off the long, two-story brick house with its high-ceilinged attic, from one of whose windows Old Glory bloomed on Decoration Day, the Fourth of July, and the birthdays of Washington, Lincoln, and Grant. The house was darkened by four porches—front, back, kitchen, and living-room—and by an ancient oak tree that dropped leaves on the roof in autumn. When you closed the front door behind you in the midsummer weather, shutting out the clip-clop of carriage horses on the asphalt street and the lazy splash of the fountain sprinkler repeating its sparkling patterns in some shady corner of the lawn, you were in a wide hallway ten degrees cooler than the world outside. Just inside, against one wall, stood an incredible piece of furniture, a monstrous oak bench whose high back supported an ornate mirror and whose seat could be lifted, revealing a gloomy chest jammed with gloves, overshoes, skates, ball bats, games, and whatnot. Wrought-iron pegs for hats and coats protruded from the back, and at either end stood a tall china umbrella stand, flowering with umbrellas and canes. Above it all hung an elaborately framed lithograph of six hunting dogs with strong muzzles, long ears, and melancholy eyes, who were to remain permanently in my memory for fond, if perhaps imprecise, reference later on, when I began to draw. These dogs hung in many a grandfather's house fifty years ago, usually over the dining-room fireplace. They were the prize hunting hounds of a famous pack that belonged to one of the Dukes of Westminster, and their names, reminiscent of old baronial halls and wild boar hunts, were Calypso, Marcano, Sereno, Lentenor, Nicanor, and Barbaro.

The parlor was the brightest room in the fourteen-room house, and it was lighted on festive occasions by a rococo crystal chandelier that threw gleams on family portraits and on the enormous framed presence of the late James Grover, Methodist minister and first city librarian of Columbus, who was shown sitting in a great chair holding a Bible in his lap. It would have taken two men to lift the almost life-size gilt-framed photograph of the handsome white-haired scholar, who knew not only his Scripture but his Shakespeare. His name, in full, was passed on to me when I was born, and I often thank our Heavenly Father that it was the Reverend James Grover, and not another friend of the family, the Reverend Noah Good, to whom the Fishers were so deeply devoted.

At the landing of the front stairs hung a copy of Rosa Bonheur's "The Horse Fair," hard to make out unless the gas mantle on the wall was lit. The upstairs hallway began here and zigzagged to the sewing room at the rear, in and out of shadow and light. There were seven bedrooms, some of them with closets as large as bathrooms, and the place seemed to us grandchildren designed for games of hide-and-seek. The vast, hot, and littered attic smelled of age and wonders, the many-roomed cellar was clean and cold and filled with barrels and boxes. In the ironing room, at the rear of the first floor, there was a trapdoor that led to storage space beneath, as if some jolly carpenter had put it there for the sake of the grandchildren who assembled on Saturdays and Sundays and invented games suitable for a house that was full of ramble and surprise. We were especially excited by Uncle Kirt's room, for it was lined with sectional bookcases containing fascinating things he had picked up in his travels for the store: a pair of six-shooters, a Sioux war bonnet, a tomahawk and arrowheads, and an opium pipe.

Grandpa Fisher, known to his wife as Will, to his brothers and intimates as Bill, to dozens of nieces, nephews, and cousins as Uncle Will, and to Mrs. Margery Albright, our old family nurse, simply as Fisher, was one of thirteen children, of whom six died in infancy or childhood. As he grew up, he was a frequent witness of his father's locally celebrated feats of strength. Bill envied his father's prowess all his life and could not be dissuaded from his conviction that he could equal the great man's achievements. He thought of himself as a fighter up to the year he died and was usually unable to argue with a man without letting go a right swing. "I ran into Jones on the street today," he would say, "and I told him what I thought of him." When he was asked how the affair turned out, he would say, "I made a pass at him," or, "I threatened to tap him." As far as we know, he never actually hit a man, but he was forever swinging his rather short and far from swift right arm. The Fisher blood had been mingled with that of the Briggses of Virginia, the Pettys of Kentucky, the O'Harras of Pennsylvania, and the Mathenys and Bells of Ohio, but to our grandfather it was only the Fisher strain that counted. If one of his grandsons got hurt while he was around,

Man with a Rose

he would shout proudly, "Show your Fisher, boy, show your Fisher!"

Some member of the family must still have, possibly in an attic, another full-length photograph of my grandfather, which shows him in his most militant attitude. Twenty-one, round-faced, and on the plump side, he is seen gripping a rifle and staring belligerently ahead. This picture was taken at the beginning of the Civil War, and it was a source of wonder to us as children that he was not in a uniform. He wore a black bearskin cap and what appeared to be a homespun suit of clothes. He used to tell us that he was a Squirrel Hunter during the war, and this puzzled us mightily until we were old enough to know that Squirrel Hunters were Home Guards. I don't know what old Jake Fisher, who kept trying to enlist in the Union forces when he was in his fifties, thought of a son who had no hankering to fight with Grant's Army of the West, but the celebrated horse-lifter probably complained about it from time to time between Bull Run and Gettysburg. It must have pleased him, at any rate, that Ulysses S. Grant was his son's lifelong idol.

William M. Fisher named his second son Grant, in honor of the General. (His first son was, of course, named William, after his father, in the immemorial American tradition.) Not even Theodore Roosevelt in his Rough Rider days, although Grandpa was devoted to him and affectionately called him Old Taddy, could light up the Fisher eyes or the Fisher teeth like the eighteenth President of the United States. There was a chromo of Grant on horseback, done in aggressive blues and browns, above the mantel in his study, and he must have read the "Memoirs of U. S. Grant" a hundred times. He began to smoke cigars when he was still in his teens, in emulation of the great smoker (he hated cigarettes and called young men who smoked them "puppies"), and he was fond of defending the General's whiskey-drinking. He always kept a bottle of rye in his house, but he had to hide it when his pious women relatives came for a visit. Once he stuck it in a clothes closet, where Cousin Nettie found it. "What is the meaning of this, Uncle Will?" she demanded. "It's rubbing alcohol," he told her, "for my bowels."

William M. Fisher's intestines were his chief worry. Americans have ever been a bowel-fearful people, and even the duel-fighting President Jackson once inquired of an English colonel who called at the White House what purgative he used. My grandfather would ask strangers the same question, hoping to hear of something new. He must have tried every laxative known to the pharmacopoeia of his time, but I doubt whether he ever took the corrosive hickory-root physic that old Jake had concocted for himself. When Grandpa was in his sixties, he heard of a woman who boxed and sold refined beach sand that was supposed to "assist the integrity of the intestinal track," and he managed, God knows how, to get down a teaspoonful of the stuff three times a day for several months. A cut-glass bowl full of sand was kept on the sideboard until Dr. Beall came to dinner one Sunday, discovered the tomfoolery that was going on, and put a stop to it, explaining that sand might be good for a chicken's gizzard, but was bad for men or machinery. He suggested a swig of lamp oil for the intestines, in place of the abrasive sand, but Grandpa regarded this as dangerous quackery and would have none of it.

Sunday was a long day in the house on Bryden Road. It began with the Lord's Prayer before breakfast, intoned in concert by everybody at the dining-room table, which seated ten and could be leafed out to make room for half a dozen more. Meals were prompt, and on Sunday morning we usually heard the clock in the steeple of Holy Cross Church striking eight as Grandpa thanked our Heavenly Father for his daily bread, or dutifully forgave, no doubt with certain reservations, his debtors and those who had trespassed against him. After the prayer, he would tuck an oversize napkin into his collar, pour half a pint of cream over two Shredded Wheat biscuits, finish them in silence, wait impatiently for the center cut of ham he had selected himself the day before, and slowly drink his first cup of coffee. He was always more interested in the children present, especially the boys, than in any of the adults, and there was never a Sunday breakfast in his home at which he didn't ask the youngest boy, "How many sheep did you kill yesterday?" This was invariably the signal for general conversation to begin. Sunday breakfast was his favorite meal of the week, and it lasted until ten o'clock, with the result that the next one, although officially known as Sunday noon dinner, was never served until two o'clock. There were few Sunday dinners in his house at which a minister was not present to say grace. The reverends were usually Methodists, for old Jake Fisher had left the Presbyterian Church after he came to the conclusion that it was snobbish and undemocratic because several Presbyterians had raised their eyebrows when they found out that he often sat down to table with the Negroes who worked on his farm. When I was a boy, the most distinguished preacher in Columbus was the late Washington Gladden, but it wasn't because he was a Congregationalist that Grandpa never had him to Sunday dinner. He was an intellectual, and hence suspect to plain, blunt men like William M. Fisher, who once said, "I go to church to hear the Word of God, not the word of Emerson." The Reverend Stacy Matheny was a frequent guest, because he was not only a Methodist but a member of the family, the oldest grandson of the late John Matheny, whose widow married Judge Stacy Taylor. (I can find no record of the name "John" having been passed on to a descendant of the ill-fated farmer who drowned in the Hocking River a hundred years ago.)

Grandpa's attitude toward men of the cloth was compounded of a mixture of respect and impatience. He believed that the best of them held the keys to the Kingdom by virtue of a purity beyond the reach of ordinary mortals, but he held that their knowledge of the ways of the world was unnecessarily childish, and, like the late Clarence Day, Sr., he was annoyed by their bland innocence in dealing with business and financial affairs. He was inclined to josh them at Sunday-noon dinner, and to attempt to instruct them in political and economic matters. Now and then he would risk the telling of a mildly vulgar smoking-car story, but he would be instantly interrupted by one of the women present. The worst suspicion he could have of a reverend was that the man might be, in his secret heart, a Democrat or a Socialist. He himself was an inflexible straight-ticket Republican, living in a strong Republican neighborhood, and he hoped that his pastors, who came and went, answering calls, were properly Republican, but he never sought to back them into an ideological corner. Politics, he felt, was not for the House of God, and he became briefly famous in Columbus one Sunday in October more than forty years ago, and got into the newspapers, when he felt called upon to announce his conviction on this point in open church. The minister, in his prayer, had begun to ask the favor and indulgence of the Lord God Almighty in the case of the holy and righteous Republican cause that year. When he reached the candidate for County Coroner on the G.O.P. ticket, and implored Providence to aid and abet his campaign, my grandfather rose in his pew and, to the dismay of his female relatives, began to shout. He roared that he had come to a place of worship for the purpose of worship and that he did not intend to tolerate a political harangue in his church. Such a thing had never happened before, and there was a vast buzzing and confusion as Grandpa stomped up the aisle and out of the church. In the week that followed, he got nearly a hundred letters, mainly complimentary, and at least twenty boxes of cigars from male admirers. The next Sunday, he was quietly back in his pew, and in time the incident was forgotten, a little to his regret, for he liked to talk about it and to have it brought up. He never asked that particular minister to his table again.

If there was one thing William M. Fisher enjoyed as much as being photographed, it was reading articles about himself, especially the incandescent kind that appeared, along with a paid advertisement, in those heavy and gaudy books with such titles as "Prominent Men of Columbus, Ohio," "Centennial Souvenir of the Buckeye State," and "Pioneers of Commerce and Industry in the Middle West." There

Man with a Rose

was a ponderous outpouring of these volumes between 1900 and 1910, when Grandpa was in his sixties and could tell his biographers that he was a director of two banks, a vice-president of the Board of Trade, a Mason, and an Odd Fellow. One of these sketches, published in 1901, contained this creamy statement: "He remained under the parental roof until twenty-seven years of age, but not wishing to devote his entire life to agricultural pursuits he determined to enter the field of commerce and embarked in the grocery business as a clerk." He used to remind us that U. S. Grant had also worked in a grocery as a young man. Bill Fisher gave up clerking, which he hated, Grant or no Grant, to take over a farm his father deeded to him, and he ran it for one year. This brief phase, according to the elegant "Centennial Souvenir" boys, was "dedicated to the shipping of grain and stock over the Hocking Valley Railroad." Young Bill soon found out that he was not a farmer at heart, and he sold his acres and opened a grocery in partnership with a man named John Wagonseller. A year after that, at the age of thirty, he bought out his partner and started a fruit-and-produce store of his own, which he called the William M. Fisher Company. When he was forty-two, he bought and moved into a larger building, and The William M. Fisher & Sons Co., after seventy years, still does business on this site.

All of us grandchildren were enchanted by the store

when we were young. You walked into a dark, cool place smelling richly of fruits and vegetables. In one room were enormous wooden bins filled with a million nuts, and kegs of grapes from Spain. Two or three black cats prowled softly about looking for mice, and occasionally we saw the darting figure of a ferret that had been installed in the store to fight off rats. In another and colder room, lighted by flaring gas jets in the years of my earliest memories, bunches of bananas hung from the ceiling, most of them green, a few turning yellow. We were always breathless and a little scared in this room, because big, hairy tarantulas were occasionally found among the bananas, which came from Honduras and Guatemala. The men in charge of the banana storeroom captured a tarantula alive now and then, and it was put on display in the front room of the store on a table, under an upturned glass tumbler. Scorpions were sometimes found in the bananas, too, and less frequently, a baby boa constrictor. The William M. Fisher & Sons Co. has three ripening and refrigeration rooms now, with cork-insulated walls and all the other modern equipment of the trade. My cousin Clifford Fisher, president of the firm, tells me that tarantulas, scorpions, and young boa constrictors are still discovered once in a while in the banana rooms. The cats and the ferret lost their jobs years ago.

The store was about a mile from the house on Bryden Road, and in good weather my grandfather always walked to work, with the red rose in his mouth. The trip sometimes took him more than an hour, for he was always meeting people he knew, or stopping to talk to people he didn't know. One of his neighbors for many years was the late Harry M. Daugherty, who made a President of the United States out of Warren G. Harding. He and Grandpa never hit it off very well, and it may have been because Grandpa, in spite of a famous aptitude for remembering figures—in the early days of the store, he kept his accounts in his head —rarely got anybody's name right and always addressed Mr. Daugherty as "Dorothy."

When Grandpa reached the store, he would ask after the families of his employees and order a basket of fruit to be sent out if one of their wives was sick or a baby had been born. Then he would inspect newly arrived shipments of Catawba grapes, Port Clinton peaches, or apples from York State. He was an authority on apples and could identify nearly a thousand varieties. He liked to take his grandsons around the place, pointing out Yellow Transparents, Duchesses, Early Harvests, Wealthies, Grimes Goldens, Jonathans, Stayman Winesaps, and McIntosh Reds, and, later in the season, Baldwins, Rome Beauties, York Imperials, old-fashioned Winesaps, and Ben Davises. It didn't take him long to make the rounds forty years ago, but today the store is three times as large, and its buyers range much farther than he ever did. Produce is now shipped from all the Central American countries, most of the islands of the West Indies, and nearly every state of the Union. Trucks roll up to the store from as far away as Florida and Texas, but in the increase of the business a neatness has been added that would astonish my grandfather. Onions and cabbages, which used to arrive loosely piled in freight cars, are now carefully packaged or put up in sacks. Nuts are no longer shovelled into great bins but are tidily packed in cellophane-covered boxes. The days of barrelled potatoes and apples are gone, and the only container that my grandfather would recognize today is the bushel basket. In his early days, Grandpa did a lot of risky speculative buying of perishable goods in carload lots, often losing heavily. He is still remembered at the store for his daring large-scale purchases of grapefruit in the years when it was only a novelty, and so sour that it had to be cut in half, lavishly sugared, and kept in family refrigerators overnight. His confidence in the coming popularity of grapefruit was not shared by his associates, but he was right, as he almost always was.

When Grandpa got to his office, he would put his hat on his desk—he usually wore a black derby—and keep it there all day, although there was a hatrack against a wall. It was a device of his to get away from bores or talkative friends. As the door opened, he would automatically reach for his derby, and if it was somebody he didn't want to see, he would rise and say,

Man with a Rose

"I'm sorry, but I was just about to leave." He would then walk to the street with his visitor, find out which way the man was going, and set off in the opposite direction, walking around the block and entering the store by the back door.

IN the late eighteen-nineties, William M. Fisher made perhaps his only major business blunder, and it was a magnificent one. He became interested in stories of gold in Georgia and, with several friends, incorporated the Dahlonega Gold Mining Company, of which he was named president. Grandpa set about the capitalization of his corporation and the promotion of its stock with his usual vigor, and persuaded a number of his friends and relatives to buy shares. He put fifty thousand dollars of his own money into the venture, and the people he had approached personally bought stock to the amount of fifty thousand. The Eldorado of the commission merchant went the way of many another such enterprise of fifty years ago. My mother still has certificates, dated November 18, 1899, revealing her to have been the proud and hopeful owner of five thousand shares of Dahlonega, a gift from her father. I don't know how many other persons held such pretty and worthless pieces of paper attesting to their golden dream, but I have known since I was a boy that Grandpa Fisher, in spite of his own severe losses, reimbursed in full the friends and relatives he had urged to invest. It is said that he couldn't sleep until the last of his friends had been re-paid. He was under no legal commitment to make good the money they dropped, but it seems that he had orally guaranteed each of them the security of his investment, and "word of honor" was, as an intimate of his once described it, "a jewel of Bill Fisher's character." He liked to make gentlemen's agreements, to shake hands on a deal, and to trust and be trusted in an amiable fashion that alarmed his attorneys. When he died, a clump of letters from the Dahlonega investors he had paid back was found in his safe-deposit vault. One of them was from a registered nurse who had sunk a thousand dollars in the Georgia bonanza. William M. Fisher's own fortune was at a low ebb after the debacle, and the dreaded words "receiver's hands" were whispered about his house, but the store didn't go into bankruptcy. There is a legend that in those dark days he would chew right up the stem of a rose and start in on the petals.

The faith that he had in Georgia gold and grape-fruit was not aroused by the gasoline engine, and he kept his horse and surrey years after his friends had turned to the automobile. The first car he bought, reluctantly, was an electric runabout. Electricity, he figured, was a natural and dependable force, whereas the gas engine was a contraption of man. He never got used to driving the electric, and approached the machine as if it were an unbroken colt. He would sit tensely erect, tightly gripping the guiding bar, and drive down the center of the street, occasionally talking to the thing as if it were alive, or shouting "Get out of the way!" at other drivers. The figure of William M. Fisher in his electric, coaxing, clucking, and shouting, became a familiar one on the East Side of Columbus. He never learned to back "her," but once when I was fifteen, he paid me a dollar to drive her out in the country and show him how. He waited till we were far from town before he changed seats with me, and then, as soon as he had taken over the steering bar, he began to scold the machine as if it were an angry horse whose ears were flat against its head. He started to back her slowly, saying, "Eep, eep!" when she veered to one side and "Awp, awp!" when she shied in the other direction. Suddenly he put on full speed, still in reverse, shouting "Whoa! Whoa!" at the top of his voice, as we crossed a ditch and banged into a barbed-wire fence. It took a garage man an hour to get us loose and on the road again. Grandpa paid him and said, in his bluffest manner, "Drop in at the store and I'll give you a watermelon." He was forever trying to cover up embarrassing situations by offering people watermelons.

SEVERAL YEARS later Grandpa bought a Lozier. He never tried to drive it himself, but he liked to have his grandsons take him out in the country, so that he could "scorch." He would shout "Get her up to forty-five!" and when that speed was attained, he would sit for-

ward, his eyes and teeth shining and his beard blowing, and bellow "Go it!" It pleased him that he could
reach, in less than two hours, the Fairfield County
homes of his wife's people, the Mathenys, and the
Jacksons, and half a dozen others. When he was a
young man he had once driven up to the farm of his
wife's brother, Jake Matheny, in a brand-new surrey
drawn by two black horses, but the Lozier was something else again. It was the sign and symbol of his
success and of the stability of the William M. Fisher
& Sons Co. There may have been more gold in his
head, as he had once ruefully put it, than in the mines
at Dahlonega, but his Lozier was the swift and noisy
proof that he had showed his Fisher and come out on
top. As he flashed through the quiet countryside of
central Ohio, he would take the red rose out of his
mouth every now and then to shout "Get out of the
way!" at benighted peasants poking along the roads
in buggies.

In his final years he rarely went to the store. He was
content to stay home and read Grant's memoirs, in an
effort to get his mind off the intellectual named Woodrow Wilson who had unaccountably defeated three
Republicans, Theodore Roosevelt, William Howard
Taft, and a fine bearded one named Charles Evans
Hughes. He would put his book down and get up and
pace the floor, muttering to himself, whenever he
thought of how the administration in Washington,
fearful of Old Taddy's popularity, had refused to let

him command a front-line division in France and bring the war to a sudden end.

On fine afternoons he would drive around town, calling on old friends and discussing the poor quality of gasoline, rubber tires, and other goods and services under the Democrats. He had never cared about any outdoor game, from croquet to football, but he was a passionate parchesi player and took on everybody who came to visit him in the evenings. Once, when he needed a single ace to get his last man home and win the rubber game from the dignified treasurer of his store, he threw three doubles in succession, and his loud protest against this antic malice struck the room like lightning.

On his seventy-seventh birthday, in September, 1917, his seven grandsons and five granddaughters came to dinner at the house on Bryden Road. Afterwards, during a round of charades or something, the doorbell rang. It was a photographer Grandpa had sent for, and we all spent the next hour posing. The last picture ever taken of William M. Fisher of Columbus, Ohio, shows him seated in the midst of his family holding a two-year-old girl, his first great-grandchild, on his lap. He seemed to be saying something to her, and since she had obviously been frightened by the exploding lightbulbs, I think I know what it was. He was saying, "Show your Fisher, girl, show your Fisher!"

CHAPTER FOUR

Conversation Piece

GRANDMA FISHER, who was sixteen years old when she was married in 1861, spent the rest of her eighty years on the go. I have no memories of her sitting down—even at Sunday dinner she was forever up and fluttering around—and Whistler would have had his hands full trying to make her pose, even for an hour, relaxed and oblivious, while her world bustled on without her. She moved about purposefully, swiftly, and silently, as if she had small oiled wheels on her shoes, lengthening the busy hours of her matriarchal days as the years went on, the fortune and responsibilities of her husband increased, and new rooms were added to the house on Bryden Road. She was thirty-nine years old when she moved into it, but she had been married just two years less than a quarter of a century. By the time I was old enough to tell her from the other women in the family her same age, a legion of relatives had grown up around her. They all called her Aunt Kate, and most of them turned to her for advice, or comfort, or help.

She kept a dozen wicker market baskets in her pantry, and at Thanksgiving and on Christmas Day they were filled with fruits and vegetables, canned goods, and jams and jellies, and piled into the family surrey. She was forever frightening us by leaping from the carriage block into the surrey before Charley Potts had brought it to a stop. She would spend most of Thanksgiving and Christmas, and many other days, driving around town and giving baskets to relatives, friends, and even strangers, who were poor in health or in pocket. She often tucked several of her favorite magazines into the baskets, *Ainslee's*, *Pearson's*, *Munsey's*, *Everybody's*, and *Country Life in America*, and frequently there was an envelope containing a check —her private bank account was practically a charity fund, sparingly used for her own pleasure or adornment. If Grandpa Fisher came home unexpectedly from the store and found her gone, he would say, "Who's she looking after now?" It could have been any one of a hundred persons. He had found out years before that it was useless to try to slow her down.

She was up at dawn every morning, even in her late seventies, setting the big house in motion, putting in phone calls, looking after her flowers in season—roses, lilacs, phlox, larkspur, hydrangeas, and her prize peonies, which she called "pinies." Her grandchildren, eleven of whom are still alive—the next to youngest boy was killed by a careless bullet—remember Grandma Fisher with great affection. She was always getting us out of the dilemmas of childhood, quietly, ingeniously, and without stern lectures, and buying the girls diavolos and woodburning sets, and the boys skates, fielder's gloves, games, or whatever else she had overheard us say we wanted. When her grandsons married, their wives got from her, in addition to a formal wedding present, some old cherished possession of hers, a piece of jewelry, a set of china, or anything else they had seen in her house and admired. If some familiar object could not be found, a search was never made for it until Grandma Fisher was asked if she had given it away. She usually had.

Kate Fisher and her husband liked a houseful of people, and their male and female relatives, three generations of them, took turns visiting Aunt Kate and Uncle Will. He had five brothers, one of whom, Jake, fascinated us grandchildren, in 1905, by building an airship which was put on display at Indianola Park. Everybody else had to pay ten cents to see it, but we got in free. It was equipped with bells and whistles that raised a racket like Hallowe'en when it took to the air, but it made only one successful flight, drifting three miles and coming down in a cornfield north of

Conversation Piece

town. It was, if nothing else, surely the noisiest airship ever built. Grandma Fisher had only one brother, Jake Matheny, postmaster of Sugar Grove, Ohio, but literally scores of aunts and great-aunts came to dinner at the house on Bryden Road: Aunt Lou, who wrote poetry and believed that everything was for the best; Aunt Melissa, who knew the Bible by heart and was convinced that Man's day was done; Aunt Sarah, who had the most beautiful face I ever saw; Aunt Molly, jolliest of them all; Aunt Lizzie, famous for her cooking; Aunt Fanny, plagued in her old age by recurring dreams in which she gave birth to Indian, Mexican, Chinese, and African twins; Aunt Florence, who once tried to fix a broken cream separator on her farm near Sugar Grove and suddenly cried, "Why doesn't somebody take this goddam thing away from me?" and Aunts Hattie, Frances, Mildred, Maude, Bessie, Katherine, Mary, Margery, and two Marthas, among others. Grandma's six children and twelve grandchildren used to gather at her house, forty years ago and longer, before setting out for picnics at Minerva or Olentangy Park, days at the State Fair, which began at eight and lasted until after dark, and the Fourth of July celebrations and Jackson family reunions at Sugar Grove. Kate Fisher was the acknowledged head of the far-flung family on these occasions, and the active and competent field commander of her army of relatives.

61

The Thurber Album

The last Jackson family reunion or, at any rate, the last one that I remember, was held at Sugar Grove, a country village southeast of Columbus, during one of the good old summertimes just before the First World War. It was far larger and noisier than the first one, which was held at Colonel Jackson's place, down Lancaster-way, just after the Civil War. One of the colonel's daughters, Lizzie, had married Jake Matheny, who served throughout the war in Jackson's 58th Ohio Volunteer Infantry Regiment, and the fact that he was my grandmother's brother made my brothers and me, and our nine first cousins, eligible to guzzle the lemonade and dig into the layer cakes at the annual gatherings of the clan, and to take part in the baseball games, the foot races, and the other goings on that lasted all day. When the reunion was held on the Fourth of July, as often happened, it went on late into the night, and the sky rockets, aerial bombs, silver fountains, Roman candles, sparklers, and pinwheels that lighted up Fairfield County for miles around were Grandpa Fisher's contribution to the celebration. He spent as much as a thousand dollars for enough fireworks to fill a boxcar of the Hocking Valley Railroad. He was pleased when somebody once told him that not even God, with His moon and stars, could put on a brighter show. Before the fireworks started, there was a banquet at noon, held outdoors unless it rained, and the food was supplied by all the

Conversation Piece

aunts: fried chicken and turkey, potato salad and a dozen other salads, as many as forty layer cakes, and enough pies, blueberry, lemon, mince, and cherry, for half a dozen Keystone comedies. There was always enough food for five hundred people, or more than twice as many as came to the annual party from Columbus and a dozen other Ohio towns.

The countryside around Sugar Grove was a deeply rural place when my brothers and I and our cousins used to go down to Uncle Jake's farm in the summertime, and nothing about it had changed much since my mother was a little girl and spent her school vacations there with her own brothers and cousins. The original tree-house in an old oak on the front lawn that was brightened by Dorothy Perkins roses and a honeysuckle hedge succumbed to time and the weather back in the nineties, but progress, in my youth, had left the home of Uncle Jake and Aunt Lizzie untouched. The deer came down from the thickly wooded hills surrounding the farm, unabashed by the horns and headlights of the first Hupmobiles. Ten acres of blackberry bushes yielded a wagonload of berries in every season, and an enormous bin in the barn held nuts in the fall that fell from six different kinds of trees. The woods were filled with wintergreen, laurel, and rhododendron, and in a genuine deep-tangled wildwood lived the biggest blacksnakes in the county. The master of these wide acres, known as Uncle Jake to a hundred youngsters, had white hair and a white beard, could bark like a dog to delight the children, and often walked about his lawn with a parrot on one shoulder and a tame raccoon on the other. Aunt Lizzie, the famous cook of the family, had a light hand with a griddle cake, wheat and buckwheat, that was known for miles around. One morning—I think it was in 1906—she made a hundred and forty-two griddle cakes in the kitchen of the summerhouse for a horde of her grandnephews and grandnieces, who remember her with a fondness that time cannot tarnish.

Charles Dickens, who was in Columbus more than once a hundred years ago, might have gone instead to Lancaster, eight miles from Sugar Grove, if it had become the capital of the state. But the old town didn't quite make it, and so the master of human caricature never drove down Fairfield County-way in a carriage, to be amazed and amused by the ancestors of the colorful characters that I knew there when I was a boy. There was a lanky farmer whose dog, wonderfully called Rain, always strayed away from home in the gloaming, and its owner would go out looking for it, crying, in a melancholy voice, "Yo, Rain!" his drawl giving the name two syllables. We would listen until "Yo, Rain" diminished and was lost in the calling of the whippoorwills. Then there was Biddleman Blazer, whom I first saw nearly fifty years ago, dressed

Conversation Piece

in a clean shirt, overalls, and shined-up boots, calling the turns of a square dance in Uncle Jake's barn and playing on the harmonica, over and over, the only tune he knew, "Turkey in the Straw." Biddleman had only a few teeth, and a mere fringe of hair, but although he lacked the fatal charm of, say, Aaron Burr, he considered himself an irresistible beau, and plagued the young Matheny and Taylor ladies with his attentions. One of them always insisted that her father and mother stay with her in the parlor when Biddleman came to call of an evening. He tolerated this a few times, and then took his flattery elsewhere, grumbling, "When I set up with a girl, I don't want to set up with her whole family." When another of his young ladies moved to Columbus, Biddleman took upon himself the considerable task of writing her an affectionate note. To his dismay, he found that what he had to say could not be confined to one page and so, after chewing his pencil for awhile in troubled thought, he wrote at the bottom, "Clarie, turn over." Clarie turned over and away from Biddleman, and the notable swain died a bachelor.

It seems to me a pity that his gravestone contains only his first and last names, for there was a lot in between. He had not been named at birth, but when he was a few months old, various members of his family wrote names on slips of paper, put them in a hat, and let the infant select one. To their astonishment, he grabbed them all, and thus became Biddleman Bistam Bastam George Washington Flinch Blazer, the "Bistam" and "Bastam" having been, I suppose, a waggish uncle's notion of the comical. I don't know when Biddleman B. B. G. W. F. Blazer died. For a long time he was the most evident of men, and then suddenly he was gone, and now there is no longer the faintest rumor, in and around Sugar Grove, of the fellow who played "Turkey in the Straw" more than ten thousand times, at square dances, and walking along the roads, and alone in his room.

It was a wonder to the folks of the neighborhood, four decades ago, that Mrs. Louis Young and her husband, figures as ubiquitous as Biddleman Blazer, didn't get into more trouble, because of their notorious absent-mindedness. They were both hard workers and endless talkers, preoccupations that can be dangerously conjoined. Louis once sat on a high limb of a tree and sawed at it, jabbering away, without realizing that the blade was between him and the trunk of the tree. He came down with a mighty crash, amid the guffaws of his friends who were lucky enough to be on hand. The Youngs were great defenders of each other's mythical awareness, a staunch loyalty natural enough in a husband and wife who lived in quandary and predicament. "Trouble is," explained Mrs. Young, known to everybody as Effie, "Louis is left-handed and was sittin' on the offside of the tree." Her listeners laughed uproariously at this. "Trouble is," said one of them, "Louis was facin' East when he should have been facin' West."

Those of us who were children when we marvelled at Effie, and are now growing old and gray, remember the day on Uncle Jake's lawn when Effie, chattering without pause, set about putting a sunbonnet on her small daughter's head and absently adjusted it to the somewhat larger head of little Grant Matheny. She was tying it under his chin when someone called her attention to what she was doing. "Smartest lawyer in Lancaster could have made the same mistake!" snapped Effie. Not long after that, she enchanted a neighbor woman who had come over to her house to get a recipe by absently looking for it in the family Bible, instead of the cookbook, searching through Leviticus, Psalms, and Proverbs in vain, babbling all the while. Effie's visitor finally had to tell her that she was following a cold trail, but nobody could ever really dumfound the great lady, and she was never without her quick verbal resources. "A man could lose his farm bettin' Effie Young don't know where things is," she snapped.

Effie had a stern contempt for tony folks who enjoyed the effete comforts of modern sanitary engineering. She once returned from a visit to a relative in Columbus to announce, "She's turned finicky since she left Sugar Grove. Got an electric toilet." To Effie

The Thurber Album

Young all mechanical things were electrical, and deserving of a wholesome woman's proper scorn and suspicion. Effie hated to get into an automobile, and once elected to walk fifteen miles on an urgent errand, although she had been offered a lift in a Model-T. Arriving at her destination, tuckered but triumphant, she announced proudly, "A body's got the feet God give 'im, ain't he?" When Effie's husband died, the undertaker from Lancaster called on her and said, in a dolorous, confidential tone, "You will want to bring him back home, of course." (After all, funeral services in those days were usually held in the family parlor.) Effie was dismayed. "Merciful Heavens, no!" she cried. "What in the world would I want with a dead man?" Family legend has it that the mortician, although usually a glib fellow, found nothing whatever to say. Effie Young often had that effect on people.

Aunt Lizzie Matheny died in 1910, and her husband two years later. Their son Stacy had been called to a church in Columbus, and the girls had married and moved away, one of them to the far West. None of us grandchildren has driven down to Sugar Grove since the First World War, and I don't know who has the Matheny farm now. All the great-aunts have been gone this many a year, and while there are still Mathenys and Jacksons in and around Lancaster, the annual reunions are held no longer, for they were sustained by a nineteenth century spirit of family soli-

Conversation Piece

darity that has not survived the women of my grandmother's generation.

Grandma Fisher died in 1925, and her passing marked the close of a way of family life in the Middle West. Her beloved *Pearson's Magazine* died the same year she did, *Ainslee's* had only a few months left, and *Munsey's* and *Everybody's* were on their way out. (*Country Life in America,* hardiest of them all, lasted until 1942.) After Grandma's death, the great, dark house on Bryden Road, which her intense vitality had lighted, seemed suddenly gaunt and cold. It was closed up, and the things she hadn't given away were divided among her children and her grandchildren. I got the lithograph of the hunting dogs and the enormous photograph of the Reverend James Grover. The dogs hang above the widest fireplace in my house in the country, but I gave the picture of Rev. Grover to the Columbus Public Library, where I think the likeness of the city's first librarian properly belongs. I hope it looks benignly down from the wall of some serene and sunny room.

CHAPTER FIVE

The Tree on the Diamond

G ROUP CIVILIZATION, they tell me, has come to the corner of Parsons Avenue and Bryden Road, where my grandfather built his house in the year 1884, well beyond stone's throw of his nearest neighbor, and I suppose the individual has taken on the gray color of the mass. But there were individuals about during the first decade of the century, each possessed of his own bright and separate values.

There was George Craft, the odd-jobs man, who claimed to be eighty, might have been seventy, but worked like a man of fifty when he put his mind and back to it. George always wore a smile and a dark-blue shirt spangled with medals and ribbons that came from curio shops, state fairs, and the attic trunks of his various employers, but George said he had won them all in the Civil War. It seems that he had been a slave

The Tree on the Diamond

and that he had freed himself. Once I asked him, "How did you do that, George?" and he broke into his loud and easy laughter. " 'How did you do that, George?' the boy says!" as if the simple question had been a Johnsonian retort. Our uncertainty about George's age was increased by his fondness for birthdays. He had several a year. "Dis is it! Dis is de real one!" he would tell us gleefully. He would knock on the front door of my grandfather's house on those festive days and say to whoever answered, "Ah wants to see Mistuh Fishah's bright face this fine mornin'!" The person who had gone to the door would call out, "It's George's birthday!" and from his study at the top of the stairs my grandfather would call back, "Give him a dime!" When George got the money, he would flash his great grin and cry, "Lawd bless de gentleman o' dis house!" When George's birthday fell in fair weather, and the walking was good, he collected lots of dimes, but he was a religious man and he sometimes punished himself for pagan thoughts or other errors of faith by decreeing an anniversary on a day of wind and rain or heavy snow. "Too bad you were born in January," my Uncle Kirt said to him once. "You won't collect many dimes on a day like this." George laughed and laughed and slapped his leg, as he did at whatever any gentleman said, and then he sobered suddenly. "Ah'm repentin' fo' mah sins, Mistah Kirt," he said. "Ah'm repentin' fo' mah sins."

The Thurber Album

When George died, he was laid to rest wearing all his medals. One of these, my uncle said, was a genuine decoration for valor, and another was the blue ribbon that had been awarded in 1905 at the Ohio State Fair for the best Rhode Island cock in the poultry exhibit.

Then there was Charlie Potts, my grandfather's stableman, whose get-up on his Sundays off was the envy of us boys. The dark-skinned Charlie had a high stack of black, curly hair, glossy with Macassar oil, or whatever they used in those days. He affected light suits, gay shirts, and flowered yellow ties; a bright bandanna bloomed in his breast pocket, and he swung a bamboo cane. He preferred to keep his Sunday destinations a secret. When we boys wanted to know where he was going, he had an invariable answer, accompanied by a mysterious wink: "If anybody should ask you, tell 'em I left you inquirin'." His room occupied a corner of the barn loft, and its walls were covered with colorful posters presenting scenes from plays of the period—"The Squaw Man," "Strongheart," "The Round Up," "The Great Divide," "The Call of the North," and "Arizona"—and photographs of Faversham, Robert Edeson, and Kyrle Bellew. When the automobile replaced the carriage, putting Charlie Potts out of a job, he took a trip to Europe on his savings. He called on us when he came back, to tell stories of what he kept calling the "rather peculiar circumstances" that attended his travels. In Charlie's

The Tree on the Diamond

idiom, the phrase fitted the commonplace as well as the extraordinary. It still does. He lives in a town in central Ohio now, and I phoned him when I was in Columbus a few years ago. "I haven't seen you for thirty years, Jim," Charlie said, "but I ran into your brother Bill, under rather peculiar circumstances, when I was spending a few weeks in Columbus recently." It turned out that he had run into Bill, as everybody runs into everybody else in Columbus, at the corner of Broad and High.

NOBODY I KNEW in the Bryden Road days stands out quite so clearly for me as Frank James, organizer, manager, captain, and first baseman of the Blind Asylum team, and jealous overseer of the craziest baseball field in the history of the game.

Few of us middle-aged men who knew Frank James as youngsters forty years ago would have recognized him dressed for burial in his full and formal name, Benjamin Franklin James. The Columbus papers revealed that elegant secret in brief obituaries when he died, a few years ago, at the age of seventy-seven. They also acquainted us with the news that Frank was part Cherokee Indian. We should have suspected this from his singularly erect posture and his fine, springy step—he walked as if the ground under him were pneumatic—but kids in central Ohio accepted the brown-skinned man as a Negro and let it go at that. I count it a happy wonder that nobody resented, in those innocent years, his sharp-tongued command of a ball club on which every player except himself was a white man.

The catcher, a man named Lang, threw a ball like a bullet, and he could take the fastest pitch of any hurler barehanded, and he could have broken his captain in two, but he always obeyed orders docilely ("Bunt it, boy, bunt it! You heah me? *Bunt* it!") and the James insults never provoked him ("What kind o' playin' is that for a grown man, Lang? What kind o' playin' is that?").

The baseball team of the School for the Blind—we called it "the Blinky," in the easy and unmalicious parlance of the young—was made up of employees of the institution. I thought Frank James was always in charge of the boiler rooms, but the notices of his death credited him with having been an instructor, and I have since found out that he taught broom-making during his last years there.

Lang was an engineer, I believe, and the rest of the players came from the kitchen, the laundry, the stable, and other corners and corridors of the gloomy institution.

When my grandfather bought a Lozier, he put Maud, the family mare, out to pasture and tore down the brick barn behind the house, leaving a clear vista across the Blind Asylum grounds all the way to Main

The Tree on the Diamond

Street. The place was to become one of the landscapes of my nightmares. Its central structure was a massive crawl of dank stone. Even the architect whose dark genius for the ungainly had created the brooding monster must have realized that it needed a touch of light. He stuck a fountain in front of it, but it turned out to be a sullen cub of the mother building, an ugly cone of rock blubbering water from a length of pipe that jutted out of the top.

We neighborhood kids used to play around the fountain, but we rarely saw the blind children there. They seemed to be in class most of the time, and from my grandfather's house the institution often looked deserted. The shouting and laughing of the ball team behind the main building on Saturday afternoons in summer seemed out of place, like the sound of a child's voice calling down an old, abandoned well. We could hear occasional noises from the building—a tray falling, a sharp voice protesting, a melancholy hand running scales on a piano lost in the wilderness of stone.

The main building sent back two brown wings, or tentacles, which invaded Frank James' outfield, as if they wanted to crush the players and stop the game. The left tentacle crept up to within fifty feet of the second baseman, and the other swung behind the center fielder, forcing him to play in and cramping the range of his action. The blunt end of this wing was separated from the stables by thirty feet of paved courtyard, on which the left fielder had to stand, an easy victim of ricocheting balls, frightened horses, and stablemen with pitchforks. If these were the stony frustrations of a Freudian dream, the gigantic tree between first and second was a hazard out of Lewis Carroll. It had the patriarchal spread of Longfellow's chestnut, and it could drop leaves on the shortstop and, with its large and sinewy roots, trip up runners rounding first. Many a hard-hit ball that should have been good for extra bases would cling and linger in the thick foliage of that ancient tree, and drop finally into Frank James' glove, or the glove of his right fielder, who had plenty of time to jog in from his position on the concrete walk beside the left wing and wait for it to come down. Visiting players screamed and cursed, and now and then they would gather up their bats and gloves, stalk off the Dali diamond, and go home, while Frank James, his hands on his hips, exasperation in his eyes, his mouth open—he was always excited and breathing hard—demanded to know what the hell could possibly be the matter with the yellow-bellies. Sometimes the finicky enemy would quit in disgust, late in the game, after the James Boys had demonstrated a special and practiced skill in bouncing the ball off walls, losing it on roofs, hitting it into the crotch of the tree, or lining it under the lowest bough, so that it would land on the concrete pavement and

The Tree on the Diamond

roll to Parsons Avenue, a hundred and fifty yards away.

THE MIRACLE MEN of Parsons Avenue played the post-office team and the city firemen and police, as well as teams made up of employees of other state institutions, and beat them all most of the time. Panting heavily, his sharp, black eyes taking in every play and every player, Frank urged his men on as if each game were the seventh in a World Series. His tongue was never silent, and he always repeated his loud commands to batters at least once: "Lay it down easy, Steffie, lay it down easy!" or "Get me a double, boy, get me a double!" or "Hit it in the tree, keed, hit it in the tree!" It was the same when his team was in the field: "Close in! Close in!" or "Lay back! Lay back!" or "Watch the bunt, boys, watch the bunt!" If a hard-hit grounder took a bad bounce on the uneven terrain, struck one of his infielders on the chest, and bounced high in the air, Frank would scream, "Ovah ya, undah ya, wheah ah ya?" Human fallibility he could not abide. "What's the mattah, keed, can't ya see 'em?" he would bawl if a player muffed a hard chance, or "Use ya brains! Use ya brains!" It is a wonder that nobody ever took a swing at him with fist or bat. If his team was far ahead and sure to win against men confused by walls and branches, Frank's voice softened and his tone grew friendly. He would let his batters use their own judgment. "Your way's mine, Emil, your way's mine," he would say affectionately. Once this same Emil, in the midst of a tight game, stepped to the plate and said to his captain, "I'll get you a home run, Frank." Instead, he popped weakly to the shortstop. "Thanks for the home run, keed!" screamed Frank. "Thanks for the home run!" Nor did his temper and sarcasm wear off. Every time Emil walked to the plate after that, Frank shouted at the opposing outfielders, "Give him room, men, give him room!"

The James Boys lost few games—not more than four or five, I believe, in all the years they played. One reason for this was that Frank could seldom be lured onto the home grounds of any of his opponents. "The boys can't get away from the institution," he explained once to the manager of a club composed of employees of the State Asylum for the Insane. "If the crazy people want to play us, let the crazy people come ovah heah."

"They are not crazy people," snapped their manager.

"You bring 'em ovah heah an' we'll drive 'em crazy," Frank retorted.

The man stared at the outfield walls, and at the tree that made pop flies out of triples and base hits out of pop flies. "I have no doubt of that," he said testily, and went away.

The Tree on the Diamond

When Frank James' team did drop a game, he revealed himself as the worst loser in the history of baseball, amateur or professional. He had no heart or philosophy for defeat. The best team had lost, and there was no justice in the world. His voice would grow husky from howling that his men should be inmates, not employees, of the School for the Blind, that they couldn't beat the Columbus School for Girls the best day they ever saw, that the whole team should give up baseball for checkers or lotto, that the Lord God had never seen a man so cruelly betrayed as Frank James. One Saturday afternoon, when I was sixteen, I heard Frank fiercely bawling out one of his pitchers for losing a game. "You threw your arm out in practice!" he roared. "I told you not to pitch more than a dozen balls before the game, but you threw your arm out." The man stared at him in astonishment. "That was five years ago, Frank," he said. "Are you still bellyachin' about that old game?" Baseball time stood still in Frank James' head and the sore of defeat never healed. Once he had a close call at the hands of a team organized by Mr. Harvey, proprietor of a drugstore on Main Street, near Parsons. The Harvey Boys were all young men of the neighborhood, familiar with the weird diamond and capable of hitting into or under the big tree. The Harveys led, 2-1, going into the eighth, and Frank heaped abuse on the head of the Harvey pitcher, a slender, quiet youngster named

Billy Allaway, who had Emil and the others missing his curves and popping up his fast ones. He struck out Frank James twice, but the raging captain continued to berate his men for going down on strikes.

"Goddam it, Frank," said one of them finally, "he fanned *you* twice."

"That's 'cause you upset me," yelled Frank, "standin' up theah an' swingin' at nothin'!"

Frank went right on belaboring the impassive Allaway—"that little boy out theah"—with quip and insult. In the ninth inning, the James Boys clumsied two runs across with the help of the enormous tree and won the game. For the first time in his life, Frank James praised an opposing player. "You pitched a good game, Billy!" he shouted. "You pitched a good game!"

Three weeks later, the Harveys took on the James Boys again, with Billy Allaway on the mound, and beat them, 3–2, in a tense and noisy game during which Frank shouted himself hoarse and seemed in danger of breaking a blood vessel. When the last pop fly of the home team had sifted through the branches of the tree into a Harvey glove, Frank James rushed up to Allaway shouting huskily, "If a man beats me he's got to play on my team." Billy pointed out that he was not an employee of the Institution for the Blind, and that this made him a ringer. "My team is my team," Frank yelled, "and if they don't want to play me they don't

The Tree on the Diamond

have to. I ain't goin' to say you're a silverware counter in the dining room, I'm gonna say you're my pitcher. If they don't want to play us they can go home. Nobody tells Frank James how to name his line-up or how to run his team." Billy Allaway won a dozen games for his new captain, and the two became great friends. Billy still insists that Frank James was one of America's great all-around athletes, a star in football, basketball, and track, as well as baseball. "He could run a hundred yards in ten seconds flat, wearing ordinary street clothes," Billy wrote me last year. "When he was forty-three he took up tennis and played it as hard, and as well, as he played everything else." Baseball was Frank's great love, though, and he believed until he died that his team, in its best years, could have licked the Columbus Senators of the American Association—on the Blind Asylum grounds, of course. It was a bitter disappointment to him that his challenge, often repeated, was never accepted by the professional club.

I SUPPOSE that shocked Nature has long since covered that crazy ball field with grass and, no doubt, crickets sing where Frank James used to stand and shout his insults and commands. Frank would have played on into his sixties, but his eyesight began to fail thirty years ago. He had thought his legs would be the first to go, but we who had heard him bawl the summer afternoons away were sure it would be his lungs and larynx. One story has it that a broken steampipe in the boiler rooms caused an injury that gradually brought on blindness, but, however that may be, he stayed on the job as long as he could see to grope his way around.

Frank James was king of that crazy ball field, but even in his heyday he was not always the center of attention. Since the diamond was the only one for miles around, officials of the institution allowed the boys from nearby Douglas School to meet their rivals there on Saturday mornings—or in the afternoon, if the James club was idle or playing somewhere else. The Avondale Avenue team came from the West Side, bringing with it, around 1908, a youngster of destiny, its captain and center fielder, Billy Southworth, who was later signed by the New York Giants. Hank Gowdy, hero of the 1914 World Series, must have played there, too, in his day, and old-timers distinctly remember Billy Purtell, who went to Chicago fifty years ago to play third base for the White Sox.

In the autumn, the field was turned into a makeshift gridiron, with one goal post, and several famous football stars scrimmaged there as boys: Chic Harley, Ohio State's immortal halfback and three-time All-American; Allen Thurman, whose long, high, spiral punts helped the University of Virginia beat Yale, 10-0, in 1915; his young brother Johnny, All-America tackle at the University of Pennsylvania in 1922; and

The Tree on the Diamond

the celebrated Raymond (Fike) Eichenlaub, plunging fullback of the Notre Dame team of Rockne and Dorais, which dazzled and smashed Army in 1913. I remember young Donald Ogden Stewart showing up one day in a brand-new football uniform and carrying a brand-new football; Bill Burnett, who was to write "Little Caesar;" Carl Randall, who went on to dance in the "Follies; " and now and then little Joel Sayre would toddle over from his home in Rich Street to watch the goings on. Long before their day and mine, George Bellows, from Monroe Avenue around the corner, practiced on the diamond—he later became, among other things, one of the best shortstops Ohio State ever had.

I like to think that the aged Frank James, nearing the end of his life, remembered and was remembered by these "keeds" of so long ago. Some of them he outlived, of course; most of the others left Columbus or moved away from the neighborhood, but at least one, Billy Allaway, was a constant visitor during Frank's last days at the School for the Blind. They would sit in Frank's small office, which held a desk and two chairs, and recall the battles of former years. "You know, Frank," Allaway told him one day, "you should have put chicken wire up in that tree." Benjamin Franklin James turned his head sharply in the direction of his guest. "Ah'm a sportsman, Billy," he said reproachfully, "an' a sportsman don't take unfair advantage."

CHAPTER SIX

Daguerreotype of a Lady

WHEN I FIRST became aware of Mrs. Albright in my world—at the age of three or four, I suppose—she was almost seventy, and a figure calculated to excite the retina and linger in the consciousness of any child. Aunt Margery, as everybody called her, was stout and round and, in the phrase of one of her friends, set close to the ground, like a cabbage. Her shortness was curiously exaggerated by the effect of an early injury. She had fractured her right kneecap in a fall on the ice when she was in her late teens, and the leg remained twisted, so that when she was standing, she bent over as if she were about to lean down and tie her shoelace, and her torso swayed from side to side when she walked, like the slow pendulum of an ancient clock, arousing sympathy in the old and wonder in the young. I used to marvel at the way she kept

her balance, hobbling about in her garden after sun-
down, with a trowel in one hand and a sprinkling can
in the other, her mouth tightening and her eyes closing every now and then when the misery seized her
knee. She scorned the support of a cane; canes were
for men, who were often feeble and tottery as early
as their sixties. It took her a good ten minutes to mount
the short staircase that led to the second floor of her
home. She would grasp the banister with one hand
and, with the other, pull her bad leg up beside her
good one, pausing every few steps to catch her breath.
She had to come downstairs backward, and this journey was even more laborious and painful. She got up
before dawn every morning except Sunday the year
around, and she rarely went to bed until after ten
o'clock at night.

Aunt Margery was an active woman who got things
done, and she did not always carry her cross with
meekness and equanimity. She was capable of cursing
her bad leg in good, round words that shocked women
of more pious vocabulary. In her moments of repose,
which were rare enough in a long and arduous lifetime, the gentleness of her face, enhanced by white
hair smoothly parted in the middle, belied the energy
of her body and the strength of her spirit, but her
mouth grew firm, her eyes turned serious or severe,
and her will overcame her handicap when she felt
called upon, as she often did, to take up some burden

too heavy for the shoulders of lesser women, or too formidable for mere menfolks to cope with. Her neighbors often summoned her in an hour of crisis, when there was illness in their homes, or a wife in labor, or a broken bone to set, for she was a natural nurse, renowned for her skill and wisdom and, as we shall see, for many an earthy remedy and forthright practice.

MRS. ALBRIGHT, born Margery Dangler more than a hundred and twenty years ago, in a time of stout-hearted and self-reliant women, came West in a covered wagon driven by her father, during the Presidency of Martin Van Buren, when she was only nine. The Danglers, before their westward venture, had lived in Long Branch, in New Jersey—she always used "in" before a state or county. The family settled for a time in Kokomo, in Indiana, and then retraced its steps to Ohio, to live in Lebanon, in Warren County, Degraff, in Logan County, and Arcanum and Greenville, in Darke County. (Judge Stacy Taylor also lingered awhile in Lebanon, but he had been gone for fifteen years when the Danglers reached that little town.) Shortly after the Civil War, Mrs. Albright came to Columbus, where she spent the last forty years of her life in the north half of a two-family frame house at the corner of Fifth Street and Walnut Alley.

Daguerreotype of a Lady

Her husband had died in Greenville the year the war ended, and she lived with her daughter Belle. When I first knew the neighborhood, at the turn of the century, Fifth Street was paved with cobblestones, and a genial City Council allowed a tall sycamore tree to stand squarely in the middle of the brick sidewalk in front of Mrs. Albright's house, dropping its puffballs in season. On the opposite side of the street, the deep-toned clock in the steeple of Holy Cross Church marked, in quarter hours, the passing of the four decades she lived there. It was a quiet part of town in those days, and the two-story frame house was one of the serene, substantial structures of my infancy and youth, for all its flimsy shabbiness.

Mrs. Albright and her daughter were poor. They took in sewing and washing and ironing, and there was always a roomer in the front room upstairs, but they often found it hard to scrape together ten dollars on the first of the month to pay Mr. Lisle, a landlord out of Horatio Alger, who collected his rents in person, and on foot. The sitting-room carpet was faded and, where hot coals from an iron stove had burned it, patched. There was no hot water unless you heated it on the coal stove in the dark basement kitchen, and light was supplied by what Mrs. Albright called coal-oil lamps. The old house was a firetrap, menaced by burning coal and by lighted lamps carried by ladies of dimming vision, but these perils, like economic facts, are happily lost on the very young. I spent a lot of time there as a child, and I thought it was a wonderful place, different from the dull formality of the ordinary home and in every difference enchanting. The floors were uneven, and various objects were used to keep the doors from closing: a fieldstone, a paving brick that Mrs. Albright had encased in a neat covering made of a piece of carpet, and a conch shell, in which you could hear the roaring of the sea when you held it to your ear. All the mirrors in the house were made of wavy glass, and reflected images in fascinating distortions. In the coal cellar, there was what appeared to be an outside toilet moved inside, miraculously connected with the city sewage system; and the lower sash of one of the windows in the sitting room was flush with the floor—a perfect place to sit and watch the lightning or the snow. Furthermore, the eastern wall of Jim West's livery stable rose less than fifteen feet away from Mrs. Albright's back stoop. Against this wall, there was a trellis of moonflowers, which popped open like small white parachutes at twilight in the summertime, and between the trellis and the stoop you could pull up water from a cistern in the veritable oaken bucket of the song. Over all this presided a great lady, fit, it seemed to me, to be the mother of King Arthur or, what was more, of Dick Slater and Bob Estabrook, captain and lieutenant, respectively, in the nickel novels, "Liberty Boys of '76."

I WAS REMINDED of Mrs. Albright not long ago when I ran across an old query of Emerson's: "Is it not an eminent convenience to have in your town a person who knows where arnica grows, or sassafras, or penny-royal?" Mrs. Albright was skilled in using the pharmacopoeia of the woods and fields. She could have brought the great philosopher dozens of roots and leaves and barks, good for everything from ache to agony and from pukin' spells to a knotted gut. She could also have found in the countryside around Concord the proper plants for the treatment of asthma and other bronchial disturbances. She gathered belladonna, Jimson weed, and digitalis, made a mixture of them, added a solution of saltpetre, put the stuff in a bowl, and set it on fire. The patient simply bent over the bowl and inhaled the fumes. She knew where sour grass grew, which you chew for dyspepsy, and mint, excellent for the naushy, and the slippery elm, whose fragrant inner bark was the favorite demulcent of a hundred years ago—the thing to use for raw throat and other sore tishas.

Mrs. Albright's sitting room was often redolent of spirits of camphor, which could be applied to minor cuts (wet baking soda or cold mashed potato was the stuff for burns); rubbed on the forehead, for headache; used as a gargle or mouthwash, in a mild solution that was never mild enough for me; and sniffed, for attacks of dizzy spells or faintness. Such attacks in Mrs. Albright's own case might have been the result of lack of sleep or overwork, but they were never symptoms of the vapors or other feminine weaknesses. A dab of camphor on the back of each hand acted to break affectionate dogs of the habit of licking. Aunt Margery had owned a long line of affectionate dogs, the first of which, Tuney—named after her brother Tunis, who was later killed at Shiloh by a ramrod fired from a nervous Southern farmboy's musket—made the westward trip from Long Branch in the wagon with the Danglers. The last of the line, Cap, a brindle mongrel who looked like a worn carpetbag, caught the secret of vitality from his indomitable mistress and lived to be sixteen, when Aunt Margery, with heavy heart but steady hand, administered the ether that put a merciful end to the miserable burden of his years. That was the year Mrs. Albright adopted, fed, and reared a newborn mouse, whose mother had been annihilated in a trap set in the cellar to catch the largest rats I have ever seen. I say annihilated because it was surely the deadliest rat-trap in the world, made of a hickory plank, a powerful spring, and a heavy iron ring that could have killed a full-grown cat when it let go. Once, Mrs. Albright cornered in the cellar the ugly patriarch of all rats, who had found a safe

Daguerreotype of a Lady

way to get at the cheese in the trap, and she whammed its life out with a lump of coal.

Shelves in Mrs. Albright's sitting room, where they were handy to get at, held alum, for canker sores; coca butter, for the chest; paregoric, for colic and diarrhea; laudanum, for pain; balsam apples, for poultices; bismuth, for the bowels; magneeshy (carbonate of magnesium), a light, chalky substance, wrapped in blue paper, that was an antacid and a gentle laxative; and calomel and blue mass, regarded by women of Aunt Margery's generation as infallible regulators of the liver. Blue mass came in the form of pills, and she made it by rubbing up metallic mercury with confection of roses. Blue mass and calomel are no longer found in every house, as they were in Mrs. Albright's day, and the free and easy use of paregoric and laudanum, both tinctures of opium, has long been frowned upon by doctors. Your druggist may have heard of balsam apples, alias balsam pears, but unless he is an elderly man, he has probably never seen one. The poultice of today has no source so picturesque as the balsam apple, a warty, oblong West Indian fruit, tropical red or orange in color. It was used for decoration, too, a hundred years ago and more, and looked nice on a window sill with love apples turning from green to red. One legend has it, by the way, that the first American tomato was eaten in 1820, by a gentleman of Salem, in New Jersey, a town not far from Long

The Thurber Album

Branch, where Margery Albright was born ten years after this startling and foolhardy act. I was pleased to find out from my pharmacist, Mr. Blakely, of Crutch & Macdonald's drugstore, in Litchfield, Connecticut, that folks in small towns and rural regions still favor slippery elm for sore throat. No housewife actually strips the bark from the tree nowadays, the way Mrs. Albright did, but slippery-elm lozenges, manufactured by the Henry Thayer Company (founded 1847) from a formula more than ninety years old, are bought by many people in wet or wintry weather. I got a box of the lozenges from Mr. Blakely myself and tried a couple. They smelled faintly like fertilizer to my snobbish city nose, but their taste was bland enough and inoffensive. I am sure they soothe the inflamed tishas of the throat. Mr. Blakely also said that people from seventy to a hundred years old drop in now and then for blue pills when their liver is kicking up. When I asked him about balsam apples, he told me he knew what they were, but he confessed that he had never seen one. It made me feel old and odd, suddenly, as if I were a contemporary of Aunt Margery's who had lived beyond his time.

Aunt Margery held that cold black coffee—not iced, just cold—was fine for torpor, depression of the spirits, and fatigue. She also used it to disguise the taste of castor oil for timid palates, but she drank the oil straight from the bottle herself, in great, gulping

Daguerreotype of a Lady

dollops that made me flinch and shudder when I was a boy. For gas on the stomach, and for gentlemen who had brought out the jugs the night before, she made a fizzing mixture of vinegar, sugar, and baking soda. Soda crackers soaked in water were excellent for thinning out the blood in cases that were not severe enough for leeches or the letting of a vein. If you fell down and broke the skin on your elbow or your knee, she kept a sharp lookout for the appearance of proud flesh. In the event of serious injuries, such as gunshot wounds or axe cuts, you had to beware of gangrum. It was easy enough to identify this awful disease as gangrene, but I was well out of my teens before I discovered what "blue boars" are, or, rather, is. Mrs. Albright had described it as a knotted groin, a symptom of the Black Death, at least one siege of which she had survived somewhere in her travels. The true name is "buboes," from which the word "bubonic" is derived, and Webster supports Mrs. Albright in her definition of the malady as a knotted groin. Then there was cholera morbus, which sounds Asiatic and deadly, but is really no more serious, I found in looking it up the other day, than summer complaint accompanied by green-apple bellyache. If you had the jumpin' toothache, there was nothing better than a large chaw of tobacco. Once, when she was sixteen, Margery Albright was out horseback-riding with a gallant of her acquaintance who bore the gloomy name of Aubrey

Hogwood. A jumpin' toothache nearly knocked her from the saddle, and Hogwood, not knowing what the trouble was, paled and stammered when she demanded his tobacco pouch. ("I says to him, 'Hogwood,' says I, 'hand me your pouch.'") She took a man-sized helping of the weed and chewed it lustily. The toothache went away, and so did Hogwood. A pallid romantic of queasy stomach, he drifted out of the realistic maiden's life. In Greenville, in Darke County, not long afterward, she married one John Albright, a farmer, whom she was destined to pull out of what I will always think of as the Great Fever.

One day in Darke County, Albright—his wife always called him by his last name—staggered in from the fields, pale and ganted—this was her word for "gaunt"—and took to his bed with an imposing fever and fits of the shakes that rattled the china in the cupboard. She was not yet thirty at the time, but already a practical nurse of considerable experience, famous in her neighborhood for her cool presence at sickbeds and her competence as a midwife. She had nursed Albright through a bad case of janders—jaundice to you and me. Her celebrated chills-and-fever medicine, with which she dosed me more than once fifty years after Albright's extremity, failed to do any good. It was a fierce liquid, compounded of the bitterest roots in the world and heavily spiked with quinine, and it seared your throat, burned your stomach, and set your eyes to streaming, but several doses left Albright's forehead still as hot as the bottom of a flatiron. His wife was jubrous—her word for "dubious"—about his chances of pulling through this strange seizure. Albright tossed all night and moaned and whinkered—a verb she made up herself out of "whinny" and "whicker"—and in the morning his temperature had not gone down. She tested his forehead with the flat of her sensitive hand, for she held that thermometers were just pieces of glass used to keep patients' mouths closed while the doctors thought up something to say about conditions that baffled them. The average doctor, in her opinion, was an educated fool, who fussed about a sickroom, fretted the patient, and got in a body's way. The pontifical doctor was likely to be named, in her pungent idiom, a pus-gut, and the talkative doctor, with his fluent bedside manner, was nothing more than a whoop in a whirlwind.

In the afternoon of the second day of the Great Fever, John Albright's wife knew what she had to do. She went out into the pasture and gathered a pailful of sheep droppings, which she referred to in the flattest possible terms. Sheep droppings were not the only thing that Mrs. Albright looked for in the pasture and the barnyard to assist her ministrations as a natural nurse. Now and then, in the case of a stubborn pregnancy, she would cut a quill from a chicken feather, fill it with powdered tobacco, and blow the contents up one nostril of the expectant mother. This would induce a fit of sneezing that acted to dislodge the most reluctant baby. Albright, whinkering on his bed of pain, knew what she was up to this time, and he began to gag even before the terrible broth was brewing on the kitchen stove. She got it down him somehow, possibly with a firm hand behind his neck and one knee on his stomach. I heard the story of this heroic cure—for cure it was—a dozen times. Albright lay about the house for a day or two, retching and protesting, but before the week was out, he was back at his work in the fields. He died, a few years later, of what his widow called a jaggered kidney stone, and she moved, with her daughter, to Columbus, where she worked for a while as housekeeper of the old American House, a hotel that nobody now remembers. She liked to tell about the tidiest lodger she ever had to deal with, the Honorable Stephen A. Douglas, who kept his room neat as a pin and sometimes even made his own bed. He was a little absent-minded, though, and left a book behind him when he checked out. She could not remember the title of the book or what became of it.

MARGERY ALBRIGHT was a woman's woman, who put little faith in the integrity and reliability of the average male. From farmhand to physician, men were the frequent object of her colorful scorn, especially the

Daguerreotype of a Lady

mealymouthed, and the lazy, the dull, and the stupid, who "sat around like Stoughton bottles"—a cryptic damnation that charmed me as a little boy. I am happy to report that Webster has a few words to say about Dr. Stoughton and the bottle that passed into the workaday idiom of the last century. Stoughton, an earlier Dr. Munyon or Father John, made and marketed an elixir of wormwood, germander, rhubarb, orange peel, cascarilla, and aloes. It was used to flavor alcoholic beverages and as a spring tonic for winter-weary folks. It came in a bottle that must have been squat, juglike, and heavy. Unfortunately, my Webster does not have a picture, or even a description, of the old container that became a household word. The dictionary merely says, "To sit, stand, etc., like a Stoughton bottle: to sit, stand, etc., stolidly and dumbly." Mrs. Albright's figure of speech gave the Stoughton bottle turgid action as well as stolid posture. Only a handful of the husbands and fathers she knew were alert or efficient enough to escape the name of Stoughton bottle.

Aunt Margery lived to be eighty-eight years old, surviving, I am constrained to say, the taking of too much blue mass and calomel. She was salivated, as she called it, at least once a year. This, according to my pharmacist, means that she suffered from mercurial poisoning, as the result of an incautious use of calomel. In spite of everything, her strength and vigor held out to the end, and I can remember no single time that she permitted a doctor to look after her. Her daughter Belle held the medical profession in less contempt, and once, in her fiftieth year, after ailing for several months, she went to see a physician in the neighborhood. He was greatly concerned about her condition and called a colleague into consultation. The result of their joint findings was a dark prognosis indeed. The patient was given not more than a year to live. When Mrs. Albright heard the news, she pushed herself out of her rocking chair and stormed about the room, damning the doctors with such violence that her right knee turned in on her like a flamingo's and she had to be helped back to her chair. Belle recovered from whatever it was that was wrong, and when she died, also at the age of eighty-eight, she had outlived by more than fifteen years the last of the two doctors who had condemned her to death. Mrs. Albright never forgave, or long forgot, the mistaken medical men. Every so often, apropos of little or nothing, she would mutter imprecations on their heads. I can remember only two doctors whom she treated with anything approaching respect. She would josh these doctors now and then, when their paths crossed in some sickroom, particularly on the subject of their silly theory that air and water were filled with invisible agencies of disease. This, to a natural nurse who had mastered the simple techniques of barnyard and

Daguerreotype of a Lady

pasture, was palpable nonsense. "How, then," Dr. Rankin asked her once, "do you account for the spread of an epidemic?" "It's just the contagion," said Mrs. Albright. The doctor gave this a moment of studious thought. "It's just possible," he said, "that we may both be right."

Dr. Dunham, one of her favorites—if I may use so strong a word—arrived late at a house on Parsons Avenue on the night of December 8, 1894. I had got there ahead of him, with the assistance of Mrs. Albright. "You might have spared your horse," she snapped when he finally showed up. "We managed all right without you." But she was jubious about something, and she decided to take it up with the doctor. "He has too much hair on his head for a male child," she told him. "Ain't it true that they don't grow up to be bright?" Dr. Dunham gave the matter his usual grave consideration. "I believe that holds good only when the hair is thicker at the temples than this infant's," he said. "By the way, I wouldn't discuss the matter with the mother." Fortunately for my own peace of mind, I was unable to understand English at the time. It was a source of great satisfaction to Margery Albright, and not a little surprise, when it became evident, in apt season, that I was going to be able to grasp my mother tongue and add, without undue effort, two and two. I have had my own jubrous moments, however. There was the time when, at forty-three, I sweated and strained to shove an enormous bed nearer the lamp on a small table, instead of merely lifting the small table and placing it nearer the enormous bed. There have been other significant instances, too, but this is the story of Aunt Margery Albright.

I remember the time in 1905 when the doctors thought my father was dying, and the morning someone was wise enough to send for Aunt Margery. We went to get her in my grandfather's surrey. It was an old woodcut of a morning. I can see Mrs. Albright, dressed in her best black skirt and percale blouse (she pronounced it "percal"), bent over before the oval mirror of a cherrywood bureau, tying the velvet ribbons of an antique bonnet under her chin. People turned to stare at the lady out of Lincoln's day as we helped her to the curb. The carriage step was no larger than the blade of a hoe, and getting Aunt Margery, kneecap and all, into the surrey was an impressive operation. It was the first time she had been out of her own dooryard in several years, but she didn't enjoy the April drive. My father was her favorite person in the world, and they had told her he was dying. Mrs. Albright's encounter with Miss Wilson, the registered nurse on the case, was a milestone in medical history— or, at least, it was for me. The meeting between the starched young lady in white and the bent old woman in black was the meeting of the present and the past, the newfangled and the old-fashioned, the ritualistic

Daguerreotype of a Lady

and the instinctive, and the shock of antagonistic schools of thought clashing sent out cold sparks. Miss Wilson was coolly disdainful, and Mrs. Albright plainly hated her crisp guts. The patient, ganted beyond belief, recognized Aunt Margery, and she began to take over, in her ample, accustomed way. The showdown came on the third day, when Miss Wilson returned from lunch to find the patient propped up in a chair before a sunny window, sipping, of all outrageous things, a cup of cold coffee, held to his lips by Mrs. Albright, who was a staunch believer in getting a patient up out of bed. All the rest of her life, Aunt Margery, recalling the scene that followed, would mimic Miss Wilson's indignation, crying in a shrill voice, "It shan't be done!" waving a clenched fist in the air, exaggerating the young nurse's wrath. "It shan't be done!" she would repeat, relaxing at last with a clutch at her protesting kneecap and a satisfied smile. For Aunt Margery won out, of course, as the patient, upright after many horizontal weeks, began to improve. The doctors were surprised and delighted, Miss Wilson tightly refused to comment, Mrs. Albright took it all in her stride. The day after the convalescent was able to put on his clothes and walk a little way by himself, she was hoisted into the surrey again and driven home. She enjoyed the ride this time. She asked the driver to stop for a moment in front of the marble house at Washington and Town, built by

Dr. S. B. Hartman out of the profits of Peruna, a tonic far more popular than Dr. Stoughton's, even if the bottle it came in never did make Webster's dictionary.

THE OLD FRAME HOUSE in Columbus and the old sycamore tree that shaded it disappeared a long time ago, and a filling station now stands on the northwest corner of Fifth Street and Walnut Alley, its lubricating pit about where Mrs. Albright's garden used to be. The only familiar landmark of my youth is the church across the way, whose deep-toned clock still marks the passing of the quarter hours as tranquilly as ever. When Belle died in 1937, in another house on Fifth Street, the family possessions were scattered among the friends who had looked after her in her final years. I sometimes wonder who got the photograph album that had been promised to me; the card table, bought for a dollar or two before the Civil War, but now surely an antique of price and value; the two brown plaster-of-Paris spaniels that stood on either end of the mantel in Mrs. Albright's bedroom; and the muddy color print that depicted the brave and sturdy Grace Darling pulling away from a yellow lighthouse on her famous errand of mercy. I have no doubt that some of the things were thrown away: the carpet-covered brick, the fieldstone, the green tobacco tin that Aunt Margery used for a button box, and the ragbag filled with silk cuttings for the crazy quilts she made.

Daguerreotype of a Lady

Who could have guessed that a writer living in the East would cherish such objects as these, or that he would have settled for one of the dark and wavy mirrors, or the window sash in the sitting room that was flush with the floor?

I sometimes wonder, too, what has happened to the people who used to call so often when Aunt Margery was alive. I can remember all the tenants of the front room upstairs, who came and went: Vernie, who clerked in a store; the fabulous Doc Marlowe, who made and sold Sioux Liniment and wore a ten-gallon hat with kitchen matches stuck in the band; the blonde and mysterious Mrs. Lane, of the strong perfume and the elegant dresses; Mr. Richardson, a guard at the penitentiary, who kept a gun in his room; and a silent, thin, smiling man who never revealed his business and left with his rent two weeks in arrears. I remember Dora and Sarah Koontz, daughters of a laborer, who lived for many years in the other half of the two-family house, and the visitors who dropped in from time to time: Mr. Pepper and his daughter Dolly, who came to play cards on summer evenings; Mrs. Straub, who babbled of her children—her Clement and her Minna; Joe Chickalilli, a Mexican rope thrower; and Professor Fields, a Stoughton bottle if there ever was one, who played the banjo and helped Doc Marlowe sell the liniment that Mrs. Albright and Belle put up in bottles; and the Gammadingers and their brood, who lived on a farm in the Hocking Valley. Most of them were beholden to Mrs. Albright for some service or other in time of trouble, and they all adored her.

WHEN MARGERY ALBRIGHT took to her bed for the last time—the bed in the front room downstairs, where she could hear people talking and life stirring in the street outside her window—she gave strict orders that she was not to be "called back." She had seen too much of that, at a hundred bedsides, and she wanted to die quietly, without a lot of unseemly fuss over the natural ending of a span of nearly ninety complete and crowded years. There was no call, she told her daughter, to summon anybody. There was nothing anybody could do. A doctor would just pester her, and she couldn't abide one now. Her greatest comfort lay in the knowledge that her plot in Green Lawn Cemetery had been paid for, a dollar at a time, through the years, and that there was money enough for a stone marker tucked away in a place her daughter knew about. Mrs. Albright made Belle repeat to her the location of this secret and precious cache. Then she gave a few more final instructions and turned over in bed, pulling her bad leg into a comfortable position. "Hush up!" she snapped when her daughter began to cry. "You give a body the fidgets."

Women who were marked for death, Aunt Mar-

gery had often told me, always manifested, sooner or
later, an ominous desire to do something beyond the
range of their failing strength. These ladies in the
very act of dying fancied, like Verdi's Violetta, that
life was returning in full and joyous tide. They wanted
to sit up in bed and comb their hair, or alter a dress,
or bathe the cat, or change the labels on the jam jars.
It was an invariable sign that the end was not far off.
Old Mrs. Dozier, who had insisted on going to the
piano to play "Abide with Me," collapsed with a dis-
cordant jangle on the keys and was dead when
they carried her back to the bed. Mrs. Albright's
final urge, with which her ebbing sense no doubt
sternly dealt, might easily have been to potter about in
her garden, since it was coming summer and the flowers needed constant attention. It was a narrow plot, occasionally enlivened with soil from the country, that
began with an elephant-ear near the rickety wooden
fence in front and extended to the trellis of moonflowers against the wall of Jim West's stable. It was
further shaded by her own house and the Fenster-
makers', and it caught only stingy glimpses of the sun,
but, to the wonder of the jubrous, it sustained for forty
summers Canterbury bells and bluebells, bleeding
hearts and fuchsias, asters and roses. There were tall
stalks of asparagus, raised for ornament, and castor-
oil plants six feet high (I doubt that she made the
castor oil that she disguised in coffee for timid palates

and drank neat from the bottle herself, but I have no doubt she could have). "This garden," said Dr. Sparks, pastor of the old Third Street Methodist Church, one day, "is a testament of faith." "It takes faith, and it takes work, and it takes a lot of good, rich manure," said Mrs. Albright, far and away the most distinguished manurist of her time.

Since there had to be services of some kind, in accordance with a custom that irked her, Mrs. Albright would have preferred a country parson, who rode a horse in any weather and could lend a hand at homely chores, if need be. She liked what she called a man of groin, who could carry his proper share of the daily burden and knew how to tell a sow from a sawbuck. City ministers, in her estimation, were delicate fellows, given to tampering with the will of God, and with the mysteries of life after death, which the Almighty would have cleared up for people Himself if He had had a mind to. It was her fancy that urban reverends were inclined to insanity, because of their habit of studying. "Studying," in Mrs. Albright's language, meant that form of meditation in which the eyes are lifted up. The worst cases let their gaze slowly follow, about a room, the juncture of ceiling and walls, and once a pastor developed this symptom, he was in imminent danger of going off his worshipful rocker. Such parsons, whether they studied or not, made Mrs. Albright uneasy, except for the Reverend Stacy

Daguerreotype of a Lady

Matheny, a first cousin of my mother's. He had been born on a farm in Fairfield County, and he knew how to hitch a horse, split a rail, and tell a jaybird from a bootjack. Mrs. Albright wanted him to read her funeral service because he was a man of few words, and he would get it over with and not whinker all afternoon, keeping people away from their jobs. Aunt Margery never discussed religion with me or with anyone else. She seemed to take it for granted that the Lord would find a fitting place in Heaven for women who devoted their lives to good works, and she let it go at that. The men would have to save their own souls, and the Devil take the hindmost.

THE REVEREND STACY MATHENY compared the late Margery Albright to the virtuous woman of proverbs, who rose while it was yet night, worked willingly with her hands, and ate not the bread of idleness. The original lady of the tribute was, of course, far richer in wordly goods than Mrs. Albright, whose clothing was not silk and purple, but in trait and toil and temper they were rare and similar examples of that noble breed of women the French call *brave et travailleuse*. I wished that some closer student of Aunt Margery could have taken over those final rites, whose formality would have annoyed the great lady as much as the lugubrious faces of her friends and neighbors. Somebody should have told how she snatched up a pair of scissors one day and cut a hornet in two when it lighted on the head of a sleeping baby; and how she took an axe and chopped off the head of a savage outlaw cat that killed chickens, attacked children, and, blackest sin of all, disturbed the sleep of a woman patient; and about the time she whipped off her calico blouse, put it over the eyes of a frightened horse, and led him out of a burning barn while the menfolks, at a safe distance, laughed at her corset cover and cheered her courage. But it would have taken all afternoon to do even faint justice to the saga of Mrs. Albright, born Margery Dangler, more than a hundred and twenty years ago, in Long Branch, in New Jersey, who departed this earthly scene June 6, 1918, in the confident hope—as old epitaphs used to say—of the blessed resurrection and the life eternal. It seemed to me, standing there in the dim parlor of the old frame house, that something as important as rain had gone out of the land.

The services came to a close with the singing of "No Night There" by two tearful women, who sang it as only middle-aged Methodist females in Ohio can sing a hymn—upper register all the way, nasal, tremulous, and loud. Mrs. Albright, I reflected, would enjoy the absence of night in Paradise only because everlasting light would give her more time to look after people and to get things done. I still like to believe, after all these years, that chalcedony is subject to cleaning, and that a foolish angel falls now and then and breaks a wing, for glory, as mere reward of labors ended, would make Margery Albright uncomfortable and sad. I trust that Providence has kept this simple truth in mind.

CHAPTER SEVEN

Gentleman from Indiana

O NE DAY in the summer of 1900, my father was
riding a lemon-yellow bicycle that went to
pieces in a gleaming and tangled moment, its cross-
bar falling, the seat sagging, the handle bars buckling,
the front wheel hitting a curb and twisting the tire
from the rim. He had to carry the wreck home amidst
laughter and cries of "Get a horse!" He was a good
rider and the first president of the Columbus Bicycle
Club, but he was always mightily plagued by the
mechanical. He was also plagued by the manufactured, which takes in a great deal more ground. Knobs
froze at his touch, doors stuck, lines fouled, the de-
tachable would not detach, the adjustable would not
adjust. He could rarely get the top off anything, and
he was forever trying to unlock something with the
key to something else. In 1908, trying to fix the snap

lock of the door to his sons' rabbit pen, he succeeded only after getting inside the cage, where he was imprisoned for three hours with six Belgian hares and thirteen guinea pigs. He had to squat through this ordeal, a posture he elected to endure after attempting to rise and bashing his derby against the chicken wire across the top of the pen.

I am not sure that my father's long, thin face, with its aquiline nose, was right for a derby at any age, but he began wearing one in hard-hat weather when he was only twenty, and he didn't give up the comic, unequal struggle, for the comfort of a felt hat, until the middle nineteen twenties, when he was in his fifties. His daily journeys to the cellar in the winter to stoke the furnace when his three sons were small became a ritual we learned to await with alarm and excitement. He always wore his derby into the cellar, often when he was in bathrobe and slippers, and he always crushed it against one of the furnace pipes, and he always said, "Damn that thing!" or nearly always. Perhaps half a dozen times in his life, when the tortured hat was knocked to the floor and rolled in the coal dust, he used "Oh, well, then, goddarn that thing!" the blackest oath he was capable of. The derby got dented in horse cabs when he climbed in or out, and later against the roofs of automobiles. Since my father was just under six feet, the hat was readily cuffed off by maliciously low doorways and the iron framework

of open awnings. At least three times, in my fascinated
view, sudden, impish winds at the corner of Broad and
High blew the derby off his head and sent it bock-
flopping across the busy and noisy intersection, my
father pursuing it slowly, partly crouched, his arms
spread out as if he were shooing a flock of mischievous and unpredictable chicks. My mother has fortunately preserved a photograph of him wearing one
of his derbies, taken about the time of the Spanish-
American War. It shows him sitting on a bench in a
park, surrounded by his wife and infant sons, looking
haunted and harassed in a derby with an unusually
large and blocky crown. In this study he somehow
suggests Sherlock Holmes trying to disguise himself
as a cabman and being instantly recognized by the
far from astute Dr. Watson, rounding a corner and
crying, "Great heavens, Holmes, you've muffed it,
old fellow! You look precisely like yourself in an
enormous bowler."

Charles L. Thurber—the initial was for Leander,
a name that somehow enchanted his mother, but dismayed his bride, and he later changed it to Lincoln—
was born in Indiana, a state known principally today,
I suppose, as the birthplace of Cole Porter and the
late Wendell Willkie. To my father, looking fondly
westward from Columbus, Ohio, where he spent most
of his life, it was the romantic land of the moonlit
Wabash, the new-mown hay and the sycamores, the

Gentleman from Indiana

house of the thousand candles, and the Lockerbie Street of James Whitcomb Riley. He grew up in Indianapolis and more than once saw Riley plain. I don't know how much truth there was in the rumors of the poet's dissipation, but my father worried about it, and when he was eighteen, he wrote to a friend, "Poor James Whitcomb Riley! He is, it seems, on the down track. It is a pitiful thing for so bright and lovable a man as he to become such a slave to drink. This is his home, you know, and he is loved here by everyone. He is our Hoosier Burns." It was a matter of early awe to me that my father knew most of the Riley poems by heart and could actually recite all of "An Old Sweetheart of Mine." Riley's celebration of the man of small worldly fortune, symbolized by the hollyhock as against the fancy roses that grow in the gardens of the rich, must have had its appeal for a youth who had gone to work while still in short pants to support a mother early widowed and always in uncertain health. My father's father is a dim figure in the annals of the family, a gentleman of retiring nature and private thought, who was thrown from a horse on a lonely ride and killed in the year 1867, when his only child was a few months old, leaving his widow to teach school for a living until frailty condemned her to a life of rocking-chair contemplation. Her son began by selling morning papers in Indianapolis, often getting up while the moon was still over the town. He had no other relatives to turn to. The Thurbers of his father's generation had originated in Boston and Providence, but most of them set out for the West when they were young, ending up in a dozen different states. My grandfather, on his way to hunt for gold in California, had fallen in love with Indiana and settled there.

Charley Thurber had wanted to be a lawyer, but he didn't have the time or the money to go to law school. When he was not yet twenty-one he was appointed to the staff of an Indiana governor. One of his young colleagues was an ambitious man with the unusual name of Kenesaw Mountain Landis. Many years later, my father ran into him at a ballpark, and they shook hands and talked briefly and vaguely of the good old days. Before the practice of law had attracted my father, he had toyed with the idea of a stage career, partly because his closest friend, a youngster named Alvah Currie, wanted to go on the stage, and finally did. Once, when they were both twelve, they waited at the stage door of an Indianapolis theatre to see the great Joseph Jefferson in person. The vigil proved too much for the restless Alvah, but his companion held on for three hours and was rewarded at last by a handshake from the Master, who later sent him a signed photograph and a letter of advice and caution that ran to at least two hundred words. My father kept the letter in mint condition until it was burned up, circa 1930, in one of the fires we were always having. As late as 1890, he still wanted to go on the stage. In a letter to my mother, written that year, he told her he was going to play the part of Mark Tapley at the "Dickens Social on Valentine's night," and he said he was reading "Martin Chuzzlewit" to be "prepared for the ordeal." To this he added, "I am also reading 'Hamlet' and the daily papers." A few years later, he prudently abandoned his dream of a theatrical career, but he may have had a nostalgic pang or two the night in 1907 when he took me to see his old friend Alvah in "York State Folks." We had the front box on the right downstairs to ourselves, and my first big thrill in the theatre was when Mr. Currie, in the second act, crossed to a mantelpiece down left, fiddled with something on it, and said out of the corner of his mouth, "Hello, Cholly." That's all I remember about the old play.

What my father turned to, finally, was politics. Presidential campaigns, in the rough-and-tumble years after the Civil War, fascinated him at an early age. A great-aunt of mine once told me that in 1884 Charley had marched most of the night in a rowdy procession on behalf of James G. Blaine, coming home early in the morning resplendent with Blaine badges and hoarse from shouting defiance of Cleveland. She said he slept lightly after he got to bed, and now and then mumbled in his dreams, and once

cheered aloud without waking up. He was only seventeen that year. Three days before the big parade, he
had written his sweetheart a love letter in which he
said, "Politics is here, as in Columbus, and I guess
everywhere else, the main and almost only topic discussed. When you answer this, Blaine will be the
President-elect, unless you are prompt. Remember
this and see how good a prophet I am." His sweetheart was a Columbus girl, and when he married her
and moved there in 1892, he found himself plump in
the middle of the loudest and toughest kind of American political activity. He ran for Clerk of the Courts in
1900, and once or twice for State Representative but,
although he wasn't an organization candidate, he was
defeated each time by only a narrow margin. Ohio
is a state notorious for its political machines and its
"slates" made up of gentlemen of pull and promise
who know how to play ball. My father was not a
machine man. He wasn't even a politician, and it's
kind of hard to explain why he stayed in politics, but,
as they say in the theatre of a part in a bad play, it was
a job. It was, in fact, a lot of jobs. He was on the staff
of two Ohio governors in the eighteen-nineties; he
was secretary to a Columbus mayor, who gave him an
enormous brass key to the city, which I envied;
around the turn of the century he went to West Point
with a Congressional committee that was investigating
the death of a plebe whose hazing had consisted of

drinking the entire contents of a bottle of tabasco sauce. He was secretary of the commission to recodify federal statutes during the first two years Theodore Roosevelt was in the White House; and he was state organizer for the Bull Moose Party in Ohio during the flamboyant Presidential campaign of 1912. The governors, and the other executives he worked for, depended on his ability to write effective speeches and tactful letters and to deal with difficult men.

I was familiar, even as a toddler, with Ohio political names, large and small—Nash, Asa Bushnell, Boss Cox, Mark Hanna, McKinley, Charles Dewey Hilles, Gongwer, Gerrish, Foraker, Farquhar, Burba, and a hundred others. As I grew older, I marvelled at the coming of President Harding out of the nowhere into the here—out of the smoke-filled room, out of the magician's hat of Harry Daugherty. Growing up in a state capital, you see all the peculiar characters who are born of struggle for office. There was Governor Willis, who hit the front pages after eating forty-eight chicken livers at a large picnic somewhere. There was the honest and colorful Vic Donahey, who said "protégé" for "progeny," roared that Bill Bryan had the guts of a grizzly bear, told a purist, "When I say 'ain't,' brother, I mean 'ain't,'" and once in my presence, broke up a long stogie into four parts, stuffed it into his mouth, and chewed it. There was the late Randolph Walton, a hound-voiced spellbinder who up into his seventies took a snow bath in his yard once every winter, clad only in shorts. There was the honorable lieutenant governor of the state, who introduced the garterless sock into the State House and who wore a shirt equipped with gold collar buttons but no collar. There was the local Republican leader who, with a tactful eye on the feminine vote, always respectfully referred to prostitutes as "whore ladies."

I remember the politicians gathering for caucus or convention in the lobby of the old Neil House, where Charles Dickens used to stop a hundred years ago. They smoked cigars, chewed unlighted stogies, began all sentences with "Look," or "Listen," or "Let me tell you," tapped one another on the chest with argumentative index fingers, shook hands a lot, laughed easily and loudly. Now and then one of them would drop into a chair and slowly smoke a cigar, with the Ohio look in his eyes—the dreamy, faraway expression of a man richly meditating on cheering audiences, landslides, and high office. My father would move among them not as an integral part of the noisy and smoky scene but as a keenly interested onlooker at a spectacle. He liked a good, hard campaign, since he had a keen love of competition, but usually at the end, whoever won, he was left exhausted and disillusioned of the hope he once had that the American Way was destined to produce a breed of men selflessly devoted to the ideal and practice of good government. He actually believed a metamorphosis might result from the florid Presidential campaign of Teddy Roosevelt forty years ago.

Ohio headquarters of the Progressive Party in 1912 were high up in the Huntington Bank Building, and the front windows of my father's office gave a clear view of the State House, across the street, squatting in the middle of its comfortable acreage. One of the candidates for a state office used to drop in not so much to find out how things were shaping up as to sit in a chair spang in front of a window, stare at the State House, smoke a cigar, and dream for an hour or two of his coming election, with the Ohio look glowing in his eyes. In making speeches, this gentleman would double his right fist and strike it into the palm of his left hand just at the moment when he assured his listeners that he was going to put an end to the dark double-dealings of the Republicans and Democrats by "cutting the umbilical cord," which, as I got it, was the lifeline that nurtured the unborn conspiracies of the two major parties. He pounded his hand and threatened to cut the umbilical cord all during the campaign. Now and then there appeared at headquarters a small man named John D. Fackler, a kind of Ohio LaGuardia, who was making things hum for Roosevelt in Cleveland and around the state generally. Walter F. Brown, who later became Postmaster General, after he was welcomed back into the Republican fold, was commander-in-chief of the Ohio forces at Armageddon, and his air of cold and quiet confidence balanced the genial ardor of the vigorous Fackler. My father, as in every campaign he got into, did most of the actual work.

At the height of the Battle for the Lord, Hiram Johnson, the Lord's candidate for Vice-President, came to Columbus. My father was assigned the task of seeing that the great man was made comfortable. Perhaps it was the weather, or indigestion, or the strain of travel. At any rate, Johnson was irritable. He snapped orders and voiced complaints. The toilet in the bathroom of his hotel started to flush at one point and would not stop, diluting the force of his pronouncements. My father had expected to meet a man immune to commonplace exacerbation, humble in his high mission, perhaps a little exalted by the nobility of his cause. Instead he met a candidate in a petulant mood. When the last gun was silenced at Armageddon, the state organizer of the Bull Moose Party got six dozen yellow Mongol pencils, a few typewriter ribbons, and several boxes of stationery. Charles L. Thurber had come a long way in disillusionment since the night in 1884 when he cheered in his sleep for the white plume of Henry of Navarre.

The interior of the Ohio State House is as darkly morose as its outside is heavily aggressive. It is almost impossible to find the governor's office, or any other, unless you have been accustomed for years to the monumental maze of corridors and rooms. Even the largest rooms seem to have been tucked away in great, cool, unexpected corners by an architect with an elephantine sense of humor. Once, when I was ten, I was lost for an hour in the stony labyrinth, looking for my father. At the time, he was keeping things in order in the pressroom, as secretary for the correspondents who covered the State House—Jim Faulkner, Ben Allen, Allen Beach, Ber Williamson, and a dozen more men of light reverence and sharp tongue, whom I held to be the highest development of the Ohio male I had yet encountered. In dull political weather, they had fun getting some of the more naive legislators to introduce bills banning short skirts for women or requiring cows to wear red lanterns attached to their tails. They joined gallery spectators in the bobwhite whistle the year the servants of the people solemnly debated the right of the quail to be protected as a songbird. When the bill was finally passed, one newspaperman, whose name I have unfortunately forgotten, wired his paper, "Out of the frying pan into the choir." I took to hanging around the pressroom as the years went on, and when, in the early nineteen-twenties, I briefly covered the State House for a Columbus paper, my highest ambition as a boy was realized; I became a member of the Ohio Legislative Correspondents Association. My father and I attended its annual banquet one year; he was an honorary member, and, I think, the only one. The meeting, held in the banquet room of a hotel, got off to a planned and orderly start, complete with toast-master and a program of speeches. Discipline did not last long. It ended precisely at the moment when the toastmaster, introducing one of the speakers, got into but couldn't get out of "formerly president of the Ohio Legislative Correspondents Association and now secretary of the Ohio Manufacturers Associa-tion." The meeting, from then on beautifully infor-mal, broke up at a late hour. At the door, as we filed out, a young reporter patted everybody's pockets, searching for his lost silver flask. My father, who never took a drink, submitted quietly to the frisking. Outside in the street, he discovered that one of his friends was missing. We found him standing all alone at the long and dishevelled banquet table, grimly finishing a trib-ute, begun in bedlam an hour before, to the memory of one of the members who had died during the year. My father was never a man to lecture the wayward. The next day, all he said to me was, "It was a daisy, wasn't it?" and let it go at that.

Everybody's father is a great, good man, someone has said, and mine was no exception. There was never, I truly believe, a purely selfish day in his life. He was sorrowfully aware, from twilight to twilight, that most men, and all children, are continuously caught in one predicament or another, and his shoulder was always ready to help lift a man's cross, or a child's, when it became too heavy to be carried alone. He tried to keep his own plights and griefs to himself, for he hated to bother anybody with his troubles, but everybody wanted him to be happy and everybody did his best to help. When he was secretary to the mayor of Columbus (he often served as unofficial acting mayor) one of his colleagues, in the midst of a political speech, suddenly digressed to talk about my father. "Charley Thurber," he said, remembering some old thoughtfulness, "is the most beloved man in the City Hall." This was conceivably the first time that adjective had ever been publicly used by a municipal employee in any American town.

My father never held a tennis racket or a golf club, and he couldn't kick a football or catch a swift pitch, but he bowled whenever he got a chance—tenpins, duckpins, candlepins, cocked hat, and quintet, a difficult game, the rules for which I was told he had helped to make up. His highest score in tenpins, 269, is the mark of a superior bowler, but he bowled for relaxation and exercise, and not from addiction. He was addicted to contests, contests of any kind. Although he couldn't draw very well, I remember his drawing the Pears' Soap baby, fifty years ago, in a contest for the best pen-and-ink reproduction of the infant in the famous advertisement. He would estimate the number of beans in an enormous jar, write essays, make up slogans, find the hidden figures in trick drawings, write the last line of an unfinished jingle or limerick, praise a product in twenty-five words or fewer, get thousands of words out of a trade name, such as, for recent example, Planters Peanuts. But it was on proverb contests and book- and play-title contests, run by newspapers, that he worked hardest. Over a period of fifty years, he won a trip to the St. Louis World's Fair, a diamond ring, a victrola, two hundred dollars' worth of records, and many cash prizes, the largest, fifteen hundred dollars, as first prize in a proverb contest.

Charles L. Thurber was a man of careful method and infinite patience. Once, when the titles of books and plays were printed so close together in a contest catalogue as to be confusing, he cut them out and pasted them on separate strips of cardboard—two thousand separate strips of cardboard. In this way he could compare them, one at a time, with each of the contest drawings, of which there were fifty or more, making at least a hundred thousand permutations in all. He liked to find the less obvious answers: "The Coming of the Tide" for a picture of two youths racing head on and shoulder to shoulder; "Richard the Third" for a drawing of three men on a bench, identified in balloons, from left to right, as Tom, Harry, and Dick. The idiotic answer that paid off on the three

Gentleman from Indiana

men was "Idle Thoughts of an Idle Fellow." Unfair and ridiculous answers are usually picked in every title or proverb contest for five or six key drawings. This is done to prevent experts like Charles L. Thurber from winning all the major prizes in every contest. My father never seemed to get on to this strategy of deceit. He approached every contest with the same light in his eye, confident that the cleverest and subtlest answers would win. His severest disappointment came in 1905, in a proverb contest conducted by the Pittsburgh *Gazette*. I was only ten, but I still remember his anguish over the answer to a drawing showing the figures of a man and a woman in a balloon: "As well out of the world as out of the fashion." The figures were tiny and murky, and he had examined them a hundred times under a hand microscope without detecting that they were dressed any differently from other men and women of the period. In his sixties he gave up his strenuous hobby, reluctantly, but soon decided to invent some contests of his own, to occupy his evening hours. He promptly sold several of them to large newspapers in the Middle West, but when one contest manager suggested that they set up a phony winner and divide the first prize money three ways, he stalked out of the man's office, and his work on contests ended that day. He was easily the most honest man I have ever known.

My father wouldn't learn to drive a car, and he

was always uneasy in one. Nobody could outwalk him. He would even go on foot to Ohio Stadium for football games, a distance of several miles from our house. When he was visiting me in New York one time, he asked me how long it would take to walk from New York to Litchfield, Connecticut. I told him I didn't know about him—he was in his sixties—but it would take me a month and a half. He looked a little wistful, but he gave up the preposterous idea and settled for a jaunt with me up Fifth Avenue from Washington Square to 110th Street, pointing out on the way a hundred things I would not have noticed myself, including a small bronze tablet bearing the Gettysburg Address, which you will still see, if you look sharp, on the facade of a building in the Twenties. If there was a dog on a roof, a potted plant on a window sill high above the street, a misspelled word in a sign, a dime on the sidewalk, his practiced eye took it in. He gave the same scrupulous attention to anyone who had something to say or something to argue. He listened intently to conversation for the unusual statement or the remarkable fact. He was never guilty of that glibbest of human faults, the habit of quick and automatic refutation. He could remember a speech or lecture almost as accurately as if he had taken it down in shorthand. If he had a hard day ahead, or an imposing task to face, he would get up early and bathe, singing, off key, "My Bonnie Lies Over the Ocean," or an old song, in the Riley dialect,

Gentleman from Indiana

called "Just One Girl." Frustration, indignation, or
deep annoyance would send him to his bureau, where
I used to watch him vigorously brushing his hair for
at least five minutes with a pair of military brushes.
When the world pressed in too strongly upon him,
he would take a train to Indianapolis and walk along
Lockerbie Street. My mother still has a letter he
wrote her from there when he was twenty-one, in
which he said, "I feel as sure that you and I will be
married as I do that we will some time end our existence here." In this letter, in which he told her that
he would be in Columbus the following Sunday, he
wrote, "I would be delighted beyond expression to
take you to church." The church he took her to was
the Methodist Church near my grandfather's house,
and soon afterward he and Mary Agnes Fisher were
married there. He ended his existence in Columbus
fifty years later, at the age of seventy-two. Among the
hundreds of letters my mother received was one from
John McNulty. "Charley Thurber," he wrote at the
end, "was a good-minded man."

The day my daughter was born, October 7, 1931,
my telegram from New York was handed to my father
while he was presiding as toastmaster at a Riley Day
banquet in Columbus. God and Nature had neatly
conspired that the birthday of his idol (October 7,
1849) and of his only grandchild should be happily
conjoined. For this small and whimsical favor I am
deeply indebted to Them both.

CHAPTER EIGHT

Lavender with a Difference

BELINDA WOOLF telephoned my mother at the Southern Hotel in Columbus one morning three years ago, and apologized, in a faintly familiar voice, for never having run in to call on her. Something always seemed to turn up, she declared, to keep her from dropping by for a visit, and she was sorry. "I've thought of you, Mrs. Thurber," said Belinda. "I've thought of you every day since I worked for you on Champion Avenue. It's been a long time, hasn't it?" It certainly had. Belinda Woolf was only twenty-three years old when she came to work for us as cook in the Spring of 1899, and she was seventy-three when she finally got around to calling her former employer. Exactly half a century had gone by since my mother had heard her voice. Belinda had thought of telephoning for more than eighteen thousand days but, as she indicated, more than eighteen thousand things had turned up to prevent her.

About a year after Belinda's appearance out of the past, I went to Columbus, and my mother and I drove out to see her. She is now the wife of Joe Barlow, master carpenter of the Neil House, where Charles Dickens used to stay, during his western trips a hundred years ago. In fifty years Belinda had not wandered very far. She was living only two blocks from our old house on South Champion Avenue. The weather was warm and we sat on the verandah and talked about a night in 1899 that we all remembered. It was past midnight, according to an old clock in the attic of my memory, when Belinda suddenly flung open a window of her bedroom and fired two shots from a .32-calibre revolver at the shadowy figure of a man skulking about in our backyard. Belinda's shooting frightened off the prowler and aroused the family. I was five years old, going on six, at the time, and I had thought that only soldiers and policemen were allowed to have guns. From then on I stood in awe, but not in fear, of the lady who kept a revolver under her pillow. "It was a lonesome place, wasn't it?" said Belinda, with a sigh, "way out there at the end of nowhere." We sat for awhile without talking, thinking about the lonesome place at the end of nowhere.

No. 921 South Champion Avenue is just another house now, in a long row of houses, but when we lived there, in 1899 and 1900, it was the last house on the street. Just south of us the avenue dwindled to a wood road that led into a thick grove of oak and walnut trees, long since destroyed by the southward march of asphalt. Our nearest neighbor on the north was fifty yards away, and across from us was a country meadow that ticked with crickets in the summertime and turned yellow with goldenrod in the fall. Living on the edge of town, we rarely heard footsteps at night, or carriage wheels, but the darkness, in every season, was deepened by the lonely sound of locomotive whistles. I no longer wonder, as I did when I was six, that Aunt Mary Van York, arriving at dusk for her first visit to us, looked about her disconsolately, and said to my mother, "Why in the world do you want to live in this godforsaken place, Mary?"

Almost all my memories of the Champion Avenue house have as their focal point the lively figure of my mother. I remember her tugging and hauling at a burning mattress and finally managing to shove it out a bedroom window onto the roof of the front porch, where it smoldered until my father came home from work and doused it with water. When he asked his wife how the mattress happened to catch fire, she told him the peculiar truth (all truths in that house were peculiar)—that his youngest son, Robert, had set it on fire with a buggy whip. It seemed he had lighted the lash of the whip in the gas grate of the nursery and applied it to the mattress. I also have a vivid memory of the night my mother was alone in the house with her three small sons and set the oil-splashed bowl of a kerosene lamp on fire, trying to light the wick, and herded all of us out of the house, announcing that it was going to explode. We children waited across the street in high anticipation, but the spilled oil burned itself out and, to our bitter disappointment, the house did not go up like a skyrocket to scatter colored balloons among the stars. My mother claims that my brother William, who was seven at the time, kept crying, "Try it again, Mama, try it again," but she is a famous hand at ornamenting a tale, and there is no way of telling whether he did or not.

My brightest remembrance of the old house goes back to the confused and noisy second and last visit of Aunt Mary, who had cut her first visit short because she hated our two dogs—Judge, an irritable old pug, and Sampson, a restless water spaniel—and they hated her. She had snarled at them and they had growled at her all during her stay with us, and not even my mother remembers how she persuaded the old lady to come back for a weekend, but she did, and, what is more, she cajoled Aunt Mary into feeding "those dreadful brutes" the evening she arrived.

In preparation for this seemingly simple act of household routine, my mother had spent the afternoon gathering up all the dogs of the neighborhood, in advance of Aunt Mary's appearance, and putting them in the cellar. I had been allowed to go with her on her wonderful forays, and I thought that we were going to keep all the sixteen dogs we rounded up. Such an adventure does not have to have logical point or purpose in the mind of a six-year-old, and I accepted as a remarkable but natural phenomenon my mother's sudden assumption of the stature of Santa Claus.

She did not always let my father in on her elaborate pranks, but he came home that evening to a house heavy with tension and suspense, and she whispered to him the peculiar truth that there were a dozen and a half dogs in the cellar, counting our Judge and Sampson. "What are you up to now, Mame?" he asked her, and she said she just wanted to see Aunt Mary's face when the dogs swarmed up into the kitchen. She could not recall where she had picked up all of the dogs, but I remembered, and still do, that we had imprisoned the Johnsons' Irish terrier, the Eiseles' shepherd, and the Mitchells' fox terrier, among others. "Well, let's get it over with, then," my father said nervously. "I want to eat dinner in peace, if that is possible."

The big moment finally arrived. My mother, full of smiles and insincerity, told Aunt Mary that it would relieve her of a tedious chore—and heaven knows, she added, there were a thousand steps to take in that big house—if the old lady would be good enough to set down a plate of dog food in the kitchen at the head of the cellar stairs and call Judge and Sampson to their supper. Aunt Mary growled and grumbled, and consigned all dogs to the fires of hell, but she grudgingly took the plate, and carried it to the kitchen, with the Thurber family on her heels. "Heavenly days!" cried Aunt Mary. "Do you make a ceremony out of feeding these brutes?" She put the plate down and reached for the handle of the door.

None of us has ever been able to understand why bedlam hadn't broken loose in the cellar long before this, but it hadn't. The dogs were probably so frightened by their unique predicament that their belligerence had momentarily left them. But when the door opened and they could see the light of freedom and smell the odor of food, they gave tongue like a pack of hunting hounds. Aunt Mary got the door halfway open and the bodies of three of the largest dogs pushed it the rest of the way. There was a snarling, barking, yelping swirl of yellow and white, black and tan, gray and brindle as the dogs tumbled into the kitchen, skidded on the linoleum, sent the food flying from the plate, and backed Aunt Mary into a corner. "Great God Almighty!" she screamed. "It's a dog factory!" She was only five feet tall, but her counterattack was swift and terrible. Grabbing a broom, she opened the back door and the kitchen windows, and began to beat and flail at the army of canines, engaged now in half a dozen separate battles over the scattered food. Dogs flew out the back door and leaped through the windows, but some of them ran upstairs, and three or four others hid under sofas and chairs in the parlor. The indignant snarling and cursing of Judge and Sampson rose above even the laughter of my mother and the delighted squeals of her children. Aunt Mary whammed her way from room to room, driving dogs ahead of her. When the last one had departed and the upset house had been put back in order, my father said to his wife, "Well, Mame, I hope you're satisfied." She was.

Aunt Mary, toward the end of her long life, got the curious notion that it was my father and his sons, and not my mother, who had been responsible for the noisy flux of "all those brutes." Years later, when we visited the old lady on one of her birthdays, she went over the story again, as she always did, touching it up with distortions and magnifications of her own. Then she looked at the male Thurbers in slow, rueful turn, sighed deeply, gazed sympathetically at my mother, and said, in her hollowest tone, "Poor Mary!"

ONLY A FEW months after poor Mary borrowed the neighbors' dogs, she "bought" the Simonses' house. It was a cold, blocky house, not far from ours, and its owner had been trying to sell it for a long time. The thing had become a standing joke among the Friole-

Lavender with a Difference

ras, a club of young married couples to which the Simonses and my father and mother belonged. It was generally believed that Harry and Laura would never get the big, damp place off their hands. Then, late one dark afternoon, a strange and avid purchaser showed up. It was my mother, wearing dark glasses, her hair and eyebrows whitened with flour, her cheeks lightly shadowed with charcoal to make them look hollow, and her upper front teeth covered with the serrated edge of a soda cracker. On one side of her, as she pressed the doorbell of the Simonses' house, stood a giggling cousin of hers, named Belle Cook, and I was on her other side; we were there to prevent a prolonged scrutiny of the central figure of our trio. Belle was to pose as my mother's daughter, and I was to be Belle's son. Simons had never met Miss Cook, and my mother was confident that he wouldn't recognize me. His wife, Laura, would have penetrated her friend's disguise at once, or, failing that, she would surely have phoned the police, for the weird visitor seemed, because of her sharp, projecting teeth, both demented and about to spring, but my mother had found out that Laura would not be home. When she made herself up, an hour before, I had watched her transformation from mother to witch with a mixture of wonder and worry that lingered in my memory for years.

Harry Simons, opening his front door on that dark evening in the age of innocence, when trust flowered

as readily as suspicion does today, was completely
taken in by the sudden apparition of an eccentric elderly woman who babbled of her recently inherited
fortune and said she had passed his house the day before and fallen in love with it. Simons was a big, jovial,
sanguine man, expert at business deals in a lighted
office but a setup for my mother's deviltry at dusk.
When she praised every room she stumbled into and
every object she bumped against—she wouldn't take
off her dark glasses in the lamplit gloom—a wild hope
must have glazed his eye, disarming his perception.
He admitted later, when the cat was out of the bag,
that Belle's idiotic laughter, and mine, at everything
that was said had disturbed him, especially when it
was provoked by my mother's tearful account of the
sad death of her mythical husband, a millionaire oil
man. But idiocy in a family is one thing, and money
is another. Mrs. Prentice, or Douglas, or whatever
she called herself, was rolling in money that day. She
upped Simons' asking price for the house by several
thousand dollars, on the ground that she wouldn't
think of paying as little as ten thousand for such a
lovely place. When she found out that the furniture
was for sale, she upped the price on that, too, promis-
ing to send her check through her lawyers the next
day. By this time, she was overacting with fine abandon, but the overwhelmed Simons was too far gone in
her land of fantasy for reality to operate. On her way

out of the house, she picked up small portable things
—a vase, a travelling clock, a few books—remarking
that, after all, they now belonged to her. Still Simons'
wits did not rally, and all of a sudden the three of us
were out in the street again—my mother who had been
my grandmother, her cousin who had been my mother,
and me. I feel that this twisted hour marked the occu-
pation of my mind by a sense of confusion that has
never left it.

My father was home from work when we got back,
and he gasped at the sight of his wife, even though
she had thrown away her cracker teeth. When these
latest goings on were explained to him, he was all
for taking his friend's possessions over to his unsold
house and returning them, with nervous apologies.
But my mother had another idea. That night she gift-
wrapped, separately, the vase, the clock, and the
books, and they were delivered to Simons' door the
next morning, before he set out for his office, each
"present" containing a card that read, "To Harry
Simons from Mame Thurber with love." It was not
my mother's most subdued performance, but it was
certainly one of her outstanding triumphs. The Frioleras laughed about it for years. It is among my mother's major sorrows that of the fifty members of that
merry club, founded in 1882, there are only three still
alive. At one of their parties fifty years ago—they
played pedro and euchre in the winter and went on

picnics and bicycle trips in the summer—my father asked his wife, apropos of what prank I do not know, "How long do you expect to keep up this kind of thing, Mame?" She thought a moment and replied, "Why, until I'm eighty, I suppose."

MARY AGNES THURBER, eldest of the six children of William and Katherine Fisher, was eighty years old in January, 1946, and I went to Columbus for a birthday party that brought together scores of her relatives. The day after the event, a columnist in one of the Columbus papers recklessly described her as "a bit of lavender and old lace." She was indignant. "Why, he doesn't even know about the time I threw those eggs!" she exclaimed. I didn't know about it, either, but I found out. At a meeting, a few months before, of one of the several women's clubs she belongs to, she had gone to the kitchen of her hostess' house, carefully removed a dozen eggs from a cardboard container, and returned to the living room to reactivate a party that she felt was growing dull. Balancing the box on the palm of her hand, like a halfback about to let go a forward pass, she cried, "I've always wanted to throw a dozen eggs, and now I'm going to do it!" The ladies gathered in the room squealed and scattered as the carton sailed into the air. Then it drifted harmlessly to the floor. Lavender and old lace, in their conventional and symbolic sense, are not for Mary Thurber.

Lavender with a Difference

It would be hard for me to say what is. Now, at eighty-six, she never wears black. "Black is for old ladies," she told me scornfully not long ago.

IN 1884, when Mamie Fisher got out of high school, she wanted to go on the stage, but her unladylike and godless urge was discouraged by her family. Aunt Melissa warned her that young actresses were in peril not only of hellfire but of lewd Shakespearean actors, skilled in the arts of seduction, and she pointed out that there was too much talk about talent in the world, and not enough about virtue. She predicted that God's wrath would be visited, in His own time, upon all theatres, beginning, like as not, with those in Paris, France. Mamie Fisher listened with what appeared to be rapt and contrite attention. Actually, she was studying Aunt Melissa's voice, so that she could learn to imitate it.

Deprived of a larger audience, the frustrated comedienne performed for whoever would listen, and once distressed a couple of stately guests in her father's home by descending the front stairs in her dressing gown, her hair tumbling and her eyes staring, to announce that she had escaped from the attic, where she was kept because of her ardent and hapless love for Mr. Briscoe, the postman. An entry in her diary of that period, dated Monday, May 14, 1888, would have puzzled the shocked visitors: "Went over to Flora's to talk over yesterday's visit. I tell you that Ira D. is cute, but I do not like him very well—he is a perfect gentleman, only he will insist on kissing me every time and I will not allow it. I can truthfully say I never kissed a fellow in all my life but once, and that was Charlie Thurber at the depot a few years ago."

Those of her relatives who drew no sharp line between life and art, the gifted and the mad, and consoled themselves with the hope that marriage would settle her down, could not have been more mistaken. Even the birth of her third son, in 1896, had little effect on her merry inventions, and her aunts must have been relieved when we left Champion Avenue and moved to Washington, D.C., in 1901. They probably thought of Washington, in those years, as a city of inviolable decorum, but it was there that we met a young Cleveland newspaperman named George Marvin, whose gaiety was to enrich our lives. He was a superior wag, with a round, mobile face, a trick of protruding his large eyeballs that entranced the Thurber boys, and a gift of confusion that matched my mother's. Uncivil clerks and supercilious shoppe proprietors in the nation's capital came to regret their refusal to sell Marvin and my mother one dish of ice cream with two spoons, or a single glove for the left hand, or one shoe. The mild, soft-spoken Jekylls from the Middle West would be transformed into Mr. and Mrs. Hyde, to the consternation of the management.

Lavender with a Difference

"Senator Beveridge will hear about this!" Marvin would shout, and they would stalk out of the shoppe, in high and magnificent dudgeon. But it was when we were all back in Columbus two years later that these comics reached their heights. Their finest hour arrived one day at Memorial Hall, during a lecture given by a woman mental healer whose ability and sincerity my mother held in low esteem. She has always been a serious and devoted student of psychotherapy, even when it was known and practiced under foolish and flowery names, and she learned long ago to detect tommyrot. Arriving after the lecture had begun, our cutups found an empty wheelchair in the lobby, and my mother, bundled up in it, was rolled down the aisle by her confederate. The lady on the platform had reached a peroration of whoosh, during which she chanted that if you had done it before, you could do it again, whatever it was, and other candy-coated inspiration to that effect. At the peak of this marshmallow mentation, my mother leaped from the chair, crying that she had walked before and could do it again. Some ten or twenty persons of the two hundred present must have recognized her, but the others were caught between cheers and consternation. The lecturer shouted, "Hallelujah, sister!" and at this point Marvin increased the confusion by bulging out his eyes, dropping his jaw, and mumbling that what he had done before he was now doing again; namely, losing his grip on reality. The crisis ended when a querulous man shouted, "Hey, that's my wheelchair!" and the culprits made good their escape.

The career of almost any actress is marked by open dates and, in the end, a long period of retirement. Who heard of the late Julia Marlowe in her last twenty years? But my mother's crowded calendar shows no season of repose, and the biographer is overwhelmed by instances and can only select a few more. There was the time she went back to Washington, in her sixties, wearing a red rose so the woman she was going to meet could identify her; they hadn't seen each other for thirty years. The train being early, or her hostess late, she pinned the rose on a sleeping dowager, twenty years her senior, who was sitting on a bench in the railway terminal, and watched at a distance the dismay of her friend when she finally arrived and the irritability of the sleeper awakened by a cry of "Why, Mame Thurber, how are you? You're looking just fine." And there was the occasion, not long ago, when she deflated a pompous gentleman, overproud of his forebears, who made the mistake of asking her how far back she had traced her own ancestry. "Until I came to a couple of horse thieves," she said with a troubled sigh. "Do you mean a father and son?" the shocked man asked, "or was it a couple of brothers?" My mother sighed again. "It was much worse than that," she said. "A man and his wife. You see, it runs in both sides of the

Lavender with a Difference

family." A hundred other hours and moments I leave to the record of another year.

With all this to take up her time, Mrs. Charles Thurber nevertheless managed to run her home like any other good housewife, hovering over the cook when we had one, following the cleaning woman around with pail and cloth of her own, and rearing three sons who were far from being mother's helpers. She was famous for her pastry and, after long study and practice, learned to make the best chocolate creams in the world. Two or three professional candy men tried to catch her secret, watching her at work like a child watching a magician, and with just about as little profit. She made her last twenty pounds of chocolates when she was eighty, and then turned to writing a cookbook of her own recipes, which she still works at, dropping it now and then to tinker with her play, whose plot and personae and provenance are another one of her secrets.

She still writes me, as she always has, fifty letters a year, and I found, going over them, that time hasn't dulled their sparkle. In one, dated December 26, 1949, she told, in fine full detail, the story of her 1933 search for Miss Bagley, which has become a family saga. Miss Annette Bagley, known to her intimates as Anna, wandered from her home in England more than sixty years ago to become a home-to-home sewing woman in Columbus. She and my mother became great friends, and then, one morning in the spring of 1895, Miss Bagley, at the age of thirty-four, took a train to Boston, where she planned to open a dressmaking shop. For several years my mother's fond letters were promptly answered, but about the turn of the century, two of them were returned by the Boston post office. Miss Bagley had dropped out of sight, leaving no forwarding address, and it wasn't until 1913 that she was heard from again. The floods of that year had inundated Columbus and she sent a worried telegram from Boston. My mother replied, by wire, that all her friends were safe, and Miss Bagley apparently received this telegram at the Western Union office in which she had dispatched her own, but a letter my mother instantly sent to the old address was returned, like the others. Twenty silent years went by.

In 1933, Mary Thurber took up the quest again, writing to the postmasters of Boston and surrounding towns, and inventing a story about the settlement of an estate. "Money," she wrote me in the 1949 letter, "always increases people's interest." It greatly increased the interest of an Anna Bagley in Malden, Massachusetts, who turned out to be the wrong one, and with whom my mother exchanged a brief and cloudy correspondence. Then she came East to take up the search in person. She was sixty-seven and she knew that Miss Bagley, if she was alive, was seventy-two. In Boston my mother set out on the old, dim trail like a trained researcher, looking up outdated phone books and directories at the Chamber of Commerce. The most recent record of Annette Bagley she could find placed her friend in Malden in 1925, so she went to Malden. Miss Bagley was not at the address listed, and the woman who lived there had never heard of her. My mother did what any good reporter would have done; she looked up old residents of the neighborhood and called on the older druggists and grocers. She learned that Annette Bagley had left that Malden house about seven years before. Someone seemed to remember that the old lady had moved to Everett Street. This street turned out to be only a block long, and my mother rang all its doorbells without success. Nobody knew anything about Miss Bagley. Then a druggist suggested that her quarry might have moved not to Everett Street but to the town of Everett, which is only a few miles from Malden. My mother transferred her pattern of search to Everett, and it was in that Boston suburb that the trail became warm. She found Annette Bagley listed in a three-year-old directory, but the elusive dressmaker was no longer at the address given. Neighbors, however, thought she had not gone far away, so her tracer continued her questioning of druggists and grocers and elderly people she stopped on the street. At twilight of the second day of her search, she came upon a small dress-making shop on a side street. "I looked through the window," my mother wrote, "and there she was, sitting and sewing with her back to me." Thirty-eight years had made a great difference in the two friends, and it wasn't until my mother asked the old lady if she had ever lived in Columbus, Ohio, that Annette Bagley recognized her.

The reason for her years of hiding was simple enough. She did not want her Columbus friends to know that her dream of a big and flourishing dressmaking establishment of her own had failed to come true. "I took her to dinner in Boston," my mother wrote, "and then to a movie. It was hard for her to believe that my oldest son, William, was forty, for when she had seen him last he was only two. I'm not sure about the movie, but I think it was 'It Happened One Night,' or 'One Sunday Afternoon,' or something like that." It isn't often that my memory outdoes my mother's, but I have always remembered the name of that movie since she first told me the story of her celebrated search for Annette Bagley eighteen years ago. It was called "I Loved You Wednesday."

Miss Bagley was ninety last year, and my mother still writes to her, and the letters no longer come back. The little sewing shop on the side street was closed years ago, of course, and the dream forgotten, but my mother is sure that, big establishment or no big estab-

Lavender with a Difference

lishment, Annette Bagley was the finest dressmaker Boston and its suburbs ever had.

IN NEW YORK, which my mother visits often, she likes to escape from her sons and see the sights of the city on her own. One morning some twenty years ago, she reached the second floor of the famous Wendel house, on Fifth Avenue, but her tour of inspection was interrupted. "I was just going by and I thought I would drop in," she told me. On that visit she made a tour of Greenwich Village by herself, but asked me to take her to what she called "the Tony's" and "the 21," whose fame she had somehow heard about. At "the Tony's" she was fortunate enough to meet one of her idols, the late Heywood Broun, and she enchanted him by casting an offhand horoscope for him that turned out to be a recognizable portrait, done in the bold colors of both virtue and shortcoming. She has always had a lot of fun monkeying around with the inexact sciences—she corresponded with Evangeline Adams, and once had Professor Coué out to dinner at our house in Columbus—and I am sure that she has already dipped into Dianetics. She embarrassed my father one time, in an impish numerology phase, by making him return a set of ominously numbered automobile license plates and exchange it for a safer one. Twelve years ago, when she entered Columbia Presbyterian Medical Center for a major operation that she took in her stride, she demanded to know the date of birth of her distinguished surgeon before she would let him operate. He solemnly gave it to her, and was pleased to learn that he had been engaged for thirty years in a profession for which his signs clearly fitted him. Later, he was astonished by her familiarity with medicine and surgery, and told her one day that she had the sound implementation of a nurse. "Of course," my mother said. "I'm Capricorn with the moon in Sagittarius."

The day she was discharged from the hospital, she decided to visit the World's Fair, and she did, in spite of heat and humidity. In a bus on the way back, she found that she had exceeded her strength, and she asked the bus driver to take her pulse. He took it with one hand, continuing to drive with the other, and reported that it was a little high but nothing to worry about. I have no doubt that she found out his birthday and still remembers it, for she rarely forgets a name or a date. She once sent me a clipping of an Earl Wilson column in which he had given Dorothy Parker's birthday as August 23rd. "Dorothy Parker's birthday is August 22nd," my mother wrote. "August 23rd is Helen Gude's birthday." A few days ago I phoned her in Columbus and asked her if she remembered her surgeon's birthday. "Why, certainly," she said. "He was born on the 30th of March. My Columbus surgeon is also Aries—April 1st."

Lavender with a Difference

In the recollections of a woman in her eighties whose mind and memory are as sharp as they ever were, the years are sometimes greatly foreshortened. When she came to New York in 1947, I found that she had made a date for tea at the Algonquin with an old friend of my father's, Charles Dewey Hilles. She said that she herself hadn't seen him for "a long time." Mr. Hilles, a celebrated Ohio Republican, died two years ago, and his long obituaries told of his having been, among many other things, an Assistant Secretary of the Treasury under Taft, Chairman of the Republican National Committee from 1912 to 1916, and a member of dozens of boards of directors. I had the good luck to be asked to the Ohio tea party, along with one John Aloysius McNulty, for many years a reporter on Columbus newspapers. We had a jolly time, and various ancient facts and forgotten dates were brought up. It came out that my mother was a year older than Mr. Hilles. "When was it," I finally asked, "that you two last met?" My mother thought about this and said, "Well, Mr. Hilles was secretary to the superintendent of the Boys' Industrial School at Lancaster, Ohio. Let me see—yes, it must have been in 1888." My mother was twenty-two in 1888, and Mr. Hilles, of course, was only twenty-one. Now, no elderly man of high and varied achievement likes to be reminded of his juvenile beginnings, and it was obvious to us all that my mother's grasp of her friend's later career was tenuous. McNulty saved the situation. "Eighteen-eighty-eight," he said, "was the year the owls were so bad."

WHEN I was in Columbus a year ago, my mother said, "Would it be possible for you to take me to lunch at the Waldorf-Astoria the next time I'm in New York?" From the tentative way she put it, I could see why she had never asked me before to take her to lunch at the Waldorf-Astoria. She was afraid that I couldn't swing it, and she hadn't wanted to embarrass me. I had taken her to every place I could think of, from the old Lafayette to Tony's and "21," but the Waldorf had never crossed my mind. I have made a conspicuous note about it on a memorandum pad, and the next time she comes to New York, I will take her to lunch at the Waldorf-Astoria, in a Hispano-Suiza if she wants it that way. It is little enough to do for Mary Agnes Fisher Thurber.

CHAPTER NINE

Snapshot of Mr. Ziegfeld

M R. ZIEGFELD, an old friend I hadn't seen for three decades, but never forgot—he was much too vital a man to forget—died not long ago in Columbus, full of years, skepticism, and wisdom. He was almost eighty and just as full as ever, I am sure, of questions, theories, and arguments. Julius Ziegfeld was a born controversialist, a man in love with the debatable aspects of life. He was an expert carpenter and all-around craftsman, who could fix anything that was broken in a house, from cellar to attic. He liked to take apart contraptions and ideas, to see what made them tick and to find out if they were soundly put together and made of good materials. He knew that the constructions and conclusions of men had a satisfying shape, and gave out a satisfying sound, only if they were right. His eyes and ears were keenly attuned to the shapes and sounds of perfection, and he gave people and ideas the same careful inspection that he gave every object he saw or heard.

"He had a carpentry shop at the rear of our home," his son Carl has written me, "which served less as a workshop than as a collecting place for all the material he gathered from the many buildings he repaired. He refused to throw anything away and even saved pipe fittings that had rusted through or that had burst from freezing. He worked on many of the old houses on Bryden Road and East Broad Street that were the homes of many of Columbus' oldest families. The owners of these houses found out that he was enchanted by old documents and they gave him yellowing papers that had lain in attic trunks for decades. These papers included land grants, appointments and military commissions, and many were signed by early Presidents. He was as proud of these documents as he was of his favorite books and never missed an opportunity to show them to a new acquaintance." Mr. Ziegfeld's library, of books and papers, had no static phase, but grew every year. He read every volume he could get hold of, dealing with American history and politics, and his arguments about the state of the Union were fortified and implemented by biographies of all the Presidents.

Mr. Ziegfeld had nine children to instruct, listen to, and argue with when they grew old enough to ap-

Snapshot of Mr. Ziegfeld

preciate the difference between opinion and fact, and knowledge and belief. Carl, eldest of the four sons, was the first of the boys to study physics and to discover what was wrong with his father's ancient, intense belief that he could build a successful perpetual motion machine. Mr. Ziegfeld had dedicated himself to this impossible project when Carl was only three years old, and he had worked on it in his spare time for fifteen years. Then one night, when all eleven Ziegfelds were gathered at table, Carl told his father what he had learned that day from his physics teacher—the fact that energy cannot be created. Mr. Ziegfeld had not gone as far in school as his oldest son, but he had read more books and thought more thoughts, and he welcomed this chance to ride into the lists against his mistaken son and his deluded teacher. Mr. Ziegfeld, born in Amsterdam in 1867, was a stubborn Dutchman, but an honest debater. He was a good listener, too, as becomes a man given to daily challenges in one intellectual arena or another, and as he listened that night, his old dream gleamed and flickered and vanished away. He jumped up from the table angrily, spluttered defiance, and left the room, but he never worked on his perpetual motion machine again; it quietly disappeared from his workshop the next day and wasn't mentioned any more.

When I was back home a few years ago, Mr. Ziegfeld called on me one afternoon, but I was out. "Too bad, too bad," he said to my wife. "I wanted to take up a couple of points with him." I had not told her about Mr. Ziegfeld, and she was puzzled by the unexpected apparition of an aged kewpie of a man, peering inquiringly over his glasses, thoughtfully running his lower lip over his upper lip, disconsolate at the lost prospect of an hour of stimulating controversy. I remembered how Mr. Ziegfeld loved discussion and dispute, and I figured at the time that he had counted on arguing with me about something or other—the decline of Man, the futility of humor, free will and determinism, the imminent triumph of the micro-organism, or the basic assumptions of Sigmund Freud. Having exhausted all his friends in every possible area of debate, he was eager to pin me in a corner, I decided, and to resume our conversations where we had left them off, more than thirty years before. I hadn't seen him since the night in November, 1916, when Charles Evans Hughes went to sleep victorious and woke up defeated.

Mr. Ziegfeld was the Democratic registrar and I was the Republican registrar that year in a voting booth on wheels that had been drawn up in front of his neat house in a tidy precinct of the south side of town, largely made up of residents with German names. Mr. Ziegfeld, son of an Amsterdam baker who brought him to Columbus when he was two years old, came from a long line of magnificent coffee drinkers. His

Snapshot of Mr. Ziegfeld

mother, he once told me, could drink as many as fifty cups of coffee on a day of crisis, when the coffee drinking began at dawn and lasted long into the night. There were other women among his ancestors—and men, too —who could outdo his mother, crisis or no crisis. One of the ladies, he said, lived to be ninety years old and averaged ninety cups of coffee a day. He was more temperate, and rarely drank more than twenty cups between breakfast and bedtime. In the Ziegfelds' corner of Holland, babies sipped coffee in their cribs, and with that kind of start Mr. Ziegfeld and his Dutch forebear who lived to be ninety must have consumed more than three million cups of coffee in their time. At my leisurely pace—three cups a day—I have estimated that I would have had to begin drinking coffee while Carthage still stood and Hannibal was alive to have a chance of approaching the record of the great Ziegfeld lady, even if I live to be a hundred. When I consider the Mississippi flow of the Ziegfeld coffee through the brown and redolent centuries, my nerves relax, my eyelids droop, my thoughts drift aimlessly about on a sweet and warm and creamy surface.

It was nice having your own house on wheels, with a wood stove in case the days got cold, and chairs made comfortable with cushions brought from the Ziegfeld home. Ours was surely the tidiest polling place in the city, inside and out. On the first morning, before I arrived—I cut classes at the university to serve as regis-

trar—Mr. Ziegfeld had washed from the tin sheath-
ing of the booth the chalk marks put there by boys of
the neighborhood the night before. All the scrawls
but one had been in the rowdy and pointless spirit of
Hallowe'en. The exception disturbed Mr. Ziegfeld
and he had left it for me to inspect. It read, in a bold,
adult hand, *"À bas le professeur."* This profanation,
so incongruous in the clear daylight of Washington
Avenue, was doubly profane to Mr. Ziegfeld because
it assaulted his Woodrow Wilson in what my colleague regarded as the radical idiom of European
back-alley political conspiracy. His eyes peered at me
over his glasses, hurt and forlorn, and his lower lip
worked vigorously. "I don't know who would do a
thing like that," he said. "I've been trying to think."
I suggested that the cynical piece of vandalism was
probably the work of some smart-aleck Republican
from the east side of town. He thought this over for a
moment and then put the outrage on a higher than
local and regional ground. "Shows Hughes has a rag-
tag following, you see?" he explained, and he went in
the house for a damp cloth.

Ours was a precinct of workingmen, so we had few
voters to register from nine to noon and from one to
five. The great body of the day belonged to the two
of us, sitting there on opposite sides of a table, with our
pencils and registration books, a copy of the election
laws, a city directory, a street map of the precinct, and

Snapshot of Mr. Ziegfeld

two cups of coffee. The iron stove in the corner had a flat top, and a gallon pot of coffee was always standing on the hot lid. It was Indian-summer weather, and the stove got so hot I had to keep propping the door of the booth open so we could get some air. Mr. Ziegfeld did not seem to mind the temperature, even when it neared ninety. Maybe it was the coffee. Maybe he was so hot inside that his skin seemed cool. I must have watched him drink seventy-five cups of coffee in the three registration days, and on Election Day, when we were locked in the booth until after midnight, counting the ballots, he drank at least thirty cups. When the enormous pot of coffee was empty, Mr. Ziegfeld would go into the house and get another one from the kitchen stove.

In the middle of the morning of the first registration day, Mr. Ziegfeld, already full of coffee, leaned back in his chair, cut a chew of tobacco from a plug, and said, "You want to argue about politics?" I didn't want to argue about politics. I had brought along a book, and I wanted to read. Mr. Ziegfeld looked upon me as a green young Republican brand that he could snatch from the burning. His round, pink-cheeked face assumed the firm, benevolent expression of a man who is about to remove a painful splinter from a child's finger. But there wasn't going to be any political argument. "I'm going to vote for Wilson," I told him, lowering my voice, I suppose, since, after all, I was the sworn Republican registrar in that voting booth. Mr. Ziegfeld almost lost his glasses. He turned slowly toward his spittoon and made it ring—he was an expert marksman. His eyes were sad when he looked at me, like the eyes of a toymaker who has opened his shop to find it ransacked of toys and tools. Finding a ready-made convert meant nothing now; he had lost an antagonist, and he stood suddenly on the awful edge of a dreary desert of acquiescence and accord. He spat again and peered at me. "Do you mind if I state the principles?" he asked. I forget what the principles were, but he stated them for an hour, pausing abruptly every now and then with his head cocked on one side, as if he were listening to something faint and far away. "What's the matter, Mr. Ziegfeld?" I asked him, finally, during one of these trances. "Tryin' to figure out who wrote that on the booth," he said. "Can't think of anybody in this community who knows French, except that young Herman Miller, who goes to the university, but he's a law-abiding citizen, you see?" I assured him again that the miscreant was undoubtedly some well-to-do cynic from east of Parsons Avenue who had wandered by on some dubious errand or other. "Mebbe, mebbe," he said, but I could see that he was not convinced. He sat in silence with his eyes closed for awhile, and then came out with a pronouncement he had been shaping in his mind. "People write on the voting booths in their own precinct," he told me. "A man's mind works that way."

We could hear the clock in the tower of Holy Cross Church strike the hours, and one morning, while its deep tones reproached the town for idleness and evil, Mr. Ziegfeld gave me the old peer and a new quession. "You want to argue about God?" he asked. I could see that he was eagerly prepared, if only for the sake of the argument, to knock down whatever frail defenses of divinity I might set up in the way of flower bells and sunset touches. What I needed was the backing of old Melissa Bailey, a great-aunt of mine, full-panoplied in the righteous armor of fundamentalism and implemented with all the terrible weapons of Holy Writ. She could find chapter and verse to turn the keenest thrust of any blasphemer. Her finest achievement as a student of the Bible was her discovery, in Revelations, of a downright denunciation of the motorcycle—my cousin Earl had a Harley-Davidson. But I didn't have the support of Aunt Melissa that day. I got out of the argument adroitly, I think. "I have the simple faith of a child," I said. That did it. Mr. Ziegfeld sagged in his chair and sighed. He looked out of the window for a long time and then back at me. "You want to defend Teddy Roosevelt?" he demanded. I made a pass at this one, just to see what would happen. It came out that Mr. Ziegfeld didn't even believe that the hero of San Juan Hill could ride a horse.

WHEN THE CHURCH clock struck nine on Election Night, we locked the door of the booth, opened the ballot box, piled the ballots on the table, and began to count them. There were, as I remember it, fewer than two hundred, and our task seemed simple enough until, a third of the way through, we came upon one that had been marked in red crayon. Mr. Ziegfeld was an experienced registrar, and he knew what to do about this departure from the use of the regulation black pencil. "Election laws clearly specify that the ballot must be marked with an ordinary pencil, supplied for the purpose," he told me. I noticed that the voter had made his illegal marks for the Republican ticket. We put the ballot aside. A few minutes later we came upon an even more outrageous violation of the election laws—a ballot across the face of which the voter had scrawled in enormous letters the single word "Nuts." In every other way the ballot was in proper order. It was a vote for the straight Democratic ticket, and just what the epithet was meant to imply was not clear to me, but it didn't puzzle Mr. Ziegfeld. "The gentleman was expressing an opinion," he said. "Seems to me his intent as a voter is plain enough, you see?" I agreed with this but pointed out that the statutes definitely stated that all ballots defaced in any manner must not be counted. I had gone over the little rule book carefully, and while Mr. Ziegfeld was familiar with the clause covering illicit ballots, my statement of it presented him with an opportunity for one of his longest and most eloquent statements of principle, dealing in general with the letter and the spirit of legislation, legal contracts, and the like. He drank three cups of coffee before we made our inevitable decision about the vulgar man's vote and placed it on top of the other disqualified ballot. It must have been about eleven-thirty when we reached a ballot that stood out as indisputable proof that the culprit of the Gallic legend was not a resident of the east side of town. We stared together at a ballot neatly marked in favor of Mr. Hughes and all the other candidates of the Republican Party for national and state offices. Across the top of this ballot was written in strong black letters *"À bas le professeur."*

We would have been there all night if I had not persuaded Mr. Ziegfeld to abandon the idea of comparing the writing on the ballot with the signatures of all the voters we had registered. I contended that the election laws did not empower us directly or by implica tion to try to determine the identity of any voter, no matter what he had written on his ballot. Mr. Ziegfeld concurred in this after a long and solemn interval of chewing, but he insisted that he had a moral duty, as a resident of the neighborhood and a man in whom the precinct reposed its confidence, to expose the fellow who expressed his political beliefs in a language and manner alien to the best traditions of the democratic process. Mr. Ziegfeld's glasses slipped lower and lower on his nose as he warmed to this unusual point of debate that had fallen in his lap. Since we had jumbled the ballots in dumping them on the table, there was no way of determining whether our rascal had voted early or late. The coffee by this time was beginning to run low, and since we had counted all the ballots and duly recorded the results, I suggested that we should, as promptly as possible, turn in our books to the Board of Elections, as required by law. Mr. Ziegfeld stood up, went to the stove, and poured the last cup of coffee. I began to clear up the table and get ready to leave. I was tired, but I wasn't sleepy. I must have put away at least eighteen cups of coffee myself that day. "I've got an eight-o'clock class at the university," I said, and regretted it. I was afraid he might sit down again and state the principles of higher education, but he stood beside the stove drinking the coffee, lost in his own private man hunt. "I'll turn in the records," he said. "Done it for years. You go home and get your sleep." I shook hands with Mr. Ziegfeld, told him what a wonderful and instructive time I had had in our house on wheels, and left him standing there, pondering and sipping.

It has occurred to me that there may have been more

than one reason for Mr. Ziegfeld's call on me that afternoon in Columbus a couple of years ago. One day, during the thirty years that followed our discovery of that mysterious and irregular ballot, Mr. Ziegfeld must have found his man. He probably wanted to tell me who it was that had written on the booth and on the ballot *"À bas le professeur."* I'm sorry I missed the old boy. Even after all these years, I would still kind of like to know who it was myself.

Julius Ziegfeld had honest and workmanlike hands and mind. He lived a good, long life, full of stimulating arguments, and the incomparable pleasure of building things, and fixing things, so that they looked right and functioned properly. There used to be a sign on the house of another artisan in this neighborhood that delighted me. It read "Watches and Sewers Repaired." Whenever I think of it, I remember Mr. Ziegfeld, who could also repair anything, no matter how heavy and simple, or small and intricate. His sign, if he had had one, might well have contained, in the lower left-hand corner, something like this: "Points Argued, Principles Stated, Opinions Changed."

Three of his children still live in Columbus, but the six others are scattered across the country from New York to California. Two of his sons are professors of fine arts, one is a consulting engineer, and Carl is district manager of a large manufacturing company. One of his daughters is a school teacher, and another is associate editor of a magazine. He lived long enough to see them grow into maturity and go their separate and successful ways. If he were alive, he would like nothing better than visiting them all in turn, repairing whatever might be broken in their houses, correcting whatever might have gone wrong with their opinions, and stating the principles of education, the fine arts, engineering, magazine editing, manufacturing, and management. There were many things in his world, tangible and imponderable, that he could not change to suit his own dreams and convictions, such as the faulty law of physics that does not tolerate the creation of perpetual motion, but he tested them all with his own mind or hands before he was convinced. I regret that I missed him that day in Columbus, but I'm glad that a small chance and permutation of politics brought us together in the house on wheels thirty-five years ago. The gallery of the unforgettable people that I was lucky enough to know during my Columbus years would be poorer without him.

CHAPTER TEN

Man with a Pipe

I HAD ONLY two male teachers before I entered Ohio State University, in the fall of 1913, one of them an amiable chemistry man named Gullum, who sympathized with my profound disinclination to make deadly bromine gas, even under a hood, in the high-school laboratory, and the other a professor of physics, Mr. Hambleton, who used to stare out a window while I was reciting, as if the flight of a sparrow or the swaying of a poplar bough were more relevant to his subject than anything I could possibly say. One day, in the physics class, I proudly announced my own system of computing the rate of acceleration of a falling object. Mr. Hambleton impatiently tried out the elaborate Thurber method on the blackboard a couple of times, chewed one end of his mustache when he saw that it worked, and then turned his bleak smile on me and said, "Young man, you would go from New York to Boston by way of Detroit." Some years after that, I told this story to Joe Taylor, at the end of one of his English classes at the university, and he said, "A straight line can also be the dullest distance between two points." I had met a little late, but not too late, a male teacher who was not a captive of old, inherited exactitudes, and who never laid down a formal rule for getting to Boston, or to Kew, or to Carcassonne, or anywhere else.

I saw Joe Taylor for the last time more than twenty years ago. I had come out of a restaurant on Fifth Avenue with a colleague of mine, and I suddenly beheld Professor Taylor walking toward us hurriedly, with a distracted look on his face. We stopped and talked, and it came out that he had arrived in New York a week early for a meeting of the Woodberry Society. It was not his fault, but that of the late John Erskine, secretary of the society, who had sent out the invitations and got the date wrong. I wanted him to have dinner with me, but he said he had to pack and take a train back to Columbus. He wasn't sure that he would be able to return for the meeting the following week, but we made a tentative date in case he did come back. When he left us, my colleague turned to me and said, "Who is that wonderful man?" He didn't come

Man with a Pipe

back, and three years later he died, in Columbus, at the age of sixty-four.

I WILL ALWAYS remember my first view of Joseph Russell Taylor, in one of his English classes at Ohio State, more than thirty-five years ago. He was round of face and body, with yellow hair, pink cheeks, and fine blue eyes. He usually wore a brown suit, and he always brought to class the light of the enchanted artistic world he lived in, of whose wonders he once said, "It is possible that all things are beautiful." He was a poet and painter as well as a teacher, and he believed that the materials of art were in all the activities of men. His classes were popular from the beginning, and in the nineteen-twenties as many as a hundred and twenty-five men and women crowded into his lecture room. On the opening day of one of his classes in 1914, he began by saying to us, "I do not expect you to take notes in this class." Forty of the fifty young men and women present wrote that down in their brand-new notebooks with their brand-new fountain pens. Standing at the lectern, possibly lost in contemplating two of his favorite fictional heroines, Henry James' Mme. de Vionnet and George Meredith's Diana—for whom he had named his own daughter Diana—he seemed oblivious of the aimless scratching in the notebooks. I don't know what experiment he was trying that day, but it didn't work. He should have known that the things he had to say were always worth recording. Some of his former students, after thirty years and more, still have at hand the notes they took in his courses, including that one in 1914.

His influence was not confined to students who hoped to become writers or teachers of English. A dozen years before my day at the university, he had tolerated the occasional classroom inattention of a young man who was given to drawing, in his notebook, prizefighters without faces, and other unique figures. The student was a Columbus boy named George Wesley Bellows, whose parents had been dismayed, rather than delighted, by their son's devotion to the idle practice of drawing pictures. Luckily for him, his professor not only was something of a painter himself but had taught drawing for several years before he became a teacher of English. Close students of Bellows' life have recognized Joe Taylor's lively and lasting interest in his young friend's talent, and most of them feel that without this encouragement the artist might never have become a professional. Joe Taylor was, for one thing, a friend of Robert Henri, Bellows' first influential teacher, and he seems to have brought the two men together. In the Gallery of Fine Arts in Columbus, there hung for a time an oil portrait of the sympathetic professor sitting in a chair and holding a pipe in his hand, done by his former student nearly forty

Man with a Pipe

years ago. When its subject was first shown the finished study, he said, "That is a painting of Joseph Russell Taylor by a young artist, but it will one day be known as Bellows' 'Man with a Pipe.' " He was a great pipe man, and once asked me, after I began to write for a living, if I smoked one when I worked. I told him that I did, although I didn't, and it seemed to please him mightily, for some obscure reason. "Good!" he said with satisfaction.

It may be that he tried to discourage note-taking on that far-off morning because, at the time, his appraisals of some authors were undergoing continual mutations. "Don't quote me outside class," he told us more than once, "because my judgments are subject to change." One of his significant reversals of literary opinion, in my years at the University, involved the novels of Joseph Conrad. "Conrad is merely a spinner of yarns," he said one day, and then, some weeks later, "I have changed my mind about Conrad. He is Henry James in the waste places." I don't know for sure what contributed most to this critical shift, but it is likely that he had been impressed by the recently published "Victory," which many Conradians now consider the Master's finest work. It contained, in Lena of the far-away island, a lady highly suitable for Joe Taylor's gallery of beloved heroines. The fictional ladies of Thomas Hardy, on the other hand, never won his heart, but he later revised his early feeling that they were merely milkmaids in romances written for milk-maids.

Joe Taylor was a great feminist, and he liked Mere-dith for giving his women characters equal stature with his men, and Henry James for his high and subtle development of the ladies in his novels. He was al-ways referring to or quoting from Wordsworth's trib-ute to the "perfect woman, nobly planned; to warn, to comfort, and command." He used to write on the blackboard—not always in poetry class, either, be-cause his lectures unconventionally overlapped—the years in which Robert Browning and Elizabeth Bar-rett Browning had done their best work, and contend that their true excellence had flowered during their marriage and might otherwise have languished.

Every now and then, he would stray from the subject in hand, abandon his notes, and discuss what was uppermost in his mind, or fresh in the news, or going on around the campus. One day, he announced that Theda Bara, then at the height of her vampish fame, would have no effect upon him, emotionally or artis-tically, if she should bang into his presence with her great eyes bulging and her dark hair in exaggerated disarray. "You can't get passion into a story with ex-clamation points," he said. Sometimes he would bring a cheap novel to class and show how its hasty and care-less author was trying to palm off "italics" for genuine emotion. "General Stonebridge was a man of iron," one of these novels began, and Professor Taylor then quoted some of the staunch fellow's vapid conversation and said, "A character of iron does not speak in words of tinfoil."

Ludwig Lewisohn, who in my time was teaching German and German literature at Ohio State, was disappointed to find no "vicious faces" on the campus. Joe Taylor, however, was interested not in a search for depravity but in finding signs of spiritual increase and of fine sensibility in the world about him, and he never gave up the wistful hope of instructing the unvicious in the literature of living. Perceptive and congenial young minds can scarcely be said to have flourished like wild flowers in that time and region, but the good professor did his best, and he had a lasting effect on the minds and hearts of scores of men and women. Professor Lewisohn, who liked and admired few men at Ohio State, brought Joe Taylor into his novel "Roman Summer." "But it must not be supposed that John Austin was a fool," the passage reads. "At college he had fallen under the influence of a teacher of intense but limited and stagnant tastes: a small ruddy gnome of a man who had, long ago, been a favorite pupil of George Edward Woodberry, a protégé of Richard Watson Gilder in the genteel days of the *Century* and had published a volume of late Victorian verse. His literary eminence was a legend in the city. Young Austin had taken all of the courses offered by his teacher. He was not unaware now of the man's limitations. What allied him to that teacher still was an unconquerable love of beauty and fitness and precision of speech." Lewisohn's years at Ohio State were unhappy ones and, coming from him, this qualified tribute is praise indeed.

"I know that some of you restless young men are eager to get on to classes that teach you how to make a living," Professor Taylor said once, taking out his watch and laying it on the lectern. "It is now only ten minutes till economics, or chemistry, or engineering." Many a restless male student gave fresh attention to this kind of talk. They listened when he said that the word "beauty" could not be applied to campus cuties, because beauty in a woman cannot be purchased with the scant coin of twenty-one years of life. With local references like this, he deftly led the anti-literature boys and girls in and out of Meredith and James, quoting the former's "My heart is not made of the stuff that breaks" and the latter's "When she touches a thing the ugliness, God knows how, goes out of it" in support of his fond thesis that beauty in a woman is a product of maturity. If the interest of the male students began to wane, he might talk about Chic Harley, the great Ohio State halfback of the period, pointing out that Harley's graceful running with a football brought true beauty of line and motion to a game that had been, only a few years before, a turgid

Man with a Pipe

struggle of monolithic masses. If Theda Bara didn't snap the boys out of daydream or apathy, Chic Harley invariably did. Once, Joe Taylor fascinated his young listeners by comparing Charles Dickens to the late Billy Ireland, who was then cartoonist for the Columbus *Evening Dispatch,* and one of the best in the country. Dickens was to Joe Taylor—at least at that moment—only a greatly gifted caricaturist.

Professor Taylor went to all the football, baseball, and basketball games, and I had the good luck to have a seat near his in Ohio Field the exciting day in 1920 when our team defeated Wisconsin by virtue of a fifty-yard pass from Workman to Stinchcomb, thrown just a second before the gun ending the game was fired. In the bedlam that instantly struck the stands like a hurricane, I caught sight of Mr. Taylor yelling at the top of his voice and slapping a strange man in front of him with his hat, time and again. He knew which of his students were varsity athletes, whether in football, baseball, basketball, or track, and many of them, including an old track man named Tracy Pittenger, remember him with special fondness. "My track career came to a sudden end out at Champaign, Illinois, when I was running at the Illinois Relay Carnival in March of 1922," Pittenger wrote recently. "I broke my leg, and along with it my heart. The following week, after I had my leg set in a cast and was hobbling from one class to another, I was about to pass Joe Taylor, going in the opposite direction. There was a moment of hesitation as we came almost face to face. I saw in his face, in just a split second, a look of complete understanding, and there were also two little tears (one in his eye and one in mine). What he did then will stand out forever in my memory. He lifted his hat and passed on his way. I will always be grateful that he didn't stop and tell me he was sorry, because what that little gesture told me was more than any words could have told. Especially when the gesture was performed by a man who never should have been required to remove his hat to any man."

The Pittenger story was written for a detailed history of Ohio State athletes and athletics, now in preparation at the university, where intercollegiate sports are rated of enormous importance. I can easily believe that Joe Taylor raised his hat to Pittenger that day—after all, A. E. Housman, one of Joe's idols, also had a warm and rueful affection for lightfoot lads—but I very much doubt the reality of the tear in his eye. Joe Taylor's eye was not made of the stuff that weeps easily. He had too much temper and toughness of spirit for the sentimental, and a fine way of getting mad, rather than merely sorry, when things went wrong. One day in 1917, I happened to look out a window of the Ohio Union Building and I saw my favorite professor practicing on a putting green about thirty yards away. He kept missing the cup by a wide margin, but he finally sent the ball to within a few inches of the hole. He went back several yards to try again, and I could see his confidence in his step and in the set of his shoulders. His next attempt was the worst of all, the ball swerving a good three feet to the left of its objective. Joe began to pound his putter on the ground, and then he walked to a tree and banged it six or eight times against the trunk. He then went back and kicked the ball, picked it up, and stalked away. Not long after this, incidentally, a young man named Robert Tyre Jones put on an identical tantrum at the Merion Cricket Club, outside Philadelphia, but he went on to the greatest glory in the history of the game. Joe Taylor, I must report, never got very much better at golf, but he was an excellent swimmer and played a good dogged game of tennis.

JOSEPH RUSSELL TAYLOR, born in Circleville in 1868, was so deeply attached to Ohio that no offer of fortune could have lured him away. He had no desire to win public renown, like Billy Phelps, of Yale, or Copey, of Harvard, and he was not flattered when his students began to call him Joey, in a mistaken attempt to institutionalize him. His ideal teacher, and one of the strongest influences in his life, was the late George Woodberry, in whose celebrated English literature classes at Columbia in the nineties young Taylor had sat enchanted. (Joe had entered Ohio State when he was only fifteen, and so he was still a youngster when he graduated.) Woodberry was not only a great teacher; he was also a poet, and he was interested in the athletes as well as the young literati who flocked to his classes. It was not easy to trace the Woodberry influence in the Taylor lectures. It showed up more in his profound and stubborn belief that he was, like Woodberry, first of all a poet. At Columbia he wore a Van Dyke beard, wrote poetry diligently in his spare time, and signed himself "J. Russell Taylor." He soon took off the beard and restored the "Joseph" to his name. Two skillful sonnets of his were published in a book called "Columbia Verse 1892–1897." After college, he sold poems to the *Atlantic Monthly, Harper's, Scribner's,* and *The Century,* and in 1903 they were published by Houghton, Mifflin in a volume called "The Overture." He later brought out several long poems, one of them wistfully entitled "Our Dancing Days."

He went to Europe twice, to visit places that made his heart leap up: the Nether Stowey of Coleridge, and Shelley's Tremadoc—where he had the luck one morning to hear a skylark singing—and, best of all, Tintagel, on the rocky coast of Cornwall, where the legendary ruins of King Mark's Castle stand, and Tarascon, in Provence. Of Daudet's "Tartarin of Tarascon," he once wrote, "It is, in my judgment, France's greatest contribution to literature in the nineteenth century." Tintagel was, for him, even more hallowed ground, because it was associated with Tristram, whose "I come from Lyonesse and a gentleman am I" he often quoted, in a dozen unexpected contexts of his own. He spent many years working, at night and in odd hours, on a monumental essay about Tristram, which I was privileged to read after his death. It ran to nearly half a million words, and was lighted and adorned by his own extensions and permutations of the great legends. He didn't believe that the poets, from Matthew Arnold to Edwin Arlington Robinson, had done full justice to the romantic figure of Sir Tristram, and he held that Wagner had made of him nothing more than a tenor. I can still hear Professor Taylor telling his classes that Tristram's lady, Iseult, was, beyond peradventure of doubt, a redhead. You didn't have to agree with him about this, or about anything else, and if, in written examinations, you set down judgments exactly opposed to his, it made no difference in your grades, as long as your points were sincerely argued.

He came back eagerly to Ohio from New York, or from Europe, for he was always, be sure (as he might have put it), a wandering and not too comfortable Ohioan wherever he went, forever remembering home. Since his dearest literary shrines and settings were so far away, his deep affection for his native state seemed to me at first a wonder unmixed (to use another of his phrases), but I came to realize that he had the true devotion of the poet to his own region, like Wordsworth's to the Lake Country of England, or Burns' to Scotland. Joe Taylor's notebooks and diaries show that he had roamed all over Ohio, painting streams and meadows, silver birches and scarlet oaks, and spotting birds by their songs and colors. On one weekend of rambling, he identified a hundred and seventy-five different birds, and he would not have exchanged the upland plover or the hermit thrush of the Middle West for Shelley's skylark, or for the nightingale whose autumnal song he once heard in the Boboli Garden, in Florence. He was familiar with Ohio's wild flora, from the fungus known as fairy ring to the purple-fringed orchis, and his home was bright in season with the flowers he collected in the woods and fields. His children remember his coming home at dusk one day bringing their mother a bouquet of bloodroot and anemones, around which he had neatly wrapped a damp handkerchief to keep it fresh.

WHEN Joseph Russell Taylor was forty-one, Henry Holt published "Composition in Narration," his only textbook (if you could call it that)—a small volume of lyric essays on the art of writing, whose serenity has survived like a flower in a book. It came out in

Man with a Pipe

1909, a year remembered by most men as the year Blériot flew over the English Channel. To Joe Taylor, it was the year Meredith and Swinburne died. The book was written so long ago that it is filled with quiet, old-fashioned scenes: a gentleman calling on a lady and presenting his card at the door; beaux taking their belles to dancing parties in sleighs or horse cabs; a balloon dreamily drifting over central Ohio in the race that started during the St. Louis World's Fair of 1904. "There were voices of children on the quiet air, and there was the good smell of the fires of autumn leaves; things of immemorial familiarity; and on the south of the evening passed what a voyager, a portent, the first sail on a new sea, the angel of tomorrow!"

Joe Taylor's book darts and wanders, intensely or at a leisurely pace, down the hundred pathways of his agile thought, but his poetic prose is carefully disciplined. "Art is revision," he wrote, and he must have lit his pipe a thousand times in rewriting his chapters. He brought impulsive feeling, rather than cold mental analysis, to everything he touched—he goes so far as to call intellect "the conventional part of imagining"—but he had the good writer's dissatisfaction with imperfect statement, and the book shows his constant wariness of certainties. "The only taste that is false is that which does not change," he wrote.

As a textbook, "Composition in Narration" must

have puzzled professors looking for conventional rules and familiar rituals. It begins, "There are really only two kinds of writing: artistic, which is narration, and scientific, which is argument," and then starts off on a Taylor-guided tour of a hundred subjects. The author quotes from personal letters; talks about his father, who gave up teaching to become a minister; explores the difference between literal fact and literary truth; discusses painting and music; skillfully takes apart one of his own moods; describes a spectacular fire in Columbus, and the effect a small replica of the Venus de Milo had on him when he spent what must have been hours turning it slowly around in different lights. In the book's last section, called "References," he talks about authors he liked at the time: Henry James, above all and at greatest length; de Maupassant; Daudet; Stevenson; Anthony Hope, for his "The Dolly Dialogues;" and, finally, "Mr. Wister." Joe must have loved "The Virginian," because the Far West always appealed to him; one of his long poems, called "Thirty Ponies," was about a tribe of Western Indians. There is also this note in "References," which I can't get out of my mind and probably never will: "It is almost true also that the most perfect Stevenson story was not written by him, but by Mrs. Stevenson; 'The Nixie,' the story remains still, as far as I know, buried in a magazine of the Eighties." That wonderful "almost true" is pure

Man with a Pipe

Joseph Russell Taylor, copyright 1909. It has given me a lovely case of the nixies.

IN SPITE OF a critical taste that changed like the weather, Joe Taylor had his immutable convictions: that nothing genuine need fear the test of laughter (he thought the comic aspects of wearing a scarlet letter could have been exploited by Hawthorne); that youth cannot hold a candle to maturity (he was never entranced by Keats' celebration of young, or trivial, love forever imprisoned in shallow April); and that there is nothing prose can do that poetry can't do better. Since James' novel "The Ambassadors" seemed perfect to him, he actually persuaded himself that it was essentially poetry. (His contention that its dialogue was the very spit and idiom of its time was even more startling.) He also believed, all his life, that "the artist is the normal man," a cryptic judgment that none of his students who went on to write or teach has ever been able to follow very far without getting lost. In his later years, he kept assuring his classes that poetry should not be read aloud, and this I think I can perhaps explain. In my day, he used to read poetry aloud, with a peculiar and disconcerting lift of inflection on the last syllable in every line. Some of his students took to imitating this curious mannerism out of class. He never did get the hang of reading verse easily and effectively, and he must have come to the conclusion that it couldn't be done.

He firmly believed, from his twenties into his sixties, that politics is an impermanent factor of life and has no valid place in art or literature. "Such things as love, life, and death, and people are the permanent things," he told his students. He said that Shelley was not a true poet, because he was a rebel; apparently you can't be both. In 1917, he said, "The Germans cannot win the war, because they are wrong," and he let it go at that. Communism was wrong, too, and therefore couldn't win: "Improvement cannot be brought about by any Bolshevist revolution, or socialistic redistribution of property. We are not so desirous of an earthly paradise as to approve revolutionary and violent means of attaining it. What we want is simply the privilege of going on—not perfection but the privilege of striving." Politics, to be sure, did not include patriotism. Joe Taylor was one of the most patriotic Americans I have ever known. He never forgave Henry James for becoming a British subject, and in the preface to a long, unpublished essay that, for his private satisfaction and amusement, he called "Taylor on James," he held that the novelist could not get rid of his Americanism merely by changing countries. He predicted in 1912 that James would come back to his own land, and he must have been gratified when he found out later that the book the Master was working on when he died dealt with

Man with a Pipe

Americans in America, after a long series of novels about Americans in Europe.

For the reassurance and guidance of any militant Ohio State trustee who might figure that a man who had rejected politics must have been a dangerous fellow, I reprint, from "Composition in Narration," Joe Taylor's warm tribute to his country.

> How should you answer if I should ask you, What is the Nation? Where is it? Show it to me. Does it look like the statue in New York Harbor? Is it the fleet that recently went round the world, with peaceful guns and with dancing on the decks? Is it the flag, is it the capitol, has it the President's many-caricatured countenance? Where and what is the Nation? Is there such a thing? You would answer that the Nation exists only in the minds and hearts of men. It is an idea. It is therefore more real than its courts and armies; more real than its cities, its railroads, its mines; its cattle; more real than you and I are, for it existed in our fathers, and will exist in our children. It is an idea, it is an imagination, it is a spirit, it is human art. Who will deny that the Nation lives?

He seems to have held himself aloof from campus politics and scandals during his more than forty years at Ohio State, but in 1929 a grotesque tragedy reached out and touched him. A professor of veterinary medicine named James H. Snook murdered a university coed, and after his execution university authorities decreed that the top half of every office door in all campus buildings should be made of transparent glass. Joe Taylor was sixty-one at the time, and it had been his custom, after his final class, to lie down and rest in his office before going home. The Snook door, which made a goldfish bowl of his privacy in the English building, put an end to these periods of rest and had a disturbing physical and emotional effect on him, which he found hard to shake off. Two years later, he was sitting in his parked automobile on the campus when it was struck and knocked over on its side by a bus filled with agricultural students. He never fully recovered from the effects of this accident, and in 1933 he died, of complications, a few months before his sixty-fifth birthday. In his last year, he had painted dozens of water colors of his beloved Ohio landscape, and he must have written poetry, too, since it was such an important part of his life. I doubt whether he found any joy in the American novels of the nineteen-twenties, except, of course, those of that normal artist, Miss Willa Cather. His delight in James and Meredith never declined and he kept going back to them at the end, and, you may be sure, to Wordsworth's immortal "She Was a Phantom of Delight." His friends thought of him as one of the permanent things of life, and when we heard that he was dead, the light of that day diminished.

CHAPTER ELEVEN

ΒΘΠ

O HIO STATE University lies in a region of literacy
and slurred enunciation, literary tradition and
careless diction, vivid vocabulary and flat pronuncia-
tion. There the words "Mary" and "marry" are pronounced the same as "merry," and there, too, Gudda
is spoken ("Where's he gudda go? What's he gudda
do?"), which results from a partial immobility of the
lips in speaking. (A stone-deaf lip-reader instantly
identified me, not many years ago, as a native of Ohio,
Indiana, or Illinois. "You say most words as if you
were saying 'king,'" she said.) As a result of this regional indifference to the graces and subtleties of the
mother tongue, Ohio State's Department of English
has had its work cut out for it from the time that land-
grant university was founded, eighty-two years ago.
In my time there, the reckless use of the language

often invaded the campus itself. There was a director of athletics with a doctor's degree who pronounced "cereal" as if it were spelled "creel" and who told his freshman classes in Physical Education that creel came in a "cartoon." And there was Chic Harley, our greatest athlete, who once announced that he thought he had "brucksed" (or maybe it is "bruxxed") one of his ribs in practice. Of the professors of English who fought the good fight against Slur and its grammatical allies during my years, two others, besides Joseph Russell Taylor, stand out especially in the memory of myself and my contemporaries. They are William Lucius Graves and Joseph Villiers Denney, familiarly known as Billy Graves and Joe Denney. (For some unaccountable reason, I forgot to report, in the chapter on Professor Taylor, that he was once handed a theme entitled "The Haunted Yatch.")

William Lucius Graves (son of one Lucius Velorus Graves, who spared him the "Velorus") was the most popular professor in the history of his university. Joe Denney, like Joe Taylor, was loved and admired by the appreciative few, but Billy Graves was known for more than forty years as the friend of freshmen, the confidant of seniors, and the chum of alumni. Every night before going to bed, he wrote at least one personal letter, and most of this correspondence was with his former students, literally hundreds of them. They recognized the tall, well-groomed bache-

lor, forever young in heart, as a mere visitor in the
intellectual world, like themselves, and not one of its
awesome, withdrawn first citizens. They liked him
because he never missed an issue of the *Cosmopolitan*
magazine, and made no bones about it, and because
he sometimes openly confessed his inability to understand certain so-called masterpieces of writing that
had set his colleagues to twittering. When the intel-
lectuals were talking profoundly about "Ulysses" and
"The Waste Land," he was still praising the simple
beauties of one of his favorite books, "The Inn of the
Silver Moon," by a man named Herman Knicker-
bocker Vielé. Billy Graves, his myriad young friends
told people, was a good guy; he could go along with a
gag; he was fun to have around.

At the Faculty Club, Billy Graves stood out among
smaller and less fastidious professors like a sunflower
in a cornfield. Some of his more retiring and hard-
working colleagues looked upon him, in wonder and
envy, as a species of man of the world. One of them, a
superior scholar but a man of a single subject and
interest, was once inspired to exclaim about Billy,
with a sigh, "Knows his music, knows his art, knows
his literature!" It was generally known that Professor
Graves occasionally sold felicitous verses to *Scribner's*
and the *Century,* that he played the piano and even the
organ, and that he took in the theatres, the art galleries,
the concerts, and possibly even the cabarets on his

frequent trips to England and the Continent. His associates pictured him moving amiably about London salons, charming both ladies and gentlemen and holding up his poised end of any conversation. As a matter of fact, he was not always too comfortable in company, especially at cocktail parties, for he rarely drank a cocktail or highball, and when he smoked a cigarette, which wasn't often, he did it with a curious self-conscious air, blowing out smoke without having inhaled it. He was an attentive listener and a good conversationalist when the talk did not encroach on areas that distressed him: four-letter realism in prose, modern experiments in dissonance, and violent techniques of painting. He was most at ease at quiet dinner parties and in genteel drawing rooms, where his jolly laughter and his sparkling fraternity pin were often heard and seen. Faculty hostesses, and downtown Columbus wives, too—many of them his former students—turned to Billy Graves when they needed a pleasant and attractive male guest to seat next to a distinguished or difficult woman at dinner. (He wrote several articles about American table manners, and in one of them denounced the use of "those infernal little silver corncob-holders.") He was also known for his ability to fill in awkward drawing-room pauses with his piano playing. He had his special favorites, mainly Chaminade, but he could read new music swiftly and expertly, and fifty years ago he used to join, for quintets, a campus string quartet whose second violin, daughter of the university president, was a variously talented young woman named Dorothy Canfield. He became a lifelong friend of the late Hugh Walpole when the novelist happened into a room where the professor was playing the piano and fell under the charm of the Graves personality. For more than four decades he entertained the members of his fraternity, Beta Theta Pi, with his ragtime variations on familiar themes. One of his Beta brothers estimates that Billy visited the chapter house five thousand times between his graduation in 1893 and his death in 1943.

Brother Graves was one of the most intense fraternity men in the history of Beta Theta Pi, or of any other Greek-letter society. I found out almost as soon as I registered as a freshman at Ohio State that Professor Graves was a Beta, but I was a senior before I learned that Professor Denney was a member of the fraternity I belonged to myself. Billy often served as a state or national officer of Beta Theta Pi, and in the course of his duties travelled thousands of miles, giving the grip thousands of times, without getting tired or even bored. When he was twenty-nine, he wrote, for his fraternity's national magazine, a loving tribute called "The Miracle of Brotherhood," and it was reprinted forty years later, when he was sixty-nine. The salute to ΒΘΠ begins with a comparison of the friendship of David and Jonathan to the ties that bind fraternity brothers. He confesses that he cannot explain the miracle of brotherhood. "I could as soon tell you what sends a bobolink into the sky on a sunny May morning, to drop earthward again amid the golden bells of his own chiming song." Billy goes on to say, "As the years continue to widen the gulf between me and my active college days, I become more and more persuaded that in Beta Theta Pi, as in no single one of our kindred fraternities, there is a tenderness of appreciation for the fraternity spirit, a loyalty of regard for the fraternity ideals, and a strength of endurance in the fraternity sentiment. I have yet to hear from a Beta what I heard from a member of another great brotherhood who could not be sure of his fraternity's name, or from a second, only the other day, who told me he had not heard or thought fraternity for so long that he hardly knew what the word meant." The tribute ends with this sentence: "If I am glad of any one thing this night, it is that for me the miracle of brotherhood has come to pass, and if I am proud of anything, it is that the badge on my breast is a Beta badge."

I ENTERED Professor Graves' short-story course in the somnolent September of 1916, one of the last of the becalmed years that preceded the Liberation of Literature in the twenties. "The Spoon River Anthology" was the most daring book of the time, "This Side of

Paradise" and "Main Street" were unborn, Hemingway was only seventeen years old, and there was little to ruffle the poise and placidity of professors of creative writing west of the Alleghenies. Professor Taylor, to be sure, labored nobly to interest his students in the short stories of Henry James, and another professor came out boldly with his admiration of O. Henry, but for the most part such timeworn classics as "Markheim," "The Necklace," and "A Piece of String" were held up as perfect examples of short fiction, to be revered and imitated. A group of precocious avantgarde students got out a rebellious magazine called *Sansculottes*—it withered in the dead weather of the period—but most of the literary-minded boys and girls dreamed of selling something to the *Smart Set* for forty dollars, or at least of getting a personal note of rejection from Mencken or Nathan. In the midst of all this, Billy Graves went his own special way, introducing his classes to Fannie Hurst's "Gaslight Sonatas," Robert W. Chambers' "The King in Yellow," Gouverneur Morris' "Spread Eagle," Josephine Dodge Daskam's "The Madness of Philip," Richard Harding Davis' "Gallegher," and Quiller-Couch's "The Householder." I am told that he later found Hemingway's stories of "blood and death" distasteful, but admired "The Killers," in which there is only the threat of blood and death.

I got what was known as a "deferred pass" in Professor Graves' short-story course, which meant that I hadn't turned in enough themes. He stubbornly insisted on outlining ready-made plots for his students to follow in writing their "original" short stories. There was the one about a paralyzed woman who beseeches her daughter not to get married and leave her, and the one about the cowardly condemned youth who goes bravely to his death before a firing squad after his mother tells him that the real bullets have been replaced by blanks. It was a matter of awe to many of us that Billy Graves' mind, or the mind of any mortal, could stand up under countless variations of these monotonous situations. Occasionally he did allow his students to write short stories out of their own imagination, and he always hoped that some of them would be bought by magazines. In 1921, one of his young men made it, with a story called "Larry Pyramids," which appeared in the *Smart Set*. It had, however, never been submitted to Billy Graves. I have always wondered what he thought of it. It dealt with a Catholic who shot craps to win enough money to provide a Mass for his dead father. (In the same issue, incidentally, there was another story that must have disturbed Professor Graves. It was called "Miss Thompson" and was written by W. Somerset Maugham.)

IN FEBRUARY, 1924, Billy Graves was thrown open to the public in an article in *Collier's*, written by

Frederick L. Collins and entitled "Everywhere I Go I Find a Pal." I was only twenty-nine when I first read this remarkable piece of journalism, but its flavor has lingered with me through the years. I had forgotten its actual phrases, however, so I looked it up the other day and read it again. Mr. Collins, best known for his "The F.B.I. in Peace and War," published in 1943, had gone to Columbus in the fall of 1923 for the Ohio State-Illinois Homecoming Game —it was one of the Red Grange years—and in looking around for a local figure notable enough to be written up, he kept hearing about Billy Graves. One Ohio State graduate, in his thirties, told Mr. Collins, "He is closer to the youth of the Middle West, exerts a greater influence than any other man since Roosevelt." (The reference was, of course, to Teddy Roosevelt, since at that time Franklin Delano Roosevelt was mainly known for having recently been defeated for the Vice-Presidency of the United States.) Like many another man, Frederick L. Collins was enchanted by Billy Graves. They had lunch and went to the football game together, where Billy was affectionately greeted by scores of students and alumni.

Early in his article, Mr. Collins spoke of Billy Graves' "kewpie figure," and later enlarged on this. "Did I say Graves had a kewpie figure? That's not fair to the professor or the kewpies. For, if it was strictly so, the latter wouldn't be so funny or the former so nice.

He looks more as your mother always likes to have you look: 'heavier than you used to be.' Perhaps it's his complexion that's kewpyish; perhaps it's his eyes, beady and smileful, like a very wise baby's. Perhaps it's the jolly young soul that shines through his great comfortable personality. Anyhow, he's something awfully nice to play with—and he's more like a kewpie than a Teddy bear." I am sure that Mr. Collins' strange nursery mood made Billy Graves squirm, but he took it in his stride. "Well, at any rate," he laughed, "I'm not on sale in the stores."

It is hard to believe, reading Mr. Collins' report of his luncheon conversation with Billy, that the year was 1923, in the midst of the Scott Fitzgerald era. " 'I suppose, among ten thousand boys and girls,' said Billy, 'there must be some drinking and considerable "petting"—I believe that's what they call it nowadays—but either I don't see it or the boys and girls I know don't do it. I rather think that the latter is true. .... Of course, there's some rouge, and the other day I heard a girl swear right on the steps of our building. At least, she said "My God!"—and I call that swearing. But then, she had just seen the mark I had given her on an examination—and I didn't have the heart to reprimand her.' " Billy Graves, his admirers will protest, was neither as naive nor as prim as all that. He had a trick of throwing away such remarks with a laugh that took the edge off them, but Mr. Collins failed to catch this in his piece. The Collins article continues like this: "Just then we passed a tall boy and a wee girl in busy conversation. It was too dark to see their young faces, but it's never too dark to listen. The boy was saying, '. . . And Billy Graves says, "not for him!"' Graves turned around with a laugh. 'Good evening,' he said. The boy wasn't embarrassed. He laughed, too. 'I was talking about you, not to you. I was quoting one of your articles.' "

The article the wee girl's young companion referred to that day had probably been printed in either the *Daily Lantern* or the *Ohio State University Monthly*. Billy Graves was the faculty's most prolific writer. In 1900, he was asked by an editor of the *Lantern* to write a weekly piece on any subject, and he agreed to do it until school closed the following year. Forty-two other *Lantern* editors came and went, and Billy kept on writing his pieces, more than two thousand of them in all, containing a total of more than two million words. He also found time, for many years, to write a monthly piece for the alumni magazine. He discussed new books and plays; the movies, which he usually scornfully dismissed, although he liked some of the old silent films, including one based on Hergesheimer's "Wild Oranges"; professors—Kittredge was his favorite among the eminent men; dogwood, hawthorn, and white lilacs in bloom; and country rambles in every weather, on which he took along a camera and a sack of chocolates. He would accompany friends on a hunting trip, but always turned his head away when a rifle was aimed at a squirrel. There was tinkle and chime and fragrance in the Graves clear prose, which charmed some readers and annoyed others. One campus critic damned the body of his writing as "sweetly innocuous," and another curmudgeon came to the conclusion that Billy was capable only of crushes and grudges, and lacked temper and passion. Then, in 1940, Professor Graves, who called his *Lantern* pieces "The Idler's Chronicle and Comment," astounded and shocked the critics of his bland style and his mild subject matter. He came out with violent attacks on his once beloved England for having instigated, as he put it, the Second World War, sharply criticized our "pro-British Congress," mysteriously discovered the gaiety of Paris under the Germans and the city's relief at the departure of British and American tourists, and praised Charles A. Lindbergh in a brief, extravagant paragraph.

The identity of the Iago—or Emilia—who had whispered evil of England in the ear of her erstwhile ardent admirer (he had often told friends that he planned to spend his last years in some English town) remains a mystery of the Ohio State campus, or, at any rate, one of its few faculty secrets. It was taken for granted that the senescent political views and vehemence of the Idler, so alien to his younger nature, were inspired by some persuasive person he had listened to with his usual attentiveness. However that may be, every now and then, between the spring of 1940 and Pearl Harbor, one of the Professor's essays, after starting out in his familiar gentle vein, would abruptly turn into hard tirade. In the *Lantern* of May 28, 1940, his column began: "I was not looking to see, in this late and capricious spring, such luxuriance of bloom in the lilacs and the dogwood. I can remember no year in which these glorious things have flourished as they have this year. A drive in almost any direction along the country roads takes one through something like an aisle of lilac bushes, simply loaded with these exquisite fragrant blooms, waving and tossing in the spring winds at the ends of their pliant branches." The little country ramble ended with these sentences: "Somebody out on Bryden Road has a wonderful dogwood tree, now in bloom; and several on the north side of the city attract instant attention. They take second place only to those brilliant hawthorns whose colors fascinated us a week or two ago." At this point, Professor Graves suddenly began to whoop it up for Lindbergh. "It is easy to see," he wrote, "why Lindbergh will never again be a great hero to the American masses. He knows too much, he is too intelligent, too fairminded, he has too much accurate information, he has had too many contacts of the sort that demagogues avoid and would not, in their ignorance want to make anyway, lest they might learn something that would shut off their empty spoutings. . . ." From here, the Idler drifted into an amusing squib about diplomas.

The Lindbergh comment called forth an indignant, well-considered reply, running to two columns in the *Lantern,* from the able Professor Joseph A. Leighton, of the Department of Philosophy. The rest of the faculty, without known exception, joined him in opposing Graves on Lindbergh, and in defending England, France, and the international policies of the American Congress. Billy was not the equal of Professor Leighton in ratiocination or implementation, and he did not pursue the debate in the *Lantern,* but he kept repeating his views privately, so forcefully and so often that his colleagues began avoiding his company. Many of them were permanently alienated, others dismissed the Idler's beliefs as nonsense, and one man observed that every professor should be allowed one sabbatical from soundness. Since few alumni had ever subscribed to the *Lantern,* Billy's host of graduate pals was largely ignorant of his strange transfiguration.

The last column the Idler ever wrote appeared in the *Lantern* of June 3, 1943. It was a return to the kind of sweetly flavored theme that had marked his writing since the election of President McKinley. Entitled "Well! Well! How Are You?" it dealt with the coming fiftieth reunion of his Ohio State class of 1893. "We will smile and talk of ancient days," he wrote, "and afterward tell our wives or husbands how awful everybody looked. 'Poor old Billy Graves. He certainly is failing. Isn't it a shame? He used to be so...'" Three months later, William Lucius Graves, sitting in his living room and talking to his wife—he had astonished everybody by marrying, late in life, one of his former students—collapsed in his chair and died instantly of a heart attack, at the age of seventy-one. Letters of condolence came from men and women all over the country, and newspaper eulogies were filled with tribute, anecdote, and reminiscence. "Billy Graves is dead," mourned the Columbus *Citizen,* "gentle, lovable Billy Graves." There was no mention anywhere of his dark sabbatical. It must be reported, in fairness, that the well-remembered charm and affability of Ohio State's professor-plus has obliterated, like a ramble of morning-glories, his flaws and frailties. The Billy Graves legend remains as bright as ever, time having quietly erased its most prominent stain. In his final years, he had successfully removed from his name the stigma of kewpie, and this must be counted, I think, in spite of its cost, among his triumphs.

CHAPTER TWELVE

Length and Shadow

BILLY GRAVES was capable of a fine composure, seated behind his tidy desk, but Joe Denney was always standing restlessly at his lectern when his classes assembled, and he would gaze at them over his reading glasses with a look of mild astonishment, as if he were sure that they, or he, had come to the wrong lecture room. He had his real faraway moments, in class and out, but not often; his absent-mindedness was usually a whimsically studied effect. "I have either just appointed that committee, or I am just about to," he solemnly told a reporter after he became president of the American Association of University Professors thirty years ago. He knew darn well he had just appointed the committee, and he presently recited the names of its members without a miss. When he had retired as Dean of the College of Arts, to devote more time to this presidency, a scroll of tribute to him, in Latin, was read aloud at a ceremony. After alarming everybody by searching his pockets for notes that weren't there—he rarely made notes—he replied in elegant Latin, without stumbling over a single ablative absolute. In class, his air of bewilderment sometimes served as a kind of impish ambush from which his alertness would leap suddenly to pounce on a serious point, or to outwit a waggish student. One of these, a roguish young lady—she would be in her fifties now —tried to throw her fast ball past him in his Shakespeare class one morning. He had asked her "Who was Pinch?" and instead of identifying Pinch, she came out with the name of a character who is arrested in one of the comedies. Joe Denney peered at her helplessly over his glasses for a moment, and then said, "My dear young lady, if I should ever succumb to the frivolous temptation to phrase my oral examinations in slang, the question you have just answered would go like this : 'Who was tossed in the clink?' "

Joseph Villiers Denney, as his command of slang indicates, had been around, outside ivied walls. After college, he had edited an Illinois paper, the Aurora *Beacon,* and then travelled in all the states of the old Confederacy, writing special articles about the New South for the Chicago *Tribune.* His interest in journalism did not last long. He was still in his twenties when he took up an academic career, beginning as principal of an Aurora high school, and then going on to teach at the University of Michigan, and later at Ohio State. As he grew older, his journalistic sense diminished. In 1923, for example, he actually expected the unscholarly Gus Kuehner, city editor of the Columbus *Dispatch,* to print a front-page story based on the fact that the Ben Greet Players would be on the campus during the Tercentenary of the First Folio. I was a *Dispatch* reporter at the time, and Dean Denney asked me to break the news of the exciting coincidence to Kuehner, which I did. He looked at me quizzically, like a beagle examining a turtle, and said, "Goody!" When I told Dean Denney of this cold reception, he sighed and said, "I suspect that I shall never be able to excite Mr. Kuehner's imagination." He was right about that, as he was about most things.

Dean Denney was for many years the busiest man on the faculty, and he became the first to make Who's Who. He seemed frail enough to be blown away in a high wind, but this was as deceptive as his lost look, for he could outwork two ordinary professors and trot home at twilight, fresh as a daisy, to write a speech or read a book. For relaxation, he played the violin. He took on almost every administrative job in the university, and, besides being Dean for twenty years, was, at various times, Acting President, Chairman of the Entrance Board, Secretary of the Faculty, and Director of the Summer Session. Not the least of his distinctions was his academic fame as one of the most brilliant Shakespearean scholars of his day. In his spare time, such as it was, he collaborated on well-remembered textbooks and lectured on Shakespeare at Columbia and other universities. Sixteen years after his death, he remains one of the indestructible human traditions of his university and the shining figure of its fondest legend.

THE DENNEY LEGEND may have got its start one day about 1905, when he ran out of blackboard space during an examination and, without hesitation, quietly wrote the last two questions on a bare, kind of chalk-colored wall. Another professor, after a reasonable interval, might have erased the first two questions or dictated the final ones to his class, but the young Dean —he was then forty-three—was not a man of hackneyed or conventional solutions. "Braque," said a painter, hearing of the writing on the wall, "would have done the same thing." That small, impulsive gesture of nearly fifty years ago has not been forgotten at Ohio State; several gentlemen, well into their sixties, learning that I was exploring the Denney yesterdays, wrote me that they were in his class that unusual morning.

Dean Denney was also a man of unhackneyed and unconventional explanations, and one of them forms the glittering keystone of the legend. Late one night some forty years ago, he boarded an owl car after making an address in downtown Columbus, possibly at a meeting of the sedate Kit Kat Club, and absently dropped a strip of six tickets in the conductor's hopper. "Hey, Mister," exclaimed that astonished man, "you only need *one* ticket!" Returning from the Forest of Arden, or wherever he may have been wandering (he was also an authority on Edmund Burke, international law, and the American Reconstruction period), he peered at the conductor over his glasses, out of ancient classroom habit. "It is my considered intention," he began, at last, "it is my considered intention," he repeated innocently, "to—ah—lie down."

The Denney legend, like all legends, abounds in apocrypha, and professorial anecdotes common to other campuses have been hung on him, just as the incident of the streetcar has been falsely attributed to other men. He is said to have driven up to his house in a carriage with several other professors and, when his wife came to the door, to have said, "My dear, you'd better come out and get the one that belongs here." He might have said that, but the best Denney authorities regard it as pat and labored, and they point out that the man who confounded the streetcar conductor never built up any of his sallies in advance. They cite as a genuine Denney a story of his arrival home after midnight from a late faculty meeting, in the automobile of a colleague named Dr. Henneker.

Length and Shadow

Mrs. Denney called down from an upstairs window, "Who is that with you, Joe? Who has kept you out so late?" Her husband leaned out of the car, peered up at her, and said, "My dear, I do not propose to betray my good friend Dr. Henneker." This was the authentic Joe Denney, imp of the faculty, who loved to tease his colleagues, especially the pompous ones, and whose wife was always his most appreciative and inspiring audience.

Although he was affectionately known as Joe to all the student bodies that came and went during his forty-two years, he lacked the Billy Graves urge to mingle with undergraduates on their own level. He wistfully hoped every September, often in vain, to encounter a few serious students interested in impersonal communion on an intellectual level. I never saw him at Ohio Field (he knew football, though, and once said, "There is no forward passing in learning; you have to cover the ground the hard way"), and his heart did not leap up when he beheld an athlete in his class. One athlete, executing a trick play, once scored ten points on a certain examination question, and Joe Denney didn't forget it. The question went something like this: "Write all you remember about 'As You Like It,'" and the student simply set down the sentence "I don't remember anything about 'As You Like It.'" Dean Denney felt that on this occasion he had been fairly outmaneuvered, but he was usually more than a match for the powerfully built and the fleet of foot. One such fellow, a track man, came to class fifteen minutes after the Professor had written duplicate questions on blackboards on opposite sides of the room —he often had to do that as his classes grew in popularity and size. The lightfoot lad, breathing heavily, his hair still wet with shower water, panted proudly that he was late because of practice for a coming track meet. Dean Denney studied him in silence, and then said, "In view of your labors on behalf of the glory of this institution of—ah—higher learning, I suggest that you may be happier answering the questions on *this* side of the room." The young man didn't find out until after class why everyone had laughed uproariously when he got up from his chair and crossed the room. He had mistaken his professor for one of those who pampered athletes, in a tradition that began in 1916, when Ohio State's football team won its first Western Conference title.

The teaching of Shakespeare was Dean Denney's life, and it was a hard life. In an address he once made to an assemblage of Phi Beta Kappas, Professor Denney spoke of a man driven to cynicism by "the infinite capacity of the human mind to resist the introduction of knowledge." After one of his effective pauses and peerings, he added, "Perhaps he had just finished reading a set of final-examination papers in which his best points were carefully missed, and his cherished theories, grotesquely distorted, were now handed back to him in such shocking and immoral disarray as to convict him of having 'most traitorously corrupted the youth of the realm.' " Professor Denney had a vast fondness for the "preposterous ignoramuses" of Shakespeare's romantic comedies, and he was able to endure philosophically the long procession of Dulls and Shallows that clamored to get into his Shakespeare classes.

Joseph Villiers Denney was the last of the old-fashioned apostles of the classics and humanities at Ohio State. He was a fighting apostle, too, with a swift and memorable sword arm. "Millions for manure," he once said, out loud and in public, "but not one cent for literature." This paraphrase of a famous piece of early American defiance belongs to the late Ellis Parker Butler, I am told. He was one of several Iowa authors who were asked, many years, ago, to present autographed books to the Iowa State Library. The request was made a short time after the legislature had appropriated twenty million dollars for the Department of Agriculture, and so Butler wrote on the flyleaf of the book he sent to the library, "Twenty millions for manure, but not one cent for literature." Joe Denney gave him full credit for the crack, but two generations of Ohio Staters insist the professor thought of it first. In any case, he found frequent use for it, because the Ohio Legislature was always glad to finance a new cow barn or horse building, but guffawed at the idea of a theatre on the campus. (The cramped chapel stage was used for most plays, but Shakespeare's were put on outdoors.) The legislators, many of them farmers, were often a thorn in the side of the College of Arts. There were always a few who tried to throw out the teaching of Shelley, because of the rumor of the poet's un-Ohioan love life, and if the legislature of 1917 did not instigate, it heartily approved of, the banning of German at the University. In that same year, Bible classes were held in the fraternity houses, in a cloudily patriotic attempt to substitute Jehovah's Word, in English, for the godless language of Goethe and Heine. This awkward and unpopular project, unnourished by any marked enthusiasm on the part of the Dean of the College of Arts, was soon abandoned. He resisted, during his long career, a hundred alien restrictions on the freedom of teaching at Ohio State, and his reputation as a firm and courageous crusader for teachers' rights became widely known in academic circles and resulted in his election as president of the professors' association. In his inaugural address to his colleagues, who had gathered from all over America, he boldly named their potential enemies: state legislatures, ecclesiastical bodies, and "powerful influence operating through trustees."

The powerful influence that Dean Denney was talking about began to operate at Ohio State in the

Length and Shadow

Fall of 1951. The university's trustees include United States Senator John W. Bricker, former United States Senator James W. Huffman, and Brigadier-General Carlton S. Dargusch, aggressively patriotic gentlemen always ready and eager to save America from the perils of academic freedom. Urged on by conservative forces in Columbus, the trustees decided that nobody could speak on the campus until he had been intellectually seized and searched to see if his political opinions contained anything that might corrupt the minds of students, such as Communism, or anything else modern or liberal or radical enough to warrant suspicion. The action of the trustees alarmed and angered men of good will, and aroused protests from every religious sect in America. The governor of Ohio tried to reassure everybody by jovially announcing that it was all a matter of good old plain common sense. While the trustees were qualifying freedom of speech at the university, they decided it was a matter of good old plain common sense, or good old-fashioned Americanism, to qualify freedom of research, too. To the dismay of the governor, the trustees, and the president of the university, groups of distinguished scholars, in various fields of theory and research, who had planned to meet on the campus, canceled their arrangements. The trustees and the president finally agreed to let freedom of speech and research get up on one knee, and to take the blindfold off one eye. Part of the faculty bravely spoke its mind, and further small concessions were made, confusing the situation, and failing to remove the stain. Joseph Villiers Denney, through all this, must have turned restlessly in his grave. Ohio State, trapped somewhere between Armageddon and Waterloo, needed him and his strategy of reason and his tactics of friendliness, and all the armament of his intellect and his humor. But he wasn't there, and there was nobody to take his place.

Dean Denney lived to see, sorrowfully, the disappearance of Caesar, Cicero, and Virgil from many secondary schools, and to watch his own university become one of the chief fortresses of the academic army opposed to liberal education and in favor of practical and empirical training in the useful modern sciences, crafts, businesses, and trades. I don't know what Joseph Villiers Denney would have made of an article that appeared last year in *Holiday,* entitled "Gigantic Ohio State," which proudly records that you can no longer get a degree there in salesmanship or sanitary engineering without having endured a sprinkling of culture in the form of a required course in the humanities. A "campus leader" is reported to have said, "Do they think Shakespeare is going to get me a job with U. S. Steel?" There is one man whose answer to that question I would love to hear, but he is, God help us all, no longer living.

The day he retired from the university, his devoted

colleagues, old and young, in the Department of English watched him gather up his books and papers and take a last look around his office. Ohio State University had taken enormous strides toward its destiny of giantism since he had first come there as a young instructor so many years before. No formal ceremony marked his going away, at least not that day, and there were no awkward or sorrowful moments of parting as the distinguished scholar and administrator, lecturer and wit said goodbye to his friends. He came, last of all, to the late Herman Miller, one of the younger professors with whom he was fond of engaging in banter. He took Miller's hand, gave him the famous over-the-glasses peer, and said, "Herman, after forty-two years of teaching I have come to the conclusion that the human species is—ah—ineducable." Then he winked, poked his young friend in the ribs, made a little clucking sound, and left the campus forever. He didn't have long to live, but in spite of his years and waning strength he insisted on going to Ann Arbor in 1935 to attend the fiftieth anniversary of his Michigan class. He had always had a deep affection for his Alma Mater, and he was pleased to find at the reunion many friends of his campus days. He had a wonderful time. Two days after his return home, with the echoes and memories of the reunion still lightening his spirits, he quietly died. He had not been able to make the Columbus *Dispatch* with the story of that old link between the Ben Greet Players and the Tercentenary of the First Folio, but that newspaper, like dozens of others in the Middle West and farther away, appreciated his singular achievements. "Ohio State University is in large part," said the *Dispatch* obituary, "the length and shadow of Joseph Villiers Denney." I like to think that his incomparable length and shadow have not been completely lost in the towering and umbrageous wilderness of modern Gigantic Ohio State.

CHAPTER THIRTEEN

Newspaperman—Head and Shoulders

WHEN I STARTED to work as a reporter on the
Columbus *Dispatch* ("Ohio's Greatest Home
Daily"), in the summer of 1920, its city editor, Norman Kuehner, was on vacation, and I didn't get my
first look at him until one hot Monday morning about
ten days later. He lumbered into the city room, a big
guy in his middle twenties, wearing a suit too dark for
the season, and the disconsolate frown of a hunter who
has seen nothing but warblers all day. He had big feet,
and his long legs supported a heavy torso that widened
into muscular shoulders. He must have worn a size 16
collar, and his large face was loosely built around its
most striking feature—a pair of brown eyes, whose expression, I soon found out, could change as swiftly as

island weather. They would take on a bland gaze of pure innocence, like a choirboy's, and then, a moment later, burn with scorn or turn as cold as a top sergeant's. He had the aggressive air of a man who would snap "Buy a watch!" if you asked him what time it was. As he stood at his desk, staring about the room, I noticed that he had unusually restless hands. One day, a few years later, the right one, doubled into a hard fist, probably saved his life when a rewrite man, cracking under the strain of the city editor's baiting—Kuehner was a practiced and tireless baiter—attacked him with a sharp spindle, set in a heavy metal base. Kuehner knocked him cold with a straight right to the jaw, putting all his weight behind it.

When he spotted me, that first day, sitting at a desk in a corner, his eyes darkened, and he sauntered slowly over to me with the gait of a traffic cop approaching an incompetent and unattractive woman driver. He stood behind my chair for several moments, not saying anything. I said, "Good morning," and he still didn't say anything. I had been rewriting some brief items from the *Lantern,* the daily paper got out by students of journalism at Ohio State University, and when he saw what they were, he swept them onto the floor with one swipe of his big hand, growled "This isn't a college paper," and strolled away, with the grace of a wagon. He let me sit at my desk the rest of the day doing nothing.

Newspaperman—Head and Shoulders

Norman Kuehner (he pronounced it "Keener"), son and grandson of German cigar makers, never wanted any part of his family's tedious and confining trade. From the time he was able to spell out robbery and murder headlines, he dreamed of being a newspaperman. As a boy in short pants, he carried a *Dispatch* route after school, and he was scarcely out of the eighth grade, and not yet fifteen, when, in 1909, he got a year-round job as office boy on his favorite newspaper. The gawky youth attacked his work breathlessly, fetching and carrying at a dogtrot, and always wearing a serious scowl, even when he was allowed to post the World Series scores, inning by inning, on an outer wall of the building, with a crowd looking on. One of the editors began calling the solemn youngster Gus, because of his supposed resemblance, in figure and temperament, to Happy Hooligan's morose brother, Gloomy Gus. He took this and all other kidding in his stubborn stride, developing a sardonic tone, a jaunty if callow cynicism, and a sarcastic vocabulary of his own. He soon became adept at the quick insult and the cold rejoinder. A tough front, it seemed to him, befitted a newspaperman, whose opening question to any stranger should be a chill "What's your racket?" (or whatever the idiom then was), instead of a friendly "What can I do for you?" A kind of personality carapace began to form because of this studied attitude, concealing a natural warmth and a wide area of sentiment from everybody but his family (he was especially adored by his two sisters) and his few cronies. He disliked being caught by anybody else with his armor down. "If Gus had been a dog," one of his old friends said recently, "he would have bitten off his tail to keep it from wagging."

The office boy came to work before eight o'clock most mornings, so that he could practice on one of the typewriters, making up news items of his own or re-writing actual ones of the day before, brooding and frowning over the keyboard, and pounding out his hard, blunt sentences slowly. They were figuratively stained with blood, for he was fascinated then, and forever after, by stories of crime, fire, accident, and violent death. Nothing in nickel novels or in anything else he ever read excited him half so much as the daily routine of a city detective. He took to hanging around the "cop house" on Saturday nights, picking up pointers from the *Dispatch* man who covered the police station, and now and then riding with the cops in the patrol wagon or a squad car to the scene of trouble, which he hoped would involve shooting. He learned to hit the ground fast, or to take cover behind a tree, when other boys his age were still in high school. Everybody on the *Dispatch* knew about his dream of becoming the paper's police reporter and teased him relentlessly. Then, in true Alger-boy fashion, he made it, before he was twenty years old. The police reporter quit, and Kuehner was told he could take a crack at the job. He kept at it, with lusty success and undiminished ardor, until he was made city editor, a few years later. He got along with the cops, talked their language, and stood up under the heavy banter common to city policemen from San Diego to Bangor. They liked the kid, and found out that he could lead with his left and cross with a fast right, and that he never lagged behind on even the roughest assignment. All policemen like to get their names in the paper, in full and correctly spelled, and Kuehner obliged them: "The arrest was made by Detective Sergeant Jolas K. Menschkey and Patrolman Wilson G. Shellenbarger." He was right behind the cops when they smashed down a door, or chased a man into a dark areaway. The young police reporter was usually out of breath, often sleepless, but never bored. He remembered these years fondly all the rest of his life.

Norman Kuehner came up to the city desk the hard way, bringing a curt philosophy with him. "You get to be a newspaperman by being a newspaperman," he told all reporters who went to work for him, with a special emphasis for college men. "You can't learn how by studying journalism in college under a broken-down ex-editorial writer for the Hohokus *Bugle*." (J. S. Meyers, then head of the Ohio State Department of Journalism, was, as it happened, formerly a managing editor of the Pittsburgh *Post* and editor of the Pittsburgh *Sun*.) Kuehner was by this time the owner of a rare collection of edged inflections, falsettos, and mirthless laughs. He stood up straight to talk to reporters and towered over most of them. They all got, in their turn, the full Kuehner treatment, beginning with a first day of idleness, during which they were ignored as completely as if they weren't there. Then came the practically impossible assignments. If a new man handled one or two of these successfully, or came back with honorable scars showing that he had tried, the city editor softened a little, like an iceberg in April weather. One cub reporter, sent to get a statement from a hospital patient whose room was closely guarded, borrowed an interne's white jacket, got hold of a stethoscope, and managed to reach the patient's bedside before he was unmasked and ejected from the hospital by way of the laundry chute. Kuehner thought he had made a good try, and grunted something to that effect. His praise was laconic and slow in coming, but it was genuine. He could forget, finally and grudgingly, the misses you made, but he always remembered your triumphs. If he growled "O.K.," it meant that you were doing pretty well. The final accolade came when he shambled over to your desk, with the look of a man in a dentist's chair, and said in a low voice, "Nice goin'," turning away quickly before you could thank him. He disliked the whole handbook of amenities, and every sign and symbol of intimacy. He rarely called anybody by his first name, and made up nicknames of his own for his staff. One man was Farmer, another Parson, and still another, who had been a lieutenant in the first war, Loot. He had a vast range of nasty intonations when he yelled at them, and a few friendly and affable ones. Some of the college men that he rode hard gave up and walked out, unable to tolerate the Teutonic weight that he constantly gave to "choinalism" and "collctch," and similar words. He could say "Phi Beta Kappa" so that it sounded like a Girl Scout's merit badge. Liking Kuehner wasn't easy, and a lot of people never managed it, but if you did, the feeling stuck—I don't know exactly why.

I made the grade with Norman Kuehner (he was Gus only to old-timers) when I went out one day and brought back a photograph of a boy who had been drowned. Such photographs had great news value to the city editor. He had been maliciously hopeful that I wouldn't be able to get a picture. "This kid's old man threw our police reporter out of the house on his can," he had told me. "Go out and give him the old college try. They must have told you how to get around tough characters by talking pretty." I brought back a group photograph in which the ill-fated youngster appeared. "Yeah," Kuehner said disconsolately, swallowing the ironic gags he had been thinking up for me, "it'll blow up O.K." He stared out a window.

"What are you—sticky-fingered?" he asked. I explained that I had not gone to the boy's house but had got the picture from his high-school principal. He gave a short, spastic laugh that started in his belly and died in his throat. It might have meant anything.

For several weeks I had been finding in my assignment box the dullest or the hardest assignments he could put his mind to. The next day, I started out of the office to follow up the story of a train wreck that had occurred north of town the evening before. Kuehner's assistant had stuck the assignment in my box. As I passed the city editor's desk, he growled, "Where the hell do you think you're going?" I told him. "Forget it," he said, glaring slowly around the room. His dark glance lighted on a college man who had started to work only a few days before. "We'll let the Phi Beta Kappa handle it," he said, and bawled at him, "Hey, Phi Beta Kappa, come here!" The torture of the new cub reporter had begun, and mine had ended. Up to that point, Kuehner had called me Hey or You, but he had found out that I had once written a libretto for a campus musical comedy, and he began calling me Author, and kept it up as long as I knew him.

When he was city editor, and even after he became managing editor, he liked to sit up until after midnight seeing the Sunday paper to press and, if he was in an amiable mood, telling yarns to whatever reporter was handling the late watch. If a phone rang, Kuehner would shout, "There she blows!" and scuttle over and answer it, hoping that hell was popping somewhere and that he could rush out and look at a dead body or a burning building. I had thought, during my first few months, that his deep absorption in death was morbid, but I changed my mind about this later on. Kuehner was a man of guts and action, but death did something to him he didn't like, and he was forever seeking the chance to swagger up to it, with a chip on his shoulder, and stare it coldly in the eye. One night, when he was sitting the watch with a young reporter named George Smallsreed, the one he called Parson, he got the news that a man who had been shot through the head was lying in the emergency ward of the Mount Carmel Hospital. He got in his car with Smallsreed and exceeded the speed limit getting to the scene. Smallsreed knew that Kuehner would have liked nothing better than to see a young reporter turn green, or faint, at the sight of gruesome death, but he managed to get through the ordeal. "When Kuehner had satisfied his curiosity at length," Smallsreed told me recently, "he looked at me innocently with those big brown eyes and said, 'Let's go out and get a hamburger, Parson.' I went with him, but I didn't eat anything." One reason Kuehner took young reporters along with him on jaunts of this sort was, I suppose, to find out whether they had what he considered the

stuff of a newspaperman in them. To Norman Kuehner, no one was a genuine newspaperman if he cringed
at the sight of blood or in the presence of human ex-
tinction. (Smallsreed turned out to have the stuff of a
newspaperman in him, all right. About a year ago,
he was made editor of the Columbus *Dispatch*.)

One Saturday night when I was sitting the late
watch with Kuehner, I was emboldened for some reason to tell him how I had once run out of front-page
copy at three o'clock in the morning when I was getting out the *Lantern,* and was saved by the fortuitous
appearance in the night skies of what Professor H. C.
Lord, roused out of bed, called the most brilliant
aurora borealis seen in Ohio since the Civil War.
Kuehner tossed his cigarette to the floor, with one of
his slow, deliberate gestures, and ground it out under
the heel of his No. 11 shoe. "God never helped me put
this paper to bed," he said sulkily, "and nobody is ever
going to cover Heaven for the *Dispatch* while I'm city
editor." He had got sore, in his abrupt fashion, because I had brought up the touchy subject of college
journalism, and also because I seemed to him to be
floating around in the supernatural, a region that made
him embarrassed and uncomfortable. I never brought
up college journalism again, or the question of provi-
dential happenings either, but it was an act of God
that gave me the chance, a few weeks later, to write a
story for a midnight extra, when the old City Hall in

Newspaperman—Head and Shoulders

Columbus caught fire during a council meeting I was covering.

The managing editor rounded up the crew that got out the extra, for Kuehner had refused to budge from his bed when I telephoned him, around eleven o'clock. "Listen, Author," he snarled, "you're on an afternoon paper. Remember?" And he hung up on me. The next day, he found out that I had saved from the fire, along with somebody's overcoat and somebody else's watch, a large stack of blueprints, not having stopped to realize that they could be easily reproduced, and his abdominal laughter and his kidding went on for weeks. He kept calling me Chief, and demanding to know why I hadn't saved any used carbon paper or rare old thumbtacks. The City Hall fire never completely burned out in his grouchy elephant memory. He wished he had been on hand when the building started to burn, not only because he enjoyed fires but also because he loved to thumb his nose at danger. During the terrible Ohio floods of 1913, he was at the wheel of the last press car to escape from the rising waters on the west side of town, and he drove it across the Town Street Bridge, up to its hubcaps in water, reaching the other side just twenty minutes before the bridge was swept downstream by the flood. When somebody praised his courage, he dismissed it with an impatient wave of his hand. "Twenty minutes is twenty minutes," he said. He was not yet nineteen years old.

The Thurber Album

About a year after the City Hall fire, the *Ohio State Journal,* the city's morning paper, came out on Sunday with a front-page story about a "ghostly wreath" that had suddenly and mysteriously appeared on a windowpane in the bedroom of a house on Oregon Avenue in which a woman had just died. The *Journal* continued to play up the story, and on the following Sunday published a half page of photographs showing curious crowds staring up at the window, and lines of automobiles passing along the street. The cars came from all over central Ohio, the story said, and as many as five thousand passed the house each day. This was too much for Kuehner. The next morning, he ripped the page out of the paper, sauntered over to my desk, and said, "I seem to remember that you cover Heaven for us. Get up there and crack that miracle and bring me back the pieces." The miracle cracked easily enough, for the wreath turned out to be nothing more than an accumulation of iridescent oil, common in the manufacture of certain kinds of glass. This I learned from a representative of the Columbus branch of the Pittsburgh Plate Glass Company, who drove me up to the house in his car. It was early in the day, and no curious people were standing around and no cars were driving slowly by. The husband of the dead woman, his grief obviously lightened by the fame that had fallen upon his house, led us up to the bedroom, where the glass expert inspected the windowpane. He told us that this particular formation of oil must have been accidental, but added that artisans could make deliberate designs out of the oil and that he had seen vases of roses, and even Scottish terriers, imprisoned in glass. The owner of the house clung obstinately to the theory of divine manifestation, even after the truth had been explained to him, and he was tight-lipped when he led us downstairs to the door, and the index finger of his right hand pointed solemnly in the general direction of Heaven. He was still standing in the door, with his arm raised on high, when we drove away.

Kuehner displayed the cracked pieces of the miracle prominently on the front page that afternoon, and that was the end of the ghostly wreath and of all the wonders connected with it except one—why the oil, which had always been on the glass, had not been discovered before. Kuehner had an answer for that one. "Look, Author," he said, "you got an old miracle around the house for years, and nobody knows about it, and then there's a death, and somebody spots it, and you tell everybody it's brand-new and you never saw it before in your life. Catch on?" I asked him what he would have done if it had transpired that the wreath had actually been sent down from Heaven. He never failed to have a fast comeback for everything. "That would have made it a *Journal* rewrite," he said sourly, "and I would have given it a paragraph on page thirty."

The Thurber Album

A city editor of the old school, Kuehner had hard and fixed ideas about how a news story should be written. "Write a flowery introduction in the first paragraph," he told one cub reporter. "In the second paragraph, tell who, when, where, what, and how. Then, in as few paragraphs as possible, relate the most important details. Write an equally flourishing conclusion. Spend the next five minutes finding the sharpest pair of shears in the office, and cut off the first and last paragraphs. You'll have a helluva good news story." He had a noisy antipathy to "literary" writing, or anything that smacked of style, even in feature stories, and his criticism when he encountered such a monstrosity sounded like the roll of thunder. "*This* story is in *bloom*!" he howled at the author of a flamboyant article, and on another occasion he bawled at a reporter, "You did this damn story with *feeling*," giving the word all the force of an obscenity. He liked short paragraphs, hated long sentences, and never used a semicolon in his life.

Kuehner was addicted to the ancient journalese vocabulary—"declared" or "stated" or "asserted" for "said," "assigned" for "given" (as in "no reason could be assigned for the deed"), and all the rest, including such headline verbs as "nab," "bam," "flay," and "flout." Because of his iron insistence on the old platitudes of the trade, several of us were astonished one Saturday night when he attacked a verb form also disapproved of by schools of journalism but almost invariably used in Middle Western newspapers of that day. The late Arthur Johnson, then editor-in-chief of the *Dispatch,* was having a last look at the proofs of the Sunday paper and came across a man who had "suffered a broken arm" in an auto accident. "You don't suffer a broken arm," Mr. Johnson said. "You sustain a broken arm." Kuehner gave him a disdainful look worthy of a professor of English, and raised his right arm above his head. "If you ever break your arm in an auto accident, Johnson," he said, "and you can do this with it, you are sustaining a broken arm." I have no idea where Kuehner found out that small grammatical truth, for he was never known to look up anything in a dictionary.

The use of what Kuehner regarded as unusual or fancy words exasperated him mightily. When a reporter wrote that certain conditions "obtained," Kuehner snapped at him, "What did these conditions obtain? It doesn't say here." In Kuehner's lexicon, conditions "prevailed" or "existed." On another occasion, a fancy reporter from Otterbein, or Wittenberg, or somewhere, used the word "vouchsafe" in a story, and Kuehner never let him forget it. If the man went out to interview someone who turned out to be a "no comment" man, Kuehner would snarl at him, "What's the matter, wouldn't the guy vouchsafe anything?" The old-fashioned vocabulary of the press and the parlance of the police were enough for Kuehner, and he had no interest in enlarging his own knowledge of words. If he ever read a book after he became city editor, he never mentioned it to me, and he liked to brag that he had not seen a play since he was a little boy. His life outside of working hours was circumscribed by the streets that led from his office to his home.

I was in Norman Kuehner's house only once, during Christmas week, nearly thirty years ago, but I have a lasting memory of the city editor at home. He seemed oddly relaxed, as if the *Dispatch* were a tight collar he had taken off at his front door. His forehead was cleared of its office scowl, and there was a new and amiable note in his voice. Time ticked slowly and pleasantly in Kuehner's living room and, for the first time in his presence, I did not feel a sense of deadline tension and urgency. For his two young sons, to whom he was intensely devoted, he had decorated the Christmas tree, and he had helped his wife arrange under it a fine old German crèche, some of whose pieces had belonged to early generations of Kuehners. When he looked at it, he wore an unfamiliar smile, as comfortable as a bedroom slipper. This was Norman Kuehner, husband and father, good family man, and considerate host. Every morning after he had breakfast, he put the tight collar back on, gathered up his office scowls and snarls, and underwent the transformation that turned Norman Kuehner, head of the family, into Gus Kuehner, city editor. One morning when he arrived at work, he bumped into a reporter who was leaning over a table, telephoning, with his rear end projecting into an aisle. "Get you a bed!" snarled Kuehner. "Get you a bridge!" snarled the reporter. Kuehner was back in his element again, his other element.

The ex-police reporter had no fondness for women on newspapers (he sometimes called them "slob sisters"), and he wished to God they would stay home and let him alone. As far as he was concerned, one good homicide was worth ten thousand society pages, including Sunday's, and a brisk running gun battle more important than a warehouseful of "woman's angle" feature stuff. He coldly ignored the fuss that was made when a Columbus girl named Mary Catherine Campbell was elected Miss America at the second Atlantic City Beauty Pageant (she won it again the following year), but he was out in the streets yelling with everybody else in town when the conquering Hank Gowdy returned from the famous 1914 World Series, and he always had space for the exploits of Eddie Rickenbacker after he came home to Columbus from the First World War. He didn't care about games—football, baseball, or any of the others—but he was one of the first to recognize the extraordinary local news value of a youngster named Chic Harley when that All-American halfback began to burn up the Western Conference in 1916. Such prominent females as Helen Wills, Gertrude Ederle, Amelia Earhart, and Babe Didrikson left him cold. In his opinion, there hadn't been an athletic gal worth looking at since Annette Kellerman.

He worked at sharpening and tempering small insults that drew tears from one or two of the less hardened women in the office. With four or five pointed words, he could take apart feminine looks, hats, perfumes, or talent. One day, after reading a woman reporter's story in which the salient facts appeared near the end, he stalked over to a male reporter's desk, carrying the typescript, and snarled loudly, "Turn this lady story upside down." The lady in question was not there at the time, but she heard about the incident and wept. "I love Norman," she sniffled, "but he is absolutely unbearable." On another occasion, he was prowling about the city room in an aggressive mood when he spied a girl reporter, a blue-eyed one named Dorothy, sitting with her legs crossed and one slipper dangling from her toes. He grabbed it off and tossed it out a window. She went down to the street, one shoe off and one shoe on, and found that the slipper had fallen through the open iron cover of a sidewalk elevator shaft and dropped into a second sub-basement. When she got it and told Kuehner where it had gone, he said, "Good shot," without looking up at her. Dorothy didn't cry. The *Dispatch* women, however, didn't bother him half as much as certain Columbus ladies who kept fluttering into the office on dull or hysterical missions and demanding to see the city editor. One of them, a periodic visitor, claimed that she could predict earthquakes by means of griping pains in her intestines. Kuehner used to hide from her in the men's room, gloomily smoking cigarettes until she had gone. Another lady, head of a citizens' committee to bring down the price of milk, kept bothering him until he turned on her once and snapped, "Don't talk to me, lady, talk to the producers." She ran a gay arpeggio of giggles. "You *are* funny, Mr. Kuehner!" she cried. "Just imagine me talking to those cows!" This may have been the first and only time in the life of Norman Kuehner that he was left, for more than three seconds, utterly speechless.

Norman Kuehner got the biggest exclusive news story of his career one day in 1929. He had the title of assistant managing editor then, but he was still a police reporter at heart. Five days earlier, the body of an Ohio State coed named Theora Hix had been found on a rifle range five miles north of the city, and Kuehner had followed every line of the murder story in all three Columbus papers. A lot of evidence pointed at James H. Snook, professor of veterinary medicine at the university. The county prosecutor had been unable to break the suspect down, but every time Kuehner's phone rang, he was sure he was going to hear the news that Snook had confessed. He hoped to hell the story would break for the afternoon papers. It was a little past noon, on Kuehner's fateful day, when the *Dispatch* man at the police station phoned him and said, "Shelly just told me he's going to eat lunch at the usual place today. Made quite a point of it." Shelly was Wilson G. Shellenbarger, an old friend of Kuehner's, who had been a patrolman when young Gus covered the cop house, and was now chief of detectives. The "usual place" was a restaurant at Spring and High Streets where Kuehner sometimes had lunch with Shellenbarger. He was excited, but he kept his voice low and casual as he said into the phone, "O.K., I'll wander over there," and hung up. He stuck some folded copy paper in his pocket and hurried to the restaurant.

When Shellenbarger showed up, he told Kuehner that Snook had confessed a few hours earlier but that the story was going to be held for the morning papers. He explained that William C. Howells, Columbus representative of the Cleveland *Plain Dealer*, had been allowed to visit Snook in his cell that morning, together with another newspaperman. Snook had repeated his confession to them, and Howells had agreed to take the stand at the trial, and corroborate the state's evidence, if the prosecutor would hold the story for the morning papers. Shellenbarger wanted to give his old friend Kuehner a break, and he did. He poured out all the facts in the case, including the details of the long and gaudy affair between the college girl and the professor, that led up to the murder. Half an hour later, Kuehner hurried back to his office with a dozen pages of notes and began to hammer out his story. He was about half finished when the county prosecutor's office phoned to announce that a conference of newspapermen would be held there at three o'clock that afternoon. Smallsreed was sent to represent the *Dispatch,* and told to stick close to the prosecutor until four o'clock. When he got back, at five minutes after four, with an official carbon of Snook's confession, he was handed a copy of the *Dispatch's* late-afternoon edition, which had just hit the street. Kuehner's long and vivid story, interspersed with photographs, covered the whole front page.

Kuehner's big story was unsigned, and there was no mention of Shellenbarger's part in it. It wasn't until two years later that Smallsreed found out who wrote the story and where it came from. Kuehner didn't get any glory at the time, but he had the deep satisfaction of knowing that he had scooped the world on one of the biggest murder stories of the century. The ex-police reporter of the Columbus *Dispatch* had had his greatest hour.

I had left the *Dispatch* six years before the murder of Theora Hix, and my going disgruntled Kuehner, because he felt sure I would end up in New York, and he hated New York. He had a standard lecture that he delivered to all reporters when they started to work for him. It was brief and clear. "If you've got any idea of going to New York to become another Oscar Hammerstein," he would growl, "quit now. This is no place for you." He might have used more aptly, for his purpose, the name of Dana or Greeley or Bennett, but he had a high respect for them, in spite of their unfortunate New York background. To him the name "Oscar Hammerstein" was derogatory, like Phi Beta Kappa, and he gave it, in a mincing tone, his best disparaging accent. He would turn his sarcasm on New York City at the slightest provocation. Once, when the telegraph editor showed him a full column of stuff sent out by the Associated Press in New York on the death of James Huneker, Kuehner glared at the copy and shouted across the room at the drama editor, "Who the hell is James Huneker?" The man replied, "He's a famous figure in the world of art," and Kuehner bawled, "What the hell world is *that*?" The death of Huneker got three lines in the paper that afternoon.

I saw Norman Kuehner only once—in 1927—after I left the *Dispatch,* but I was to hear his voice again the next year, when he called me up in New York. Late one afternoon, the telephone in my office rang, and when I picked up the receiver and said "Hello," a big voice, heroically but unsuccessfully trying to disguise itself, growled, "Why the hell don't you come

Newspaperman—Head and Shoulders

back home where you belong?" Kuehner had been assistant managing editor of the *Dispatch* for only a few months, and he had reluctantly come to New York to attend a convention of newspapermen. The meetings were over, and he was waiting restlessly in the Pennsylvania Station to take a train back to Columbus. I don't think he had ever been in New York before, and he was anxious to get the hell out. One of the last things he said, before he hung up abruptly, was "Where do you get your ladyfingers now, Author?" This was a deathless Kuehner gag, going back to the day, seven years before, when he had found out that I often dropped in, after work, at a photographic studio near the *Dispatch* where newspapermen gathered and afternoon tea was served. The male tea drinker, Kuehner stoutly believed, could easily be capable of such other feminine vices as running up a pair of dimity curtains in secret, or playing with embroidery cloths. I explained that New York was far more effete than Columbus, and that I had gone in for *babas au rhum*. He made a critical sound with his lips and put up the receiver.

Exactly ten years later, I got a letter from him, the only one he ever sent me. A lot had happened to Norman Kuehner, I found out, between the day he telephoned me and the day I got his letter. In 1936, the managing editor of the Columbus *Dispatch* gave up his job suddenly, for reasons that have never been clear to me. He had got into a melancholy state, lost weight alarmingly, and found it hard to keep his mind on his work. There was a persistent rumor outside the *Dispatch* that the paper had decided its editors should all be college men. It is easy to see how the great disparager of college men on newspapers might have cracked under such a cruel, ironic blow. He got a job in the press department of the Landon headquarters in Chicago during the Roosevelt-Landon Presidential campaign, and once telephoned Smallsreed from Chicago to growl, "You still working on a newspaper? This is the life, and there's dough in it." His voice sounded strained and unconvincing. There was only one life for Norman Kuehner, and that was on a newspaper, and all his friends knew it. After Landon's defeat, Kuehner drifted back to Columbus and worked for two years in the Unemployment Compensation Commission, in a building that was near the *Dispatch* and a million miles away. His letter to me, in 1938, contained the names of half a dozen Oscars, or former Columbus newspapermen who had come to New York to work, and he wrote, in his old peremptory manner, "Contact them and tell them I got to have a job. I'll do anything from turning a lathe to trimming ladies' hats." He never came to New York again, the New York he despised, because he got a job with the Curtiss-Wright Corporation in Columbus, and he kept it until he died. He worked the "suicide shift," from midnight until eight in the morning, and kept at it doggedly for three years. In the summer of 1943, he wrote one of his sisters that he had high hopes of going back on the *Dispatch*. This warmly affectionate letter to "Dearest Irma" was the last he ever wrote. The suicide shift had worn him out, and he had only four months to live.

On Christmas Day, 1943, I arrived in Columbus, and after I had checked in at the Deshler, I bought a copy of the *Dispatch* at the newsstand and found, in flipping through it in my room, the story of the sudden death, from a heart attack, of Norman Kuehner, at the age of forty-nine. He had been living alone in an apartment, for his wife had died the year before, one of his sons was a sergeant in the Army and the other a corporal. Kuehner's body might not have been found for days if he hadn't collapsed while he was filling his bathtub with water. The tub overflowed, and attracted the attention of the people living on the floor below. This was the only item in the story of the death of Norman Kuehner, aircraft worker, that would have interested Gus Kuehner, newspaper editor.

I went to his funeral, and found there only a handful of the hundred men and women who had worked for him or with him. The service didn't take long, and nothing was said about Gus Kuehner, police reporter, city editor, and managing editor. I was driven back to my hotel by a sportswriter named Bill McKinnon, one of Kuehner's oldest and closest friends. McKinnon had sat beside him, thirty years before, in the Apperson Jack Rabbit that tore across the Town Street Bridge up to its hubcaps in water. "I saw him two weeks ago," McKinnon told me, "and he said, 'I sure would like to get that paper out just once more.'" I don't know exactly what happened to Norman Kuehner, as I have said, and I am sure he wouldn't want me to pry into it. I can hear him saying, in one of his exasperating tones of voice, "Lay off it, Author. This story's cold."

I have discovered, in talking to some of Kuehner's old friends and associates, that the anxiety dreams of several of us still center in the city room of the old Columbus *Dispatch* building. In one of my own recurring dreams, I am pounding away at a story I can't handle, because my notes are illegible and the type bars make no marks at all on the gray copy paper. The hands of the clock on the east wall of the city room, facing the reporters' desks, are frozen at a quarter after one, fifteen minutes past deadline, and there is a large, amorphous figure just over my right shoulder, standing there gloomily, saying nothing—the ghost of Norman Kuehner. Some of us, the ones who liked him, will never get him out of our dark subconscious, or, for that matter, out of our bright and fond memory.

CHAPTER FOURTEEN

Boy from Chillicothe

BILLY IRELAND got on a train, somewhere in Ohio, one summer day thirty years ago, sat down, and began looking out the window. Shortly after the train started to move, one of the men aboard set off on a slow walk through the coaches, examining everybody's face politely but carefully. When he had had a look at all the male passengers, he came back to where Ireland was sitting, and spoke to him. "Every time I get on a train, I search for the most interesting-looking man aboard. You are far and away the most interesting-looking man on this train, and I would like to sit down and talk with you." This collector of special personalities said his name was Charles J. Finger, and that he was a kind of writer. Billy told me about the incident a week later when I dropped in at his office. He was the cartoonist of the Columbus *Dispatch,* and everybody on the paper liked to watch him draw his daily cartoon, or his Sunday page in color called the Passing Show. I didn't know anything about Charles J. Finger, but I looked him up. It turned out that he was the editor of *Reedy's Mirror* and general manager of a group of railroads in Ohio. He was in his early fifties when he introduced himself to Billy Ireland, and he was writing the first of the twenty-four books that he finished before his death in 1941.

The man Charles Finger picked out that day thirty years ago as the one most likely to charm and instruct him had silvery hair, although he was only forty-two years old, twinkling—it's the only word for them—blue eyes, and a healthy pink complexion, all of which conspired to give his round face a kind of genial glow. He was rotund, and not tall, like the jolly figures of myth, from Santa Claus to the beaming, plump Mother Nature who often appeared in his cartoons. He became the *Dispatch* cartoonist in 1899, when he was only nineteen years old, and worked on the paper for thirty-six years. When he died, at the early age of fifty-five, he had long been one of the city's most loved landmarks, and it was almost as if the statehouse had been quietly taken down during the night and moved away.

William A. Ireland was born in Chillicothe, in Ross County, Ohio, in 1880 and grew up there during the

Boy from Chillicothe

nostalgic era of horses and buggies, covered bridges, and dusty country roads that mired carriage wheels in the rainy season. These roads were always in his mind. I ran into him one day in 1922, walking along East Broad Street in Columbus, and his face wore the particular Ireland smile that meant he had just heard, or remembered, a good Ross County story. "This farmer down there," he began, "drove over to a preacher's house in Chillicothe one day, with the mother of his five children and the kids themselves, running in age from six months to eleven years. 'Me and Elviry want to git married,' he said. The parson was surprised and said, 'These, I take it, are the children of a previous marriage.' The farmer shook his head. 'No, they ain't, Reverend,' he said. 'Y'see, me and Elviry's been plannin' to drive over here an' git hitched ever since I met her at the huskin' bee back in 1909, but the roads has been too bad.'" Billy could turn any topic in the direction of his old home town. Once, when a friend told him that his work shone like a beacon light, he shook his head. "My kind of light," he said, "is an old lantern a farmer carries around his barnyard after dark." He meant, of course, a Ross County farmer and a Ross County barnyard and, if lanterns are made there, a Chillicothe lantern. Ross County people ("My kind of folks," he called them) turned up, gently disguised, in some of his cartoon characters: the Jedge and Uncle

Jerry, Tish Lybold and Uncle Lafe Newberry, and Teck Haskins, from the village of Yellow Bud up near the Pickaway border.

Young Billy Ireland was a regular small-town kid and the leader of his gang. He pitched horseshoes, played marbles and Run Sheep Run, flew kites, made slingshots, carved jack-o'-lanterns and fished for bass and catfish in the streams and pools, and swam with the rest of the fellas in a part of Paint Creek called "Yaller Hole." I don't think he ever did a Passing Show with quite as much pleasure as he got out of drawing a similar page for the Chillicothe *News-Advertiser* one day in November 1931, on the occasion of that paper's hundredth anniversary. He went back to the years between 1886 and 1899 for his material, and the page was crowded with drawings that came out of the memories of his youth: a covered bridge with a sign on it reading "$10 fine for driving through this bridge faster than a walk"; Billy and four other little boys walking naked into the town after the Marshal had seized their clothes in a futile effort to keep them from swimming in "Yaller Hole"; a travelling medicine show, complete with a colored banjo player, entertaining a crowd on the Courthouse Square; eight-year-old Billy shaking hands with the great P. T. Barnum at the circus grounds "way out on East Main Street"; a bunch of the fellas belly-bustin' down Water Street Hill on their sleds; the same bunch gaping at a Saturday matinee performance of "Bessie's Burglar" in Clough's Opera House; a balloon ascension and parachute jump at the Ross County Fair. "We never smell leaves burning in the Fall without thinking of a little brick house at the corner of Sixth and Paint Streets" was lettered above a fond drawing of the cartoonist's birthplace. In the lower righthand corner young Ireland, aged nineteen, was shown leaving town for Columbus, and carrying a straw suitcase—"the unhappiest moment of this period." The page is signed "Bill Ireland of the old Paint Street gang." (His oldest friends called him Bill, but he was Billy to everybody else.)

Billy Ireland was a precocious craftsman with a piece of chalk when he was only seven years old. He would lie on his stomach and draw pictures, of locomotives and Indians mostly, on the smooth, flat flagstones in front of the Courthouse, and on other suitable surfaces around town. He never took a drawing lesson in his life, but he got a lot of encouragement from his astonished elders, especially a sympathetic teacher, Miss Jennie Winn, who gave him a set of paints and crayons. Miss Winn was also a writer of sorts, and when a St. Louis newspaper agreed to publish some short nature pieces she had written, she got Billy to illustrate them. They were used in the newspaper, whose editor actually bid for the permanent services of the illustrator without realizing that he was a child in short pants. Everybody in Chillicothe soon knew about Billy, the boy artist, and when he was only seventeen, he got a job on the *News* there. He worked on copper plates covered with a coating of chalk, and the process was tedious and difficult. He would lay his original ink drawing on the plate, and carefully cut through its lines with a sharp stylus, reproducing them on the chalk, which often chipped or crumbled, so that he would have to begin all over again.

Ireland was not yet twenty when he got three different offers from papers outside Chillicothe, one in Cleveland, one in Pittsburgh, and the other the *Dispatch* in Columbus. He accepted the *Dispatch* offer because Columbus was not so big as the other cities, and because it was not very far from Chillicothe. Columbus people were soon talking about the young man's cartoons, which were signed with a shamrock. They showed observation, inventiveness, and a warm humanity, and they had the power of provoking a smile or, more rarely, a frown that was not easy to lose. Unlike his local contemporary, Harry J. Westerman, of the *Ohio State Journal,* whose style and symbolism were oblique and allusive, so that people sometimes phoned the *Journal* to ask what he was driving at, Ireland had a direct representational approach to the ideas and happenings, predicaments and phenomena, wonders and curiosities that amused or amazed him. His draftsmanship was clean and brisk, and no arty or pretentious line ever got into his daily cartoon, or his Passing Show. Nobody else could draw a weather-vane, or a rocking chair, or an old-fashioned ice-cream freezer with his fine affectionate touch. He wanted to be known as a newspaperman, and not as an artist. "I don't know what they mean by style," he would say, not realizing that he had a style all his own. It was the product of a unique comic sense, and a profound love of "scratching," as he called his painstaking drawing. He sat at his drawing board with the eager concentration of a man watching a tennis match, and he would lean back every now and then, with his head on one side, to chuckle over some hilarious figure in progress. His daily cartoons were widely reproduced, both in America and abroad, but his Sunday page in color was his great dedication.

The Passing Show was largely regional in character, and often purely local, but it somehow managed a universal appeal and it became nationally popular among connoisseurs of comic art. Irvin Cobb and George M. Cohan knew and liked the Sunday feature, and Will Rogers, who came to be a great friend of Ireland's, went around telling people, "I take two newspapers, the New York *Times*, and the Columbus *Dispatch* for Billy Ireland's page." The "janitor" of the Passing Show, as its creator modestly called himself, slaved lovingly over it for nearly thirty years, turning out more than twelve hundred lively extravaganzas of Midland life, in its robust and happy aspects, and its strange and wonderful moods and manifestations. Trying to "make" the Passing Show became a challenge and a pastime. People stopped the amiable janitor on the street with suggestions, or came to his office, or wrote him notes. He was regularly informed of the grotesqueries and peculiar goings on in a dozen different states. Readers sent or brought to his office enough freaks of nature to fill a museum: oddly shaped vegetables, enormous hen's eggs, turtles with dates carved on their shells (one 1869 specimen was proved to be a young impostor), coins, arrowheads, and other relics turned up by farmer's ploughs, an oak bough with a horseshoe embedded in it, a plank into which the quill of a chicken feather had been driven by a cyclone, and a vast assortment of other odds and ends. When he got an idea he liked, his pleasure was as exultant as a Ross County rooster's cock-a-doodle-doo. One day, a week after he had drawn a "snuggle puppy," a variant of the common lounge lizard or parlor snake, somebody suggested that the female of the species must be the "cuddle kitty." Billy had put his hat and overcoat on and was about to go home, but he went back to his drawing board instead, and drew a cuddle kitty that Tenniel would have envied.

The *Dispatch* cartoonist was most at home and most effective in the intimate domain known as human interest, which takes in everything from the calling out of the fire department to rescue a cat in a tree to the assumption of royal guardianship over the destinies of five infants born to the same mother on the same day. In this congenial region Billy's imagination played brightly upon the familiar antics and quandaries of Man and Beast. When he turned to the animals of house and field for his devices, as he often did, he could achieve a peculiar combination of warmth and sharpness that none of his contemporaries could quite match. He looked up the rigging of ships or the harness of horses, to get it meticulously right, but he drew domestic animals, and most wild ones, from memory. The morphology of the rhinoceros and the hippopotamus came readily to his mind, but he had difficulty spelling their names. He wasn't even sure, in fact, of "Holstein" and "Guernsey," and I once asked him how he could draw cows from memory as accurately as he did, when he couldn't even spell their names. "If you'll look closely at those cows," he told me, "you'll see that they're misspelled, too."

On Mother's Day, 1932—Dorothy Parker called it "This Year of Hell"—one of his most widely copied cartoons came out. It presented the world as a forlorn calf, lost in a bog of desolation and fear, its head raised on high and bawling "Mother" at the unresponsive skies. Two years later, after he heard the glad news of the birth of the quintuplets, he drew another cartoon that became one of his most popular. It showed various females of so-called lesser species and their young: a possum, with nine; a bird with a nestful of open bills; a sow with a litter of seven; a rabbit with thirteen; a turtle with twenty-two; a quail with her multiple brood; a black bass with twenty-five; and a frog with countless polliwogs. (Billy didn't live long enough to be cheered by the Middle Western hound dog that gave birth to twenty-three puppies a dozen years ago.) The caption went like this: "What's all this excitement about having five babies?"

My own favorite Ireland cartoon is one of a half dozen that he made between 1920 and 1933, dealing with a number of proud dirigibles that came to grief in wind and storm in those years. There was a mouse-faced dirigible, in center foreground, peeking timidly out of a hangar, obviously dubious about the wisdom of emerging, while high up in the sky, unseen but sensed by its prey, a mammoth cat, made of clouds, was crouching and getting ready to pounce. His cartoon about the crash of the Shenandoah, on September 3, 1925, was more conventional, but there is an interesting story connected with it. He had been about to go out that day for a round of golf in a foursome of long standing, about which he once said, "If I can't play with these boys in Heaven, I don't care whether St. Peter lets me in or not," when he got word that the Shenandoah had been blown to pieces in a thunder-

storm at five o'clock that morning over the village of
Ava, less than a hundred miles from Columbus. He
had once seen the cabin lights of the Shenandoah as
it drifted dreamily over Columbus in the night, like
a ship out of the Empire of Imagination, and its end
disheartened him. He called off his golf game, drove
to his office in his car (it was a Packard his doting
publisher, Robert F. Wolfe, had given him for a
Chrsitmas present) and drew the cartoon that had
occurred to him. In its upper lefthand corner the
heroic figure of a warrior in armor, labeled "The
Elcmcnts" and carrying shield and broadsword, stared
down in contemptuous triumph at the broken figure
of winged Man, lying in the right foreground. I had
forgotten this one until it was recalled to me recently,
but I have never forgotten for long the cloud cat and
the dirigible mouse.

Billy Ireland preached and practiced a simple
theory of his own about newspaper cartooning: "If
you can make a man laugh you can spit in his eye."
For three and a half decades he made a constantly
increasing audience laugh, but he would spit in his
reader's eye only when he wanted to alert him to a
public danger or a civic nuisance, or to enlist him in
some cause near to his own heart. His drawing pen
became an influential instrument in his city and his
state. He was largely responsible for restoring the log
cabin birthplace of U. S. Grant to a site near Point

Pleasant, Ohio, where the President was born. The cabin had been on vulgar display for a long time in the State Fair Grounds. He led the campaign to put the quail on the songbird list in Ohio, and he was on hand and joined in the whistling of the bobwhite song the day the legislature passed the protective bill. Billy called the quail "the little old lady in the Paisley shawl," and there is a legend that he hired a freckle-faced youngster in a tattered jacket to sit in the gallery and start the bobwhite whistling. His ridicule of the Ku Klux Klan, in the early twenties, was a significant force in the disintegration of the Klan's local Klavern. Klansmen used to stand, in full bedsheet regalia, on street corners, with lighted cigars protruding from the mouth-holes in their robes, and Billy's caricatures literally kidded them to death.

When it came to exposing political shenanigans, Billy could hold his own with the best of them, and he had a hand in the defeat of Governor Frank B. Willis when that Republican ran for a second term. Willis, a flamboyant man of gusty appetite, once committed a public indiscretion that the cartoonist, although he was a great eater himself, could not condone—the governor ate forty-eight chicken gizzards at a picnic. The Ireland cartoons, all during the gubernatorial campaign, showed Willis' private car followed by a string of boxcars labeled "Chicken Gizzards." In the larger and grimmer field of national

politics, William A. Ireland was no Thomas W. Nast,
but he had his outstanding successes in the big arena.
He never won a Pulitzer Prize, though, probably
because of his well-known accent on comedy. Pulitzer
Prize judges usually bypass the Irelands and give
their awards to more consistently solemn fellows.
Moreover, for more than twenty years of Billy's
thirty-five as a cartoonist, there wasn't any Pulitzer
Prize, and some of his finest serious work was done
during the First World War, which ended four
years before the annual awards were established.

In September 1917 he drew a cartoon called "The
Leper of Potsdam," showing the Kaiser sitting in
front of a hovel and whimpering, "I only murdered
Belgium because I had to," while hooded female figures representing the virtues and decencies of humanity file by in a mournful procession, averting their eyes
or raising their hands in horror. It was reprinted in
papers all over the country, and it brought its creator
a remarkable letter from the celebrated Jay N.
("Ding") Darling, which Mrs. Ireland, who still lives
in Columbus, has preserved. "Your 'Leper of Potsdam' is a wonderful cartoon," Darling wrote. "I think
it is really better than any cartoon I have ever seen on
any subject or at any time—and I am more or less of
a fan on the subject. It fascinates me with its perfection and I cannot let it slip by without extending
my congratulations." Ding, incidentally, was one of

thirty newspaper artists who drew special cartoons in honor of Billy Ireland in 1924, on the occasion of his twenty-fifth anniversary on the *Dispatch*. They were reprinted in a big Sunday supplement that Billy didn't know anything about until the day it came out. He was once given a silver loving cup inscribed to "The First Citizen of Columbus" and he got many other honors during his long career, but this homage from his colleagues was the tribute he prized most.

Another letter in Mrs. Ireland's collection is one that William Jennings Bryan wrote her husband on May 30, 1912, a month before the Commoner maneuvered the nomination of Woodrow Wilson at the Democratic Convention in Baltimore. Billy had done a cartoon predicting that Wilson and Champ Clark of Missouri would be the principal candidates for the nomination, but indicating that it would probably go, in the end, to Bryan. He had sent the original of the cartoon to Bryan, and I will let Old Silver Tongue take it from there. "The labyrinth cartoon has arrived," Bryan wrote, "and I hasten to thank you for sending it. I have seen no other cartoon, dealing with the uncertainties of the Democratic situation, that equals it in conception and execution. It has faults, of course. It proves you a false prophet and the picture of me would convict you of libel in any court of justice, but with the exception of these minor defects it is a work of art. It reminds me of a motto which I once saw over the stage of a theatre, namely, 'Fiction hath in it a higher aim than truth.'" Ireland liked both Bryan and Teddy Roosevelt, but he could never see beneath Al Smith's citified brown derby to discover the Happy Warrior's character and ability. He once exclaimed about Franklin D. Roosevelt, " I think he's going to be my kind of President," but he soon changed his mind, and his last daily cartoon, published on Memorial Day, 1935, twenty-four hours after his death, called up the angry spirit of a soldier from each of our wars to protest against something F. D. R. had said about the Soldiers' Bonus Bill.

It seemed to me, when I was on the *Dispatch* in the early twenties, that Billy was always in his office, working on his Passing Show or a cartoon. The door was open and anybody could walk right in; he had learned to go on drawing when he had visitors, and there was a constant stream of them through the years: admirers, sightseers, gag men and cut-ups, Ross County folks and other friends, youngsters who wanted to become cartoonists themselves, and co-laborers of established reputation in his own vineyard. He looked at all the sketches the would-be artists brought him, and his opinion was either an enthusiastic "Keep at it!" or a gentle "What else can you do, son?" In 1925, Milt Caniff, now famous for his "Terry and the Pirates," but then a freshman at Ohio State, came to Billy and asked for a part-time job in the *Dispatch* art department. "Draw something that will make me laugh," Ireland told him, "and I'll get you the job." Caniff went to his room off the campus and drew a panel of cartoons telling, in the figures and idiom of fairy tale, the story of his own life. The final panel revealed that it was up to King Ireland whether or not the Dragon of Life slew Prince Milt. Billy not only laughed at it, he loved it, and Caniff got a job working on layouts after class, at seventeen dollars a week.

Most of Billy's contemporaries, both comic and serious artists, were friends of his, close or casual, from Rudolph Dirks, the Katzenjammer man, and George McManus, creator of the immortal Jiggs, to George Bellows, one of his earliest fans, who gave him a lithograph, lovingly inscribed, that still hangs on a wall in the old Ireland residence on Woodland Avenue in Columbus. Bellows' two daughters (Billy also had two, just as pretty) were admirers of their father's idol, too, and must have made him sign his name and draw his shamrock for them when they were little girls, for they were dauntless autograph hunters then. They once accosted McManus in a restaurant after somebody had pointed him out to them. He asked them who they were, and when they told him, he turned over his menu, handed it to them, and said, "*You* sign *your* names for *me*." I told Billy this story when I was in Columbus, two years before he died, and he sighed and said, "The comic strip boys have all the charm, and something else the rest of us haven't got —money."

Among his best friends in his own profession were two men who shared his genius for capturing intimate, recognizable scenes from American family and neighborhood life, H. T. Webster and the late Clare Briggs, a Middle Western boy himself, whose style and subject matter greatly resembled his own, and whose death in 1930, also at the age of fifty-five, was one of the severest blows of Ireland's life. Billy's friends knew him not only as a brilliant cartoonist, but a wit who could hold his own in any company, and a gifted story teller, impersonator, and amateur actor. He belonged to the Salmagundi Club in New York and always dropped in there, and at the Players and the Lambs, on his way to his summer home on Cape Cod. His colleagues would go out of their way to visit him in Columbus. "Billy Ireland was one of the most entertaining companions I have known," Webster wrote me recently. "I visited him once during Prohibition and old Bob Wolfe, who had to be away at that time, gave Billy the key to his liquor vault. This struck me as the acid test of affection and esteem, and that we produced no noticeable dent on the stock made both of us a little ashamed. Wolfe had fitted Billy's office with a large ornate and expensive desk, but Billy kept corn in it to feed the pigeons and continued using his battered old drawing table. Wolfe was so devoted to Billy that he was always ordering him to forget his work and take trips with him." Ireland's foremost idol among American draftsmen was Charles Dana Gibson, and it was Webster who brought the two men together. "We were both ardent admirers of Gibson," Webster said in his letter, "and once when a few of us, including Gibson, were asked to a dinner in Chicago, I maneuvered to get an invitation for Billy, who joined us en route. Meeting Gibson was one of the big moments in his life and he told me he was all for making Dana king of the United States."

Neither Robert F. Wolfe nor any other of Billy Ireland's friends had to work very hard, as a rule, to persuade him to take a trip with them. "The motto of America," he once said, "is 'Let's Go,' " and he was an inveterate goer. On a thousand fair Sundays he set out early for automobile trips with his cronies that lasted all day. He liked to drive down to Chillicothe when the redbud, dogwood, and lilacs were in bloom. "I get hill hungry," he would say. If there was a maple sugar "b'ilin' " or an apple butter "stirrin' " going on anywhere, he wanted to be there, and he would travel to the ends of Ohio to look at a covered bridge he hadn't seen before, or watch cheese being made in a new way, or attend a county fair, or stand around for awhile in an old blacksmith shop. He knew all the roads of Ohio, and they appeared in maps and sketches drawn for "The Gipsy Trail," a corner of the Passing Show that recorded his Sunday travels. The streets of Columbus, however, also held a deep fascination for him, and his eyes would gleam like a boy's when he looked at a steam shovel in an excavation, men in helmets using acetylene torches on a streetcar rail, a scissors grinder sharpening something on his whetstone, a hook and ladder turning a corner, or a hyacinth on a window sill. He regarded the skillful worker in any field, from hedge trimming to watch repairing, as a fellow craftsman, and a workmanlike job always held his attention and brought out his sincere praise. The accomplishment of a creative task, such as the erection of a hen house, or the painting of a flagpole, seemed to him to call for a celebration. He once led the merry-making that attended the building of a bird house in a friend's backyard. There was a washing on the clothesline at the time, and Billy admired it as he admired everything that was neatly done. He promptly looked up the washwoman and said, "Edna, that's the prettiest washing out there I ever saw." Edna never forgot that, and often talked about it. It was still fresh in her memory, fifteen years later, when she heard the sad news that Mr. Billy Ireland was dead.

He hated illness and idleness with the ardent impatience of the outdoors man and the ceaseless creative artist, and he refused, with amiable stubbornness, to go to a hospital for a necessary operation when he developed an exophthalmic goiter during his forties. His friends were worried, and pleaded with him, but he wouldn't listen. Then his publisher, a man used to getting difficult things done, led a friendly conspiracy to trick Ireland into the operation. Dr. André Crotti casually suggested one day that an oxygen treatment would be good for his patient and Billy agreed to submit to that. The next morning, as the oxygen was being administered, it was gradually replaced by an anaesthetic gas. When Billy's "lamps went out," as his old friend Hazard Okey puts it, he was carried downstairs to the dining room, which had been swiftly and secretly converted into a makeshift operating room, complete with a battery of nurses and technicians. To Dr. Crotti, a distinguished thyroid surgeon, this was just one of hundreds of goiter operations, but he must have been a little uneasy as to how his friendship with the cartoonist would come out of it. The friendship survived without a scar; Billy was bewildered, but grateful for what had gone on behind his consciousness, and he took it as a good joke on himself.

William A. Ireland died in his sleep, at his home on Woodland Avenue, one night in late May, as his favorite season of the year was coming to a close. He had suffered several minor heart attacks, but he had had no intimation that he was going to die, fifteen years short of his three score and ten, and his friends were glad of that. The bereaved Columbus *Dispatch* devoted most of its front page, under an eight-column headline, to its great cartoonist, and there was a deep layout of photographs of him, six columns wide. One of them showed him with John T. McCutcheon, of the Chicago *Tribune,* at some tree-planting ceremony; in another he was seen riding in the cab of a locomotive and wearing an engineer's outfit and his best Sunday "Let's Go" smile. It was a souvenir of the day he had been the honored guest of the Pennsylvania Railroad on one of its Middle Western trains, and had been allowed to handle the throttle for awhile, as the locomotive hit a clip of seventy miles an hour.

Billy Ireland's church was the American outdoors, with its far-flung congregation of folks. He rarely went to indoors church, and once said, "I'd rather see the sun shining on trees and streams than elbowing its way through stained glass," but he was an Episcopalian, and so there were formal services at his home. So many people came to the funeral that hundreds could not get inside the house. The ones that stayed outside were careful not to trample the double row of iris in bloom that lined the walk to the front porch. Hazard Okey, a deacon of long standing in the outdoors church, waited in the front yard, and when a catbird in a bush began to sing he opined, "Billy's probably hearing that bird and not what the parson's saying in there."

Billy Ireland had wanted to be buried in Chillicothe, and he was taken there in a motor hearse followed by an imposing procession of automobiles, of which at least a dozen were needed for his close personal friends, he had so many. The car just behind the hearse was the red one of the chief of the Columbus Fire Department, and Billy's friends commented that the idea of the swiftest and most impatient motor car in town leading the way to Chillicothe would have made the chief's old friend smile. He was buried on a green slope of Grandview Cemetery. The redbud and dogwood and lilacs had long since gone out of bloom, but the sun was shining and the day was pleasant, and the flowers of June were coming into blossom. His grave overlooks the town of Chillicothe, the valley beyond, and Mt. Logan and its adjacent hills. More than a hundred years before, this very scene had inspired the artist who designed the great seal of the state, which shows a benevolent sun rising between the hills and shining upon the proud symbols of Ohio's agricultural wealth. Billy Ireland loved that seal and its story, and often talked about it. It represented for him not only his beloved Ross County, but his Middle West and his United States of America. A dozen publishers, including Hearst and Pulitzer, had tried to get him to leave Ohio for New York or Chicago, or some other big city, but Billy always turned them down. "I'm a buckwheater, and I belong in buckwheat country," he wired the owner of one newspaper, and to another he sent this simple message, "I want to live within burying distance of Ross County." The Gipsy Trail of the boy from Chillicothe had come to its end, many years too soon, but in the right weather, and at the right place.

CHAPTER FIFTEEN

Franklin Avenue, U.S.A.

B OB RYDER, editor and paragrapher of the *Ohio
State Journal,* always had a black Cadillac, with
Ohio license plates 844, a number that was assigned to
him year after year, but he preferred to drive from his
home on Franklin Avenue to his office on East Broad
Street in his electric runabout. He gave up the old
electric in the early twenties, after it had become one
of the last ones in town, because he thought it was beginning to attract attention, and he disliked nothing
so much as being conspicuous, or even noticed. A tall
man, almost six feet two, with red hair, blue eyes, and
a pleasant smile, he was recognized by everybody in
Columbus when he rode in the electric, a straight-
stemmed black pipe between his teeth, his knees almost
as high as the steering bar, but he had the delusion
that almost nobody knew him by sight. When pass-

Franklin Avenue, U.S.A.

ersby stopped to stare at him as he unsnarled himself and stepped out of the car in front of the Journal Building, he would feel furtively for his black bow tie, to see if its ends were dangling, or if he had forgotten to put one on. He almost always wore, conceivably as protective coloration, a blue serge suit, white shirt, and one of the dozens of black bow ties he owned, but he was much too striking a figure to manage the invisibility and anonymity he craved. I saw him a hundred times, but I met him only once, forty years ago, when I was a junior in high school. I had written some paragraphs for the school paper, in flagrant and callow imitation of the master, and sent them to him. He read them, as he read everything that came to his desk, and reprinted one in the *Journal*. Later my father introduced me to Bob Ryder, and I still remember that great day.

Robert O. Ryder, editor of the *Ohio State Journal* from 1904 to 1929, the liveliest years of its one hundred and forty-one, reached the third floor of the Journal Building, where he had an office overlooking the statehouse grounds, promptly at five o'clock every afternoon. Frequently the clock of Holy Cross Church, five blocks away, was striking the hour as he began his invariable office routine by crossing to the pigeonhole box on a wall of the city room, to pick up the letters addressed to him personally, or to the editor. Then he would stuff the editorials and paragraphs

263

he had written at home into a pneumatic tube and shoot them down to the composing room. He was adored (I have spent some time looking for the right verb, and that's it) by the members of the *Journal* staff, who greeted him each afternoon, in a sudden silence of typewriters, as if they hadn't seen him for a long time. When the clatter started up again, he would walk among the desks, as unobtrusively as possible, to compliment whatever reporter or reporters had written something for the morning paper that he especially liked. One reporter named John McNulty, who worked for him thirty years ago, wrote me the other day, "To imagine such a man as Bob Ryder coming over to my desk, almost sheepishly, and leaning over and saying, in manner as if he were being very bold, 'That was a good story you had this morning, John,' is to imagine the unbelievably happy jolt." (An imperishable Columbus legend, by the way, tells what happened after McNulty was fired from the *Journal* by a managing editor whose ulcers were acting up. "The next day," an ancient journalist has written me, "McNulty walked into Bob Ryder's office and said, 'Mr. Ryder, now that I have been fired I suppose there is a vacancy on the staff.' Bob told him that was correct. 'Well,' said John, 'I'd like to apply for the job.' He got it.") Ryder's department was the editorial page, and he left the news to the managing editor and the city editor, but he never missed anything that was printed in the *Ohio State Journal*.

When Ryder closed the door of what he always called his "elegantly appointed" office behind him, the first thing he did was to refill his pipe with Bull Durham, the only tobacco he ever smoked. ("Other men find that Bull Durham is so fine-grained that it pulls through the stem," says McNulty. "Perhaps it pulled through for Bob Ryder, too, but he would never complain about that because he wouldn't want to worry the Bull Durham people.") The editor's office was, in fact, far from elegant. He didn't own a typewriter—he wrote all his copy in longhand with a pencil—and there wasn't even a desk in the room. He sat at one of two long tables placed side by side, with lamps in the center. For visitors, there were several comfortable leather chairs that had come from the old Neil House on High Street, so that the room looked more like the lobby of a small hotel than the office of a working newspaper editor. One end of Ryder's table always held a stack of exchanges, newspapers from all parts of the state, from which he clipped items for a Sunday column of his called "Round About Ohio" that dealt with the appearance of flowers in January, snow in May, mysterious showers of rocks upon farmhouses, strange animals "lurking and prowling about and acting huge and feral," and other peculiar happenings in the eighty-eight counties of "this glorious old Commonwealth of ours." Ryder knew scores of Ohio newspapers almost as intimately as he knew the *Journal* itself, and in his paragraphs he kept up a running banter through the years with the editors of many of them.

The other table in Ryder's office belonged to a soft-spoken associate editor named A. E. McKee, part of whose job was the tactful handling of difficult callers, such as Constant Reader, Vox Populi, Pro Bono Publico, and Irate Citizen, who were forever dropping in to amplify and underline in person arguments or complaints they had written in letters to the editor. The *Journal,* in Ryder's years, printed more letters from readers than any other paper its size in the country, as many as three columns daily and two solid pages on Sunday. They discussed politics, Prohibition, religion, and such minor subjects as whether the robin, when it cocks its head on one side, is looking or listening for the earthworm. A local printer, obsessed by the horrors of vivisection, once sent in a pasted-up communication five feet long. Ryder waded patiently through it and picked out some of it to print. No letters were barred from the *Journal* except the libelous, the obscene, and the plainly insane. Even the arguments of a vociferous Columbus communist were occasionally published.

The *Ohio State Journal* man, as he liked to be known, wrote thousands of editorials in his day, and

Franklin Avenue, U.S.A.

literally tens of thousands of paragraphs. The editorials were logical and temperate expressions of his liberal convictions, and the paragraphs formed a light and humorous chronicle of the goings-on in his Franklin Avenue neighborhood, a typical American middle class community. He wrote everything with painstaking care, and gave as much thought to a paragraph about the neighbor women of Franklin Avenue— "They always succeed in making a girl who is as pure as the driven snow sound less interesting than one who is no better than she ought to be"—as he did to the detailed examination of a complicated act of Congress. The *Journal* editor worked with the intensity of the born scholar. He had once taught Latin in a Columbus school, and he was an inveterate reader of history and the classics. Expressions like *"similia similibus curantur"* popped up in his paragraphs now and then to startle readers who did not have his erudition, but his style and most of the things he had to say were clear and precise, and he had no real affectation. At home and in the office, he put in from ten to twelve hours a day, including most Sundays, for twenty-five years, building up, a sentence at a time, what finally became a veritable mountain of prose. There must have been fifty thousand paragraphs in the end, running to a million and a half words. He burned himself out in his constant devotion to what he fondly called "this old Palladium of Liberty," and his doctors ordered him to retire in 1929, when he was only fifty-four years old. The following year he moved to California and died there in 1936, a few days after his sixty-first birthday.

Robert O. Ryder was born and brought up within the sound of various campus bells. He was the son of the Reverend William Henry Ryder, who taught Greek language and literature at Oberlin, where Robert and two of his brothers were born. In the late seventies the family moved to Ann Arbor, Michigan, another college town, and the elder Ryder became pastor of the First Congregational Church there. In 1888, he took the chair of New Testament Interpretation at the Andover Theological Seminary in Massachusetts, and when he died there in 1908 he had long been recognized as one of the outstanding scholars in his field.

William Henry Ryder's sons inherited their distinguished father's intellectual gifts, and all of them majored in the classical languages and were graduated from college with high honors—Bob went to both Williams and Yale. Frederick, the eldest son, known as Jack, taught at the old Columbus Latin School, later became the founder and principal of the Columbus Academy, coached the Ohio State football team, on the side, from 1892 to 1896, at a salary of three hundred dollars a season, and ended up on the Cincinnati *Enquirer* as one of the best known sports writers in the country. Another of the boys, Arthur, was for many years a learned professor of Sanskrit at Stanford. When Bob got out of Yale, in 1897, his brother Jack took him on as a teacher of Latin at the Columbus Academy. His career there was short-lived, however, because the Spanish-American War broke out after he had been at the Academy one year and his big brother Jack, as adventurous as Bob was sedentary, enlisted immediately and closed down the school. Bob tried to get in the army, too, but he was rejected as being underweight for his height. He had often accompanied Jack when the athletic Ryder dropped in at the *Ohio State Journal* to turn in a sports item, and he had come to know all the *Journal* men. He asked for a job and was set to work as a reporter.

The young Latinist soon decided that printer's ink was headier stuff than Horace's Falernum wine. He wrote feature stories and covered local beats until he was assigned to the statehouse. His pieces about the legislature showed a flair for humor. Once in reporting a brawl between two legislators who kept calling each other "liar," he ended his account with "Both gentlemen were correct." (Later he wrote, "Nothing is less interesting than avoiding personalities.") His irreverent note about the brawl, out of place in a straight news story, was an early sign of his editorial leaning.

He had become a reporter at the beginning of an important era in American journalism. The last years of the old century, and the first years of the new, were exciting ones for newspapermen, with the war, the Philippine Insurrection, the death of Queen Victoria and the coronation of Edward VII, the flamboyant rise of Colonel Teddy Roosevelt of the Rough Riders, the assassination of President McKinley, W. J. Bryan and the monetary issue, Imperialism, the prophetic experiments of the Wright brothers at Kitty Hawk, and, in Ohio, the noisy political feud between Mark Hanna and Senator James B. Foraker. There was also young William Randolph Hearst with his Yellow Journalism and screaming red-ink headlines and, as if to balance this, the founding of the sound and responsible Associated Press, to which the *Ohio State Journal* became one of the first subscribers.

In 1901 Bob Ryder was made city editor of the *Journal* and he persuaded his superiors to avoid the infection of Hearst's Disease. The *Journal* did not play up crime or other sensational news, and its headlines and typography remained conservative. The influence of the quiet, unemotional city editor increased, and when the ownership of the paper changed hands in 1903, he was promoted to managing editor, and then, before he was thirty, to editor. The new publishers were Robert F. and H. P. Wolfe, Democratic sons of a dyed-in-the-wool Democrat named Andrew Jackson Wolfe. Previous owners had promoted Republicanism at the expense of unbiased news, and

Franklin Avenue, U.S.A.

when the powerful Republican Party in Ohio found out that the Wolfes were Democrats, it howled its indignation to the moon and the sun. The Wolfes agreed that the *Journal's* ancient political tradition and policy should be preserved, and this led to a quandary. Ryder, it came out, was also a Democrat. The Wolfes had almost despaired of working out the problem when their editor came up with the solution. His father-in-law, Colonel E. S. Wilson, had published, for thirty years, the staunchly Republican *Ironton Register,* and Ryder brought him to the *Journal,* gave him the nominal title of editor, and insisted on being called managing editor himself.

Colonel Wilson wrote glowing editorials in praise of the Grand Old Party, cherry pie, sunsets, and other glories of God and Man, presided at banquets, addressed meetings, joined clubs, and in general acted as the *Journal's* official, and unquestionably Republican, spokesman. As the gregarious gentleman from Ironton became a prominent and familiar public figure, his shy son-in-law gradually began to withdraw from the company of men. He had enjoyed stag parties as reporter and city editor, and used to walk home late at night from so many of them that he started an editorial campaign for owl car service in Columbus, and succeeded in getting it. For awhile he had gone to the theatre, and he had even been seen at parties ornamented by the disturbing presence of women. But his social life, like Carthage, had to go, on behalf of his dedication to the editorial page. Once in a long while he would slip away to a prize fight or a ball game, and he took his wife to see Maude Adams in "Quality Street" and Otis Skinner in "Your Humble Servant" when they placed the Hartman Theatre, but that was the measure of his entertainment. On Sunday he sometimes took Mrs. Ryder to the Faculty Club on the Ohio State campus for a quiet lunch with a former *Journal* man. Afterwards, in the spring and early summer, they would drive to Greenlawn Cemetery, of all places, for an afternoon of bird watching.

Bob Ryder wasn't a crusader, but he slew many a dragon in his time, quietly, by the light of his study lamp, and their bones lie scattered through the back files of the *Ohio State Journal*. It wouldn't be easy to reconstruct the monsters now, because nothing is so old and unfamiliar as the menaces of yesteryear. Corruption in government was the Questing Beast that the redheaded Palamides in the blue serge suit pursued most relentlessly. He believed that dishonesty in public office, from municipal to federal, was more dangerous than incompetence, and he rode past the blatherskites to get at the rascals. ("We often wonder what other feasances there are besides mal, mis, and non," he wrote in 1923.) He was the spearhead of a successful drive against the practice that gave constables and justices of the peace in Ohio a percentage of

Franklin Avenue, U.S.A.

court fines—a famous victory that led to similar re-
forms in other states. The *Journal* editor was also the
first in Ohio to attack the Ku Klux Klan. His vigorous
editorials denouncing it went on until the local Klansmen folded their robes and disappeared, at least from
public view.

Bob Ryder's Franklin Avenue, celebrated in ten
thousand paragraphs, is one of several quiet residen-
tial streets on the East side of Columbus that were
built up by the well-to-do middle class in the years between the Civil War and the end of the century. Time
has changed and commerce crowded the region, and
it has suffered from various infections of Progress, but
in the good old days, Franklin Avenue proceeded tranquilly eastward toward Franklin Park, amidst the
placid and rhythmic sounds of horses' hoofs, and carriage wheels, and the scrapers of white wings. (The
Franklin Avenue man was a G. A. R. veteran with a
handle-bar mustache, and a habit of whistling at his
work.) The avenue was the proper setting for the
home of Robert O. Ryder. He lived, for twenty-two
years, at number 1041.

The neighborhood was strongly Republican when
I was a boy. Youngsters grew up there in the vague
belief that Democrats kept Confederate flags in their
attics, and were probably guilty of living in sin, and
responsible for the sinking of the *Maine*. During
Presidential campaigns the parlor window of almost

273

every house displayed large posters bearing the frank, open countenances of the patriotic Republican candidates for President and Vice-President. There are oldsters in Columbus who could recognize the photographs of these Republican Vice-Presidents, in the period between 1884 and 1908: Levi P. Morton, Garret A. Hobart, Charles W. Fairbanks, and James S. Sherman. Ancients of especially good memory might even recall the two Republicans who were defeated for the Vice-Presidency in those years: John A. Logan and Whitelaw Reid. If Democratic families had the temerity to put likenesses of their candidates on their window panes, in the tough final decades of the last century, Republican kids would throw eggs at them.

In 1901 the dauntless Ryder, who lived on Fair Avenue then, another Republican stronghold, came out boldly for a Democratic candidate for governor. The man was defeated, but it was a minor reverse for the *Journal* editor. His greatest disappointment came in 1928 when Al Smith was overwhelmingly defeated for the Presidency by Herbert Hoover. The *Ohio State Journal* had declared for Hoover, but Ryder's admiration of Smith shone out more than once on its editorial page. He respected Smith's sound common sense in opposing Prohibition and, in his paragraphs, occasionally poked fun at Hoover's "noble experiment." The *Journal* came out for Hoover, all right, but Ryder's editorials, between the nominations in

Franklin Avenue, U.S.A.

July and the election in November, subtly managed to throw a warm clear light on the figure and stature of Al Smith while directly praising his opponent. Ryder had become a kind of spy in his own camp, and he had a lot of fun acting his dual role. After Hoover's election Ryder wrote three editorials about the defeated candidate. "Governor Smith made a gallant fight," said one of these. "Though he is crushingly defeated, his frankness and courage have impressed the country. . . . Did you notice how prompt he was with his congratulations and how generous?" On another day: ". . . We wonder if Al is not pretty happy, for all the defeat of his high ambition. He is a great human being, and a great human being, we imagine, would not count the loss of the Presidency as of supreme importance while he held the love and devotion of those who knew him best." Finally Ryder wrote: "It would be a tragedy if the country should hear no more from this clearheaded, honest-minded, frank-spoken, liberal leader of the useful minority."

During the campaign, the Socialist Labor nominee for the Presidency, Verne L. Reynolds, had been allowed to speak from the City Hall steps in Columbus. Ryder went to listen, and described him in an editorial as "an earnest, kindly appearing man." This editorial went on to say: ". . . we wish to compliment our city authorities for permitting Mr. Reynolds to speak where he listed and our local chapter of the D. A. R.

275

for not raising a fuss about it. Radical vocal attacks
on the established order do no harm, while the at-
tempted suppression of them does harm, with its de-
nial of the right of free speech and its making of mar-
tyrs. . . ."

Newspaper paragraphing, the daily grinding of
gleams and sparkles of humor and satire from the
grist of human nature and the news of the world, is a
special and demanding comic art. Its practitioners
must keep regular hours, like the office worker, and
they can't indulge in the relaxing frailties and postures
of temperament. The best paragraphs, to be sure, come
out of the quiet mind and the tranquil time, but the
true paragrapher has had a tough training in reporting and editing, and he can write in any mood or
weather. The art, alas, no longer flourishes as it once
did, in the hard and gritty soil of today's editorial
pages, and the great paragraphers of the halcyon years
are either dead or grown old and retired, men like
Bob Ryder of the *Ohio State Journal,* Ed Howe of the
Atchison *Globe* (Ryder affectionately called him old
Ed Howe) and Bob's favorite Ohio contemporaries,
Jack Warwick of the Toledo *Blade,* J. S. Mires of the
Liberty Press, and Dusty Miller of the Wilmington
News-Republican. Will Rogers was a part-time newspaper paragrapher, but his stuff appeared in a fancy
box off the editorial page, so he can't be included
among the elite, and neither can the dialect boys, like

Franklin Avenue, U.S.A.

Abe Martin, or the column conductors, such as Franklin Pierce Adams and Bert Leston Taylor, who printed poetry, of all things, and stuff from contributors. Ryder, at the top of his form, was probably the best of all the genuine paragraphers, and his "output," as he lightly referred to what he wrote, was more widely reprinted than that of any of his colleagues except Howe. The old *Literary Digest* used a great deal of it, and so did the *Journal* man's favorite newspaper, the late New York *Morning World,* and a hundred others. When Harold Ross, an editor steeped in newspaper traditions, started *The New Yorker,* he insisted on having a column of paragraphs, and he hired Howard Brubaker to write them. They appeared, of course, only once a week, and thus were six times as easy to do as the daily stint of the old guard. I suppose there are first-rate newspaper paragraphers still around, but the heyday of the craft, as far as I am concerned, came to an end when Bob Ryder left the *Journal* and Ed Howe died. The famous Kansan had started the Atchison *Globe* in 1877, when Bob Ryder was two years old, and he wrote his last paragraph in 1937, a year after Ryder's death. (Howe once said, "I want to go to bed some night after a hard day's work and never wake up again." He got his wish one night in his eighty-fourth year.) Both Ryder and Howe had slaved over their paragraphs the way a poet slaves over a sonnet. "A good paragrapher," Ryder once wrote, "is one that can make something that was ground out sound as if it were dashed off."

For a man who practically never went anywhere, Ryder miraculously managed to take in the manners, customs, and foibles of everybody in town: girls standing briefly on tiptoe to kiss their young men in uniform goodbye at the Union Depot during the First World War; nice old ladies driving down the center of Broad Street in their elegant Baker electrics; the neighbor women on Franklin Avenue, gossipy and suspicious—"The night has a thousand eyes, and the neighbor women at least twice that many ears."—stylish stouts trying to look naturally slender; and all the other people, male and female, "good, bad, and indiscreet," of his community, a diligently observed and faithfully reported microcosm of the America of his time. His paragraphs dealt directly with the larger scene, too, and commented wisely and sharply on national figures in the news, the reformers and the inspirationalists, the pompous and the bigoted, who came and went, from the arduous regime of Teddy Roosevelt to the dark extremity of Herbert Hoover. He deftly punctured the vainglorious pronouncements of gloomy social prophets, now forgotten, such as the one who proclaimed that "Man is but a disease of the agglutinated dust," and another who said, "Marriage is the daughter of loneliness and desperation." The years have tarnished most of his timely and topical paragraphs, ones

like "We feel pretty sure that W. E. D. Stokes' mamma
didn't believe in spanking," but they have left others,
such as this one, untouched: "Whoever named near
beer was a poor judge of distance." Ryder's daily column also served to reveal its author's personal and
typically masculine household behavior and his likes
and dislikes. He was a ham-and-eggs, steak-and-pota-
toes husband, and he constantly reiterated his hatred
of spinach, stewed celery, avocados, garlic, and fluffy
or pallid desserts—"We often get up in the morning
feeling like a cherry pie and go to bed at night feeling
like a gooseberry fool." He invented "The Franklin
Avenue Protective Association" as a vehicle for the
expression of his distastes, as in this paragraph: "A
careful scientific experiment reveals the fact that an
unfertilized field produces only 198 crates of spinach
to the acre, whereas a fertilized one produces 507, and
the Anti-Fertilizer Club of the Franklin Avenue Protective Association will be organized at a large and
enthusiastic meeting this evening." And in July 1927
he wrote: "Another depressing reminder of the de-
cadence of the times is that they have named a new
salad after Col. Lindbergh, instead of a good five-cent
cigar."

A regular daily feature of his called "The Young
Lady Across the Way," illustrated by Harry J. Westerman's amusing drawings of a pretty but vacuous
girl, symbolizing the American woman's indifference

to what is going on in the world, was syndicated in various newspapers and published, in part, in a small volume in 1913. Ryder had agreed to syndication and book publication of "The Young Lady" in order to promote the fame of his collaborator, the *Journal* cartoonist, and not his own. The young lady of Ryder and Westerman antedated F.P.A.'s Dulcinea by several years, but she could scarcely compare to her later prototype, who became nationally known as the heroine of Kaufman and Connelly's gay comedy, "Dulcy," produced in 1921. After all, Ryder had batted out his young lady's sayings on the side, wherever *that* was, but even so, some of them are still memorable: "The young lady across the way says she overheard her father say that wheat was suffering from the activity of the bears and she never knew before that they ate it." And there was this one: "We asked the young lady across the way if she were not oppressed by the thought of social injustice and she said not particularly as she didn't have to invite people to her parties who didn't invite her to theirs and the thing evened up pretty well in the end."

Every now and then, for twenty-five years, Bob Ryder would wistfully express the hope that he would one day send "that truly great paragraph ricocheting down the echoing corridors of time." Anyone who had the leisure and strength to go through the files of the *Ohio State Journal* would come upon hundreds of truly great paragraphs, but the journey from 1929 back to 1903 would be long and tedious. Two aging fans of the old master have done some research for me and sent on about two hundred paragraphs that they picked out of Ryder columns here and there, and I have made up a column of the best of them. Here it is:

Another reassuring evidence that the feminine is eternal, in spite of everything, is that the girl in the *rose de printemps* knickers still measures a piece of tape by holding one end against the tip of her nose and counting the distance between that point of interest and the tips of her outstretched fingers as exactly one yard, just the way the woman in the red flannel petticoat used to do.

One of the more obscure problems in psychology is why an editor's wife always decides to have him get the screen door for the kitchen down from the attic and put it up on the day he is bending every energy to get the country saved by 2:50 P.M., so as not to be late at the opening game of the season.

The fashion authorities seem to differ as to the exact position of the waist line, but we imagine it will be satisfactorily located as soon as it's warm enough to put up the porch swing.

We suppose every woman who has been married a good long time has her moments of depression, as she cleans up after her husband, when she feels that she'd rather have the insurance money.

What probably will always puzzle us, as we don't dare ask anybody in a position to know, is what becomes of the five inches that the so-called stylish stout corset gets rid of.

When the neighbor women can't find out anything definite against some attractive young matron of whom they don't quite approve, they say she has no background and seem fairly well satisfied.

Our memory goes back to the time when another reason why we regarded girls as of the inferior sex was because they never seemed to have any warts.

A vociferant candidate always seems to find it easier to explain to thoughtful audiences why his opponent should not be elected than why he himself should be.

In some cases it is a difficult matter to draw a hard and fast line where convalescence stops and plain loafing begins.

About all a girl has to do to get engaged to a soldier is to be around.

A woman is either hearing burglars or smelling something burning.

One day during the summer of 1929 Bob Ryder slipped away from the *Journal,* leaving the managing editor to run the paper any way he wanted to, and got on a train for Montreal. The Hoover-Smith campaign, among other things, had taken a lot out of him, and he needed a rest. His idea of an enjoyable vacation was to hide out in a big hotel in Atlantic City, Chicago, or Canada, and spend a couple of weeks eating ham and eggs, avoiding spinach and salads, and reading or being read to by his wife, "a certain noble woman" of the paragraphs. She shared his desire to get away from people, his sense of humor (when he didn't have time to read the Ohio newspapers, he trusted her to pick out their funniest items), and his taste in books. The 1929 vacation lasted only a few hours. When they got off the train, Mrs. Ryder noticed that her husband looked sick. At the hotel he couldn't sign the register; his right hand had become helpless. They took the next train back home and he spent three weeks in bed recovering, but not completely, from a slight cerebral hemorrhage. It marked the end of his thirty-one years as a newspaperman.

In 1930 the Ryders moved to Berkeley, California, and settled down in a house on a winding street overlooking Oakland Bay. They were accompanied by Mrs. Wilson, "our dear mother-in-law" of thousands of amiable paragraphs Ryder had written about his wife's relatives. Later, a widowed sister of the retired editor and a widowed sister-in-law came to live in Berkeley. He was, as he might have put it, *plein de dames,* but his erudite brother Arthur was not far away, and two or three former *Journal* reporters, who had gone to Hollywood, came up to visit their old boss. One of them, Joel Sayre, had managed to get the startling phrase "a pregnant mule" into the *Journal* in a feature story he wrote about a talented hog caller in 1921. It was the first time the word "pregnant," an obscene synonym for "expectant," ever got into a Columbus newspaper, and many readers were shocked. For weeks after the article appeared Ryder would stop at Sayre's desk and say, with a grin, "How are all the pregnant mules today, Joe?"

It had been Ryder's intention to start writing again, but he found that he could no longer hold a pencil in his hand for more than a few minutes at a time. Once in awhile he managed to write a letter to a friend back in Columbus, and one, written in March 1931 to James E. Pollard, a former *Journal* man, who is now head of the Department of Journalism at Ohio State, described his life as it was that year and as it continued to be up to the end. ". . . I am getting along pretty well, I think," Ryder wrote, "but as the months pass it is evident that I shall never work again the way I used to. The enforced idleness is very irksome at times, as you can imagine, but this is a beautiful place. My brother, a tremendously scholarly but none the less quite human and decent old scout, is here, and I'd much rather live this way than not live at all. For the first time in my life, I am able to read almost as much as I want to, and that helps some. I have read Gibbon's

'Decline and Fall of the Roman Empire,' Motley's 'Rise of the Dutch Republic,' Macaulay's 'History of England,' all of Shakespeare, and a good deal of Milton, much of Dickens, Thackeray and Trollope, and a lot of other good old books, so you can see there are some real compensations for being laid on the shelf. The climate out here is one of them. All the lies about it are true. . . .

"I have no doubt you share my regret over the sale of the *New York World*. There are almost no honest, independent, courageous newspapers left now. The chain-store variety is rapidly attaining complete domination of the field. No wonder we elect Hoovers and do other unwise things! The business depression, if prolonged enough, may help bring the country to its senses, but to accomplish that great end I fear the hard times would have to last ten years and be much more severe than they are. Such an experience would be terribly hard on individuals but the nation as a whole would benefit by it, I think. Adversity is a better teacher than prosperity."

One night in the spring of 1936, Robert O. Ryder died peacefully in his sleep, like Ed Howe, and Billy Ireland, whose death ten months earlier had grieved his old friend and colleague. The two men had come up in Columbus journalism together. Ryder had gone to the *Journal* in 1898, and Ireland to the *Dispatch* in 1899. Each had married a girl named Florence, and their homes on the East side of Columbus were not far apart. They were the only members of "The Polar Explorers," an imaginary club they invented and elaborated on at occasional Sunday night suppers in each other's home. Ireland had been the subject of a hundred of his friend's fondest paragraphs, and the tall figure of Ryder appeared in many of Ireland's Passing Shows. Billy died at the age of fifty-five, and Bob was fifty-five when he left Columbus.

When Ryder was elected to the Ohio Journalism Hall of Fame in 1942, a year after Billy Ireland was similarly honored, dozens of men who had got their start under him sent telegrams of praise. These tributes came from the authors of a score of books, a vice-president of a New York bank, a vice-president of a national radio network, a special assistant to the Secretary of the Navy, the head of a Washington news agency, the tax commissioner of a big city, and other ex-*Journal* men who had risen to eminences in various fields that would have made their shy old editor uncomfortable. His able successor and long-time friend, J. A. Meckstroth, delivered the eulogy at the Hall of Fame banquet and said at the end, "A kindlier, fairer, or more upright man never lived." Each of the men who honored Robert O. Ryder that night would gladly take on the considerable task of resurrecting and publishing the finest examples of his work if he had wanted it that way, but they know he didn't. The *Ohio*

Franklin Avenue, U.S.A.

State Journal man was content to remain, quietly and unnoticed, in the files of the old Palladium of Liberty. The back issues of his newspaper, during his years, have been carefully and lovingly preserved. According to a Ryder admirer who went through some of them recently, not even the oldest ones have started to turn yellow. At any rate, he told me the other day, it seemed that way to him.

CHAPTER SIXTEEN

Loose Leaves

A DEPARTMENT OF ANNOTATION, AMPLIFICATION, AND AFTERTHOUGHT

Last Days of an Old Strategist

B ENJAMIN FRANKLIN JAMES, that vivid strand in the tapestry of my youth, and restless tyrant of the Blind Asylum baseball team, spent his final years, I have just found out, in the home of an old friend in Columbus. He was blind, and had to get around with the aid of a cane, an irksome burden for a man who once could run a hundred yards in eleven seconds with his overcoat on. Sight had been the keenest faculty of old Eagle Eye, but all he could do in the end was daydream and talk about battles long ago. During the Second World War he listened to the radio a lot and became a dynamic and outspoken military expert. He was forever predicting what Montgomery and Patton and the other generals were going to do, and when he was wrong, as he was most of the time, he could squirm out of his mistakes with all the eloquence he had shown on the diamond when the bases were loaded against him. "I guess Frank was what they call a rationalizer," one of his friends told me. He died in 1947, still believing that his ball club could have taken the Columbus Senators the best day they ever saw, and given the Yankees or Giants a rough time of it.

The Stoughton Bottle, and Other Lost Magics

AFTER "Daguerrotype of a Lady" appeared in *The New Yorker,* I got some interesting and pertinent letters from ladies in a dozen different states of the Union, whose pioneer women are still remembered, especially by members of their own dauntless sex. One correspondent, Mrs. Dorothy Terrill, of Wynglen Lane, Los Angeles, said she once actually saw a Stoughton bottle plain, a rare experience, since Stoughton bottles must be almost as hard to come by nowadays as Button Gwinnett signatures.

"In the year 1930," she wrote, "I moved into an old house in a small town in Pennsylvania. The house had been recently taken over by the bank after the death of an old couple who had lived there for years. Way back under the rafters in the attic of the house was a Stoughton bottle. The house was reputed to be about eighty-five years old at the time. No one knows how long it had been there. The bank told me I might have anything that was in the attic. So I came into possession of it, along with a lovely old azure vase, an antique clock and a very odd covered basket. Contrary to your opinion, it is not squat and heavy. It is rather delicate and decorative. It is a flask of pressed glass with "Stoughton" on it in fancy enamel letters. The S is white on the upper part and red on the bottom. The rest of the letters are white with blue bottoms. It has a lead top in a cork like a vinegar bottle. The bottle is about six inches high and holds about a pint."

I have always thought of the Stoughton bottle as a simple, sturdy, household vessel, something like the homely, unadorned little brown jug, but if Mrs. Terrill's was not an impostor, the Margery Albrights of the last century must have flung its name, in scornful epithet, not only at lazy oafs and hobbledehoys, but also at slickly dressed smart alecks, with macassar in their hair, and clean fingernails, who sat around doing nothing, while their womenfolks rescued horses from burning barns, cut hornets in two and cats' heads off, and kept the wheels of life in motion. About Dr. Stoughton himself, who must have designed the bottle that bore his name, I have had no report whatever

Loose Leaves

I can only sit around like a Stoughton bottle and wonder what he was like.

Mrs. Frank O. King, wife of the artist who draws "Gasoline Alley," reminded me of other ancient remedies that Mrs. Albright knew, but that I had left out of my list: "The onion and sugar syrup which cooked on the back of the hard coal burner during the winter months and was served to us when we had colds, the flaxseed poultices, the salt pork strip with its coating of pepper which was wrapped around our sore throats, and the sulphur which was blown down our throats during a diptheria runoff."

"Sassafras and slippery elm," wrote Mrs. Emma H. Woodford of Claremont, California, "were among the herbs used by the mountain folk of southwest Missouri when I lived there during the eighteen-seventies and eighties. They took calomel, too, and were frequently salivated by it. I was disappointed, however, that Mrs. Albright did not make use of dogwood, which in the Ozarks was an emetic if scraped up, a cathartic if scraped down."

Mrs. Anne Badger Schurman of New Castle, New Hampshire, wrote, "Your 'Daguerrotype' takes me back sixty odd years to my own childhood on a New Hampshire farm and a neighbor whom we called 'Aunt Phoebe Ann.' Each fall my mother and I would go with Aunt Phoebe Ann into the woods and fields to gather the herbs she would need for the year. You didn't mention several that were kept always in stock, such as thoroughwort, a horrible tasting tea for breaking up a cold, and wormwood. I don't remember what that was for, but goldthread was a small and very bitter root to cure canker."

All I know about early American remedies of the woods and fields I learned from Aunt Margery and Noah Webster. According to him, wormwood is "a European woody herb, of a bitter, slightly aromatic taste, formerly used as a tonic and a vermifuge, to protect garments from moths, and in brewing, but now chiefly in making absinthe." The name of the herb is akin to the German "wermuth," from which the French "vermouth" seems to have been derived. Many people have vermouth in their homes, but try and buy absinthe nowadays.

Goldthread is a North American herb with fibrous yellow roots, also known as dodder. It is a parasite, in some instances, which attaches itself to the surrounding vegetation and absorbs nourishment from its host. Webster doesn't seem to have found out that American pioneer women used the root of the plant as a remedy for canker. My two favorite varieties of dodder, by the way, are devil's-guts and creeping crowfoot.

Thoroughwort, also known as boneset, wild hoarhound, and agueweed, was once valued for its diaphoretic and tonic properties. The worts of America are almost as common as the Smiths. There are nineteen, for example, whose names begin with the letter "b": banewort, barrenwort, bathwort, bearwort, beewort, bellwort, birthwort, bladderwort, blisterwort, bloodwort, blushwort, brimstonewort, bristlewort, brittlewort, brotherwort, brownwort, bruisewort, burstwort, butterwort.

Just as this herbal was about to go to press, up popped Mrs. Dorothy H. Clark, of Albuquerque, New Mexico ,who wrote me that in her father's house there were several "squat, brown, earthenware, Stoughton bottles." Mrs. Clark went on to say, "In an effort to get me to drink my milk, it was occasionally cooled in one of these bottles. Liquids were, or seemed to be, much colder when cooled in them."

It is just barely possible, I suppose, that there were plain Stoughton bottles for everyday use, and fancy ones to be brought out on Sunday. I don't know. Seventy-five years ago there must have been a million Stoughton bottles in American homes, but nobody knows very much about them now. A researcher I know looked through encyclopaedias, called up antique dealers and glass makers, and even interviewed a few aged women. "I couldn't find out anything at all about the Stoughton bottle," he reported finally.

The Thurber Album

The Great Runaway

IT HAS BEEN a year since I read Professor Joseph Russell Taylor's "Composition in Narration," but I still can't get out of my mind his fascinating account of a remarkable cabhorse runaway, surely one of the most spectacular in the history of our vehicular traffic. He set the story down in spare, flat sentences, deliberately avoiding style and the devices of color and suspense in order to emphasize the difference between journalistic fact and the truth of creative narration. It goes like this:

"The young men of a Greek letter fraternity, assembled in convention in a university city, among other functions gave a dance. As they were the hosts, they sent the carriages for their guests, and the girls came otherwise unattended. At the end of the dance, three girls entered their carriage for the long drive home, and agreed to offer the fourth seat to one of the men, an undergraduate in the home college, who was a neighbor of all of them. Therefore they directed the driver of the carriage to this boy, singling him out from the group on the steps of the hotel where the function occurred. The driver closed the carriage door, and turned away on his errand; but the horses, taking the closing of the door for a familiar signal, immediately started to trot away without a driver or direction. The sudden start of many men to stop them frightened the horses, and they ran away.

"It was midwinter, the city deep in snow. It was about two o'clock in the morning, and the carriage was reasonably safe from collision. The region of the city in which the girls lived lay north; the horses ran east, in the direction of the railroad yards. A mile's run brought them without mishap into this region; and there the horses checked at a freight train that crossed the suburban street ahead of them, and turned into an open field of snow, where they circled slowly, coming back again to the street, and turning back toward the city at full speed again. In this interval, while the carriage was turning slowly, the girls opened the carriage-door, and all escaped safely to the snow. One of them, seeing what a remote and desolate place they were to be left in, sprang into the open door of the carriage again, as it passed them, and so was carried safely back to the barns, from which she was sent home under adequate protection.

"The other two remained in the unknown suburbs, five miles from home, in the middle of a snowy field. They were in evening dress, and the night was cold. They set out to walk for help; they came through streets where the street-lamps shone on foreign names in the little shop-windows; they found every house dark in this poor precinct; and it was not until they had passed many squares that they found a house in which there was a light. Here they rang, and were answered by a priest of the old church. The house was the parish house, and his own dwelling. The girls requested the use of his telephone to call for help from their friends. But the priest was inclined to disbelieve their story; it seemed to him that two women richly dressed, alone in such a place at such a time of the night, must be intoxicated or otherwise suspicious. His endeavor therefore was to hold them at the door until he himself could telephone to the police; while they persisted in their request to be allowed to use his telephone for themselves. This colloquy had proceeded for some minutes at the lighted door, when there came a halloo of many voices from down the street, and a carriage drove swiftly up to them; it was filled with men of the fraternity, and was one of many carriages that were scouring the city for them. This rescue, of course, finished their adventure."

Professor Taylor pointed out that all this could be transformed into fiction in half a dozen different ways. If he had written it himself, I am confident he would have done it from the viewpoint of that wonderful and unforgettable girl who quietly climbed back into jeopardy. She has become my favorite unsung heroine. She would probably be in her early seventies now, and I hope she is alive and well, and that she tells the tale of the Great Runaway, on winter nights, to a flock of grandchildren.

Loose Leaves

Fanny Stevenson's Fateful Sprite

FANNY VAN DE GRIFT STEVENSON'S short story, "The Nixie," which aroused one of Professor Taylor's sudden, intense literary enthusiasms, was published in *Scribner's* for March, 1888, and it is likely that Joe fell in love with it when he was a young man. It is hard to believe that he read it again in his mature years because nobody else appears to have shared his wild and wayward belief that the piece was better than any of the stories Fanny's distinguished husband wrote. I haven't had a chance to read "The Nixie," but I have learned something about it from *Voyage to Windward*, the recent and interesting biography of Stevenson written by J. C. Furnas. The story lies buried in a magazine of the eighties, all right, but its ghost, strange and mischievous, rose up to deal a final and fatal blow to the tortured friendship of Robert Louis Stevenson and William Ernest Henley.

Mr. Furnas devotes a fascinating chapter to the disastrous and complicated consequences of "The Nixie." It seems that the plot of the story had actually been devised by a brilliant cousin of Stevenson's, Katherine de Mattos, who outlined it one night at Henley's house in the presence of the Stevensons. The story, as written by Fanny Stevenson, is a fantasy dealing with "a poetic young man meeting in a railroad carriage an eerily feeble-minded young woman who turns out to be a water sprite." The idea of making the woman on the train a water sprite, or Nixie, was a dubious conceit of Fanny's. Miss de Mattos' version had made the girl an escaped lunatic. "She rejected," writes Mr. Furnas, "Fanny's eager suggestion of the nixie-motif. She also rejected Fanny's rash offer of collaboration and—being literary, too, and a great close friend of Henley and his London circle—tried her hand alone. All Henley's efforts to place her manuscript were futile. Further prodded by Fanny, Katherine grudgingly handed her the plot to do as she liked with, and Fanny's version proved salable to a magazine presumably not insensible to the value of her husband's surname. This success, where his protégée and he had failed, was well calculated to rankle in a man who had small use for Fanny to begin with."

Henley read "The Nixie" in *Scribner's* and wrote a letter to his friend Stevenson which marked the breaking point of their long friendship. "I read the *Nixie* with considerable amazement," Henley wrote. "It's Katherine's; surely it is Katherine's? There are even reminiscences of phrasery & imagery, parallel incidents—*que sais-je?* It is also better focussed, no doubt; but I think it has lost as much (at least) as it has gained; and why there wasn't a double signature is what I've not been able to understand. . . ."

Loose Leaves

The friendship between Henley and Stevenson had always been complex, but it now became even more touchy and difficult, and it failed to survive exchanges of letters typical of the men and their period, appliquéd with French expressions, subtle phrasings, and old-fashioned protestations of ancient loyalties. Stevenson later wrote a wry fable about the breaking of the ties, and I remember a poem of Henley's that begins, "What is it ends with friends?" Fanny had quite a lot to say about it all, but Miss de Mattos was content with exclaiming, "There is devilry in the air!"

Most biographers and critics take Stevenson's side in this affair, but I am an old Henley man myself, and I remain unmoved by the heavy burden of proof that lies against him. William Ernest Henley hated Fanny Stevenson's guts and so, God help me, do I. I also think it was Katherine's story, and that there should have been a double signature. Furthermore, I am blessed or cursed, whichever it may be, by an inherited gift of taste that leans towards real girls on trains, crazy or not, and away from nixies and pixies and nymphs. The story remains, however, the literal property of Fanny Van de Grift Stevenson. It was the third story she ever had printed and it was apparently her best, although nobody but my old professor thought it was wonderful.

Joseph Russell Taylor clearly fell in love with the fantasy at first sight, and he still remembered it fondly twenty years later. I salute any man who can carry into his middle years, untarnished and undiminished, those first fine affections of his youth.

Once a City Editor. . . .

I DIDN'T KNOW Norman Kuehner during his last fifteen years, and I realize that I made the mistake of foreshortening them too much. In trying to slip quietly past the explanation of his tragic decline, I succeeded only in leaving it provocatively vague. There were many reasons, I have since found out, for what happened to Kuehner, but the chief one, two of his oldest friends agree, seems to have been his regret at leaving the city desk and its intimate contact with reporters, to become a forlorn and maladjusted managing editor.

"As managing editor, Kuehner was quickly and completely lost," one man wrote me. "He did not know how to adjust himself to the job. He felt he was not equal to the necessary contacts. He was at a loss, for example, in customary chats with syndicate salesmen, who like to talk about newspaper problems generally, and about many other things. Kuehner had the same problem in all his social contacts. His life had been so long in the city room that his interests lay there always. Many times he told me, 'If only I had remained a reporter or city editor. This business of being an office man, I don't understand. I produce nothing. I can't point to anything in the paper that is mine. There is nothing to the job of managing editor.'"

"The greatest tragedy in Kuehner's life," another old friend of his told me, "happened when he was taken out of the city editor's chair. He never seemed to be the same Gus. As time progressed, Kuehner appeared to be more ill at ease and to withdraw into a shell. In his latter days he rarely came out of his office. I remember having a long talk with him at lunch and advising him to circulate more around the building, take renewed interest in the mechanical operation, engage in more public relation functions. He had seemed happiest in the days when he sat at the city desk, edited copy, and sent reporters out on stories. Once away from that, he was out of his element and he apparently knew it. But didn't you find that underneath that crustiness, much of which must have been a continuous act, was a wonderful layer of kindliness and humaneness? You touched upon it in the description of his home life. I remember during the early days of radio he ran around to dime stores buying parts for me and others in the office for homemade sets."

I did mention the basic kindliness and warmth of Kuehner's nature, but perhaps without enough emphasis. City editors of his complicated kind are hard

to get down on paper. They have a curious occupa-
tional urge to keep their insides to themselves most
of the time, and they are likely to be different things
to different people. "I never saw his rough side," another colleague of his wrote me, and a woman reporter
who worked for him before I did told me, "He was
always gentle and sweet to me." A devoted member
of Norman's family recalled that he was a sensitive
little boy, easily depressed when his mother scolded
him. "Tell me good words," he would say to her when
he was only six, and he wouldn't start off for school until she did.

It is probable that I stood out in Kuehner's mind,
during my first months on the *Dispatch,* as the veritable incarnation of College Journalism, but our
friendship in the end was genuine and lasting. Nobody
liked him more, or remembers him with greater fondness.

An O. Henry Mystery

NOT LONG after Billy Ireland got to Columbus in
1899, he met a doctor named John M. Thomas. They
were both young and unmarried—Billy was not yet
twenty—and they lived at a boarding house at 383
Oak Street. Dr. Thomas had been appointed physician
at the Ohio Penitentiary in Columbus through the

efforts of a young state representative from Marion named Warren Gamaliel Harding. One evening, in 1899 or 1900—the years since then have worn the story smooth, like a legend, and obscured some of the dates and facts—Dr. Thomas brought home "a great many" manuscripts that had been written by William Sydney Porter, who was then a prisoner in the penitentiary. The manuscripts, which were in longhand, mysteriously disappeared and were never found. Billy Ireland took the blame because they had been in his possession last. Dr. Thomas had given them to Billy to read and the cartoonist had put them on a table in his room. Somebody, possibly a maid who wanted to dust the table, placed them on a washstand one day, and they were never seen again. The tale has its various versions. One holds that Billy had not had time to read the manuscripts, another tells that he did read them and recognized their merit, and there is an odd, persistent rumor that he deliberately threw the stories in the wastebasket because Dr. Thomas had told him that O. Henry didn't want them back. Still another variant of the tale has it that the manuscripts, "ten inches high," were taken out and burned by the landlady, after she got tired of seeing them around day after day. All that remains now is speculation, since the principal figures in the case are dead. My own conjectures are based on passages, here and there, in Professor C. Alphonso Smith's "O. Henry Biography," published in 1916, a curiously vague and old-fashioned book. Dr. Thomas comes into the book in several places, but Billy Ireland is not mentioned anywhere.

Porter (variously known as Will, Bill, and Sydney) had entered the penitentiary on April 25, 1898, and was released on January 24, 1901. He had been convicted of embezzling a little more than a thousand dollars from a Texas bank. Few people believed he was guilty then, and almost nobody believes it now. The record of his literary output during the thirty-three months of his confinement is incomplete, partly owing to his own failure to keep a detailed account of what he wrote there. It wasn't until October 1, 1900, two years and a half after he came to the penitentiary, that Porter began to enter in a notebook the titles of stories he had written there. Only ten were listed. He unaccountably left out "Whistling Dick's Christmas Stocking" and "Georgia's Ruling," both of which were sold and published during what Professor Smith calls "the shadowed years." How many others he may have left out is anybody's guess. On April 5, 1899, Porter wrote a letter to Mrs. G. P. Roach, his mother-in-law, that ended, "I have abundant leisure time at night and I have been putting it to best advantage studying and accumulating manuscript to use later." He never explained, in subsequent letters, what he meant by "manuscript."

Loose Leaves

Porter had been writing for more than a decade before he was sent up. In 1887 he began to turn out a large volume of jokes, squibs, paragraphs, verses, vignettes, and sketches. Some of these were bought, for a pittance, by the Detroit *Free Press,* and a magazine in New York called *Truth* paid him six dollars for one or two sketches. In 1897 he had sold a short story to *McClure's* called "The Miracle of Lava Cañon," the first one ever published. The editors of the magazine rejected some other stories of his at the same time; nobody knows how many or what happened to them. As for his penitentiary stories, Dr. Thomas informed Professor Smith that Porter wrote "quite a number," whatever that means. The doctor often found one on his desk in the morning, and he told Professor Smith that Porter had asked him to read his stories before sending them out to a magazine. Nobody at the penitentiary could give Professor Smith an accurate estimate of the volume of Porter's pieces.

It is not even known for sure whether the most famous O. Henry story, "A Retrieved Reformation," was written at the penitentiary, but one prison official, the late George W. Willard, thought that "it may have been sketched out there." This story, based, according to Dr. Willard, on the career of a safe cracker named Jimmy Connors, a fellow prisoner of Porter's, later inspired Paul Armstrong's hit melodrama, "Alias Jimmy Valentine." Others contend that Jimmy Valentine, in real life, was another safe cracker, then at the penitentiary, named Dick Price. The best authority for this belief is Homer C. Howard, who covered the penitentiary for the old Columbus *Press-Post* during Porter's years there. According to Mr. Howard, a judge ordered that a safe at the newspaper offices be opened during a stubborn court litigation, and Howard suggested that Price was the man for this job. (In the play, Jimmy Valentine opens a safe in which a little girl has been accidentally locked up.) The variants of the Jimmy Valentine story are characteristic of the uncertainties about Porter's life and work, particularly during his Columbus period. The penitentiary, for some unexplained reason, has no record that Dick Price or Jimmy Connors was ever a prisoner there.

Will Porter was a notoriously close-mouthed man, and even his friends knew very little about him. One of them, Robert H. Davis, who collaborated with Arthur B. Maurice in 1931 on a study of O. Henry called "The Caliph of Bagdad," wrote in that book: "He had a genius for taciturnity and a profound admiration for silence." Even the editors of *McClure's* didn't learn until years later that O. Henry had been in the penitentiary. His stories had been sent to a friend in New Orleans and remailed from there. His genius for secrecy explains why he never told anybody about the strange case of the vanishing manuscripts that Dr. Thomas took home that night more than fifty years ago.

In 1903 he sold "A Retrieved Reformation" to the *Cosmopolitan,* but it wasn't until 1908 that he brought out his book of short stories called "The Gentle Grafter." This book, Professor Smith wrote, "found its inspiration in the stories told to O. Henry from 1898 to 1901. The first eleven stories in this book had not before been published. They probably belong, as do some of the stories in 'Cabbages and Kings,' to the accumulation of manuscript mentioned by O. Henry in his letter to Mrs. Roach." These eleven stories may have been among the ones that disappeared, and O. Henry may have rewritten them later from memory. It is reasonable to surmise that an author might postpone the tedious task of rewriting stories that he had already done before. Certainly he didn't put off the eleven prison pieces because of a fallow period; in 1904 and 1905 he wrote a total of a hundred and fifteen short stories.

Dr. Thomas told Professor Smith that Porter could turn out a story "in from one to three hours," and such a prodigious writer might get over the loss of even a stack of manuscripts ten inches high. Perhaps they were rejections, anyway. Since he could get the professional opinion of America's leading magazine editors, I can think of no reason for his asking the advice of a young doctor and a young cartoonist on stories that he hadn't submitted to magazines.

Will Porter was a humorist, one of the best America has produced, and such a man is likely to be careless about preserving original manuscripts. "The Caliph of Bagdad," Bob Davis wrote, "slipped through his 'Little Old Bagdad on the Subway,' leaving but few tangible souvenirs of his reign. How many of the tales that were born of O. Henry exist in the original? Not a dozen, I should say. We have various letters, a sheaf of penciled pages, some sketches, numberless endorsed checks and some touching appeals to 'hurry up with the cash.' But in comparison with the great mass he turned out in typewritten and longhand manuscripts —nothing."

Billy Ireland never mentioned the lost stories of O. Henry to me, although I knew him pretty well when I was a reporter on the Columbus *Dispatch* in the early twenties. By that time he had probably got tired of talking about the incident. Behind the high stone walls of the old gray building on West Spring Street, where Will Porter spent a thousand and five nights, his name has probably been forgotten. One of the few certainties about his life there is that he invented his famous pseudonym while acting as night clerk of the prison pharmacy. There are several theories as to where he got the name: he had seen it in a New Orleans newspaper, he had come upon it in a French medical book, he got it from the actual name of the captain of the guard at the penitentiary. This last seems to me the most likely explanation. The captain of the guard was a man named Orin Henry.

The faint trail of William Sydney Porter, in and out of Columbus, Ohio, has long since grown cold. I leave the mystery of the missing manuscripts of O. Henry to a younger and more active researcher, but I warn him that the task is hard, and that it may even be impossible. "O. Henry had no conscientious Boswell," wrote Davis and Maurice, "no faithful Forster. . . . Therefore, O. Henryana today is largely a matter of memory, more or less shadowy, and often conflicting."

O. Henry lingered here a little season, left a few blurred fingerprints, and quietly departed. Most of the things he touched are lost, but his best work has not been forgotten and it won't be.

*   *   *

An old friend of Ireland's rang my doorbell one day, just as I was about to take these final pages to the printer, and told me a couple of things that I can't leave out. Billy's next to last Passing Show had suggested that Mt. Logan be turned into a state park, and not long after his death the legislature unanimously adopted a resolution to acquire the land and call it the Ireland Memorial Park. Nothing has been done about that yet, but the project hasn't been forgotten.

Billy Ireland's idea of the way a man ought to be buried, my caller told me, was simple but impractical. "I would like to have some of my friends go down to the lumber yard and get some pine boards and make a box to bury me in with their own hands. You see, after they put me down there, I'd like to get back into the ground as soon as I can and help grow a tree." When a man becomes famous there are some things he can't do, and one of them is being laid to rest in a box made of simple pine boards. William A. Ireland was buried in a satin-lined coffin with silver handles, like everybody else.

A Gathering of the Klan

THE *Ohio State Journal* had the best story, and the Columbus *Dispatch* almost nothing, about the first open-air meeting the Ku Klux Klan ever held in the city. It took place in a field north of town one fabulous Saturday night in the summer of 1922. This comic but alarming gathering of men in muslin was touched by the wayward aimlessness of the decade, but it had a sobering effect on those who witnessed it. It was far different from the flagpole sitting, Marathon dancing, and goldfish swallowing of the crazy years. The raffish element in Columbus, noisy but never large, had got over the belief that a certain cathedral in the city had been left without a steeple so that the flat top of the tower could be used as a gun emplacement during a planned Catholic insurrection, but the Klan gave a new and more active outlet to religious intolerance. For many months Klansmen had been recruited throughout the city, but they had kept pretty well under cover until the night of the open-air meeting.

The City Hall reporters of the three Columbus newspapers, the *Journal, Dispatch,* and *Citizen,* met at the corner of Broad and High Streets a few minutes before eight o'clock that evening. They had been approached earlier in the week by a thin young man with a low voice, a gray felt hat, and a love of nickel novels. He may also have been stirred, a few years before, by the Wagnerian music that accompanied the rides of the Klansmen in D. W. Griffith's "The Birth of a Nation." (The movie was banned by the Ohio censors, but many people went outside the state to see it.) At exactly eight o'clock the thin young man showed up in a Packard limousine driven by an older and more talkative Klansman, a snappy dresser, whose breath smelled of rye. The newspapermen got in the car, and its curtains were instantly pulled down. They were asked if they minded being blindfolded and the *Journal* reporter, George Bricker, now a "word man" in Hollywood, said, "This is the most fun I've had since I was ten. I wish I'd brought my water pistol, though." The thin young man blindfolded his guests with handkerchiefs. "You won't need your water pistol," said the older man. "We got a couple of thirty-eights in this car, loaded with real bullets."

The car began slowly winding in and out of a maze of streets—"So you guys won't know where you're going," the driver said. He was wrong about that. All of us knew Columbus like a book. After twenty minutes we left the sounds of the city behind. "Nelson Road," said Bricker. There was a hint of surprise in the driver's grunt. We were whirled back into the city and in and out of more streets until abruptly we came to a pattern of sounds as familiar as our mothers' voices. We were being driven over the viaduct that arches Columbus' great tangle of railroad yards and leads directly past the clamorous entrance to the Union Station. Half an hour later the Packard slowed down and began to creep along. It had become part of a long procession of Klansmen's cars. The reporters heard the racket of a motorcycle and the unmistakable voice of a cop shouting, "Keep that Marmon in line!" and "Hey, Barney Oldfield! You in the Ford! Both hands on the wheel!" He didn't say anything to the driver of the darkened Packard. "That cop wearing a bedsheet?" Bricker asked. The snappy dresser didn't like that. "Nah," he grumbled, "but we got a couple of ex-cops that rate 'em." The Packard finally came to a stop in a field with a hundred other parked automobiles. The curtains of the car were run up and the reporters were told they could take off their blind-folds. They instantly knew where they were. Less than half a mile away gleamed the bright familiar lights of the roller-coaster in Olentangy Park.

Several hundred men, dressed in white sheets with peaked hoods, were milling around, their trousers peeking out ludicrously under the sheets. One of them kept bawling, "If there is anyone here who isn't a Klansman, or doesn't intend to be sworn in tonight, they will remain at the peril of their life!" The snappy dresser told the newspapermen that this threat was not meant to include them. He had a bottle of rye in one hand, and with the other he took a .38 Colt revolver from a side pocket of the car, examined it, and put it back. About seventy-five sheeted candidates for mem-bership in the organization were lined up, and a spokesman ordered them to repeat after him the oath of the Ku Klux Klan, and then there was an awkward pause. It was time to light the fiery cross, but it couldn't be found. One hoarse voice began shouting, "Where is the fiery cross? Where the hell is the fiery cross?" and a hundred others joined in. Ten minutes later the Klansman in charge of the fiery cross was found asleep behind a tree with an empty whiskey bottle beside him. During the search, a dozen Klansmen had come up to talk to the reporters. Three of them, in spite of their robes, were identified by Bricker. He recognized the voices of two of them and the posture of the other. The neophytes were finally sworn in, and as their voices were lifted in the ugly responses, the snappy dresser kept repeating, "Boy, that's one hell of an oath those guys are takin'! They'll never forget it." The ceremonies were over before eleven o'clock, except for horseplay, a few fist fights, and some drunken singing.

On our way back to the center of the city we passed a group of Klansmen in full regalia standing on a street corner. One of them waved an upraised hand. We saw that he was signalling to a trolley car. It stopped and the Klansmen clambered on. I remembered the wild riding horsemen of *The Birth of a Nation*—cowboys, most of them, I have no doubt. And here were hooded ushers and countermen and garage mechanics and dentists and short-order cooks—crusaders in Model-T Fords, avengers in trolley cars.

The next morning the *Journal* published Bricker's colorful and accurate story of the meeting, which ran to more than a column. (The *Citizen,* which has no Sunday paper, printed a long account of the goings on in its Monday issue.) The *Dispatch* reporter, a tall, thin, nervous man, had written two columns for his paper, but his story was rewritten and cut down to a single, cautious, emasculated paragraph. The city desk had sent it on without any changes, but an editor higher up had decided that it would be discreet "to wait and see which way Columbus is going to jump." The *Dispatch* reporter, an aging and muttery writer now, still broods about what happened to his story of the open-air meeting of the Ku Klux Klan that Saturday night thirty years ago. He stops strangers now and then and croaks, to the faint sound of a distant bassoon, "There was an editor." Friends say he means the redheaded editor of Franklin Avenue, the one he wishes he had been working for that summer, who never in his life waited to see which way anyone was going to jump before he made up his own mind.

*   *   *

The death of Bob Ryder, March 16, 1936, got only one sentence in the New York *Times,* but that paper printed nearly two thousand words about the passing of Ed Howe, October 3, 1937. The Kansan was, after all, the author of twenty-eight books, and he had always spurned the Ryder cult of invisibility. When he was eighty-two, he said, for everybody to hear, "Give me two years and I'll write the greatest book in the world." He had written his best book long before that, "Story of a Country Town," which ran into fifty editions. It was praised by William Dean Howells, who probably never heard of Bob Ryder, although Howells was once a reporter and editorial writer for, of all American newspapers, the *Ohio State Journal*.

*   *   *

It seems to me, in conclusion, that Robert O. Ryder may have sent that truly great paragraph ricocheting down the echoing corridors of time when he wrote: "A hardened reformer never seems able to make up his mind which is the most beautiful word in the language, 'compulsory' or 'forbidden.' "

HERE ARE those two remarkable Taylors, Judge Stacy, upper left, and his son Mahlon, whose combined life spans have taken in the administrations of every President except George Washington and John Adams. The group picture shows a country gathering of Taylors, Fishers, Mathenys, and Bealls, and their kinfolk in 1901. Aunt Mary, the great pipe-smoker, is fourth from the right at the table.

AT THE top is the lithograph of the Duke of Westminster's hunting dogs, once as common as the Stoughton bottle in American homes.

Below are two pictures of William M. Fisher of Columbus, Ohio. One of them shows him at eighteen, and the other was taken in Grand Rapids when he was in his fifties.

THE William M. Fisher & Sons Company is seen here as it looks today, eighty-two years after its founding.

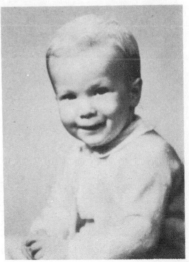

At the right is young William M. Fisher, III, great-great-grandson of the founder.

THIS photograph of Grandma Fisher in a polka-dot dress and her husband sporting a satin waistcoat was taken a year before the Battle of Gettysburg, when she was seventeen and he was twenty-two. They had been married a year.

THE LADIES in the upper row are Grandma Fisher's sisters: Aunt Lou, on the left, and Aunt Melissa. Under Aunt Lou is Aunt Hattie, late wife of Mahlon Taylor, and the other aunt is Sarah Bancroft, one of the four daughters of Judge Stacy Taylor and Mary Hollingsworth Taylor.

THE young lady with the reticule is Colonel Jackson's daughter Lizzie, about the time she married Uncle Jake Matheny of Sugar Grove. The happy couple is shown below, a long time later.

THREE gentlemen of the old Bryden Road neighborhood: Charley Potts, my grandfather's coachman, upper left, next to old George Craft, with all his medals, when he was 85, or maybe 113, and, below, the mighty Frank James, captain of the Blind Asylum team, during his last years.

THE MAN behind the gun is Billy Allaway, pitcher, marksman, and all-round athlete. Under Billy's pistol is Billy Southworth, formerly of the Avondale Avenue baseball team and the N. Y. Giants. Below him is Ray Eichenlaub, fullback of the Notre Dame team of Rockne and Dorais that gave Army the old razzle-dazzle one day nearly forty years ago.

AUNT MARGERY ALBRIGHT, sitting in her garden on a summer's day in 1912. She is holding a potted azalea, and behind the chair is her famous trellis of moonflowers, which bloomed year after year, to the wonder and amazement of the "jubrous."

HERE IS Aunt Margery with the three Thurber boys, William, Robert, and James, reading from left to right. The picture was taken about 1897. The studious gentleman is Rev. Stacy Matheny, reading a copy of *American Devotion*, which he compiled and edited himself.

THIS IS Charles L. Thurber, who was brought up not far from Lockerbie Street in Indianapolis, and married Mary Fisher of Bryden Road, in Columbus. The man with the Bible in his hand is Rev. James Grover, and this is the picture of him that hung in my grandfather's parlor.

THE two frilly tots at the top are James Thurber
and his big brother Bill. In the oval is Robert, with
an older brother on each side, wearing ties that
came from God knows where.

THIS IS Belinda, taken about the time she fired at the prowler in the back yard. Below are a photograph of Mamie Fisher, wearing her youth like a rose, and a portrait of Mary Fisher Thurber, painted only a few months ago, at the age of 85.

THE Four Leaf Clover Club, with Mary Thurber at the far right, next to Laura Poe, whose house she later "bought."

AN 1890 gathering of the Frioleras. The pretty girl standing in the middle is my mother.

THIS IS a recent picture of the house at 921 South Champion Avenue, which was either on fire or full of dogs or something at the turn of the century.

George Marvin, who enlivened things for the Thurbers after they left 921 and moved to Washington, is seen at the right in a rare somber mood.

HOLY CROSS CHURCH on South Fifth Street, whose steeple clock strikes the hours and quarter-hours and is heard from time to time in the pages of this book.

THIS IS MR. ZIEGFELD, who lived a few blocks away and could hear the old clock clearly, if he wasn't too busy with his thoughts or his tools.

HERE we have George Bellows' "Man with a Pipe," the portrait of Professor Joseph Russell Taylor he painted forty years ago. At the right is a photograph of the artist as a young man.

Professor Billy Graves was a popular broadcaster whose audiences loved to hear him read prose and poetry over the air.

Charles W. ("Chic") Harley, Ohio State's greatest halfback, sometimes called "The Only One," whose running was a cross between music and gunfire. His Frank Merriwell exploits of thirty-five years ago inspired the building of Ohio Stadium, the crowded horseshoe seen on the opposite page. The other view is of old Ohio Field, taken about the time "Chic" Harley was born.

DEAN Joseph Villiers Denny, scholar, teacher, administrator, wit and legend, whose lively exchanges with young Professor Herman Miller (at left) used to brighten the somnolent Faculty Club at Ohio State.

THIS IS Norman ("Gus") Kuehner, as he looked in his middle thirties when W. G. ("Shelly") Shellenbarger, in the straw hat, gave him the story of Snook's confession. The third man is George ("Parson") Smallsreed, another old friend of Kuehner's, now editor of the Columbus *Dispatch*.

COLUMBUS held three noisy homecoming celebrations during Gus Kuehner's years on the *Dispatch*, honoring, in turn, Hank Gowdy (below), hero of the famous 1914 World Series; Captain Eddie Rickenbacker (left), American ace of the First World War; and Mary Catherine Campbell, twice elected Miss America at Atlantic City in the 1920's.

BILLY IRELAND, the boy from Chillicothe, in his jovial or customary mood. He carried humor around with him like a Ross County lantern, to brighten his corner of time and the world.

THE LEPER OF POTSDAM

THIS IS the Ireland cartoon about Kaiser Wilhelm that won the admiration of "Ding" Darling and was widely reprinted in America and abroad.

ANOTHER of Ireland's most popular cartoons, published on Mother's Day in 1932, the darkest year of the Depression.

THE Ryder with the pipe is Bob, editor of the Old Palladium of Liberty, informal historian of Franklin Avenue, U.S.A., and wise observer of the goings on in what he called "this old vale of tears and laughter."

The other Ryder is his remarkable brother Jack, scholar, headmaster, athlete, football coach, soldier, sports writer, and learned authority on Tacitus, Juvenal, Hans Wagner, and Rube Waddell.

THE Young Lady Across the Way, wide-eyed daughter of Bob Ryder and Harry Westerman, who never got anything quite right or knew exactly what was going on in the world.

AND HERE, last but far from least, is William Sydney Porter, who became O. Henry in Columbus, Ohio, more than half a century ago. He moved on to his beloved Bagdad-on-the-Subway, lingered there a little season, and quietly departed, leaving a few blurred fingerprints around. Most of the things he touched are lost, including the mysterious manuscripts that disappeared from the house on Oak Street in Columbus, one day in 1899 or 1900.